# World's Best Travel Experiences

## 400 EXTRAORDINARY PLACES

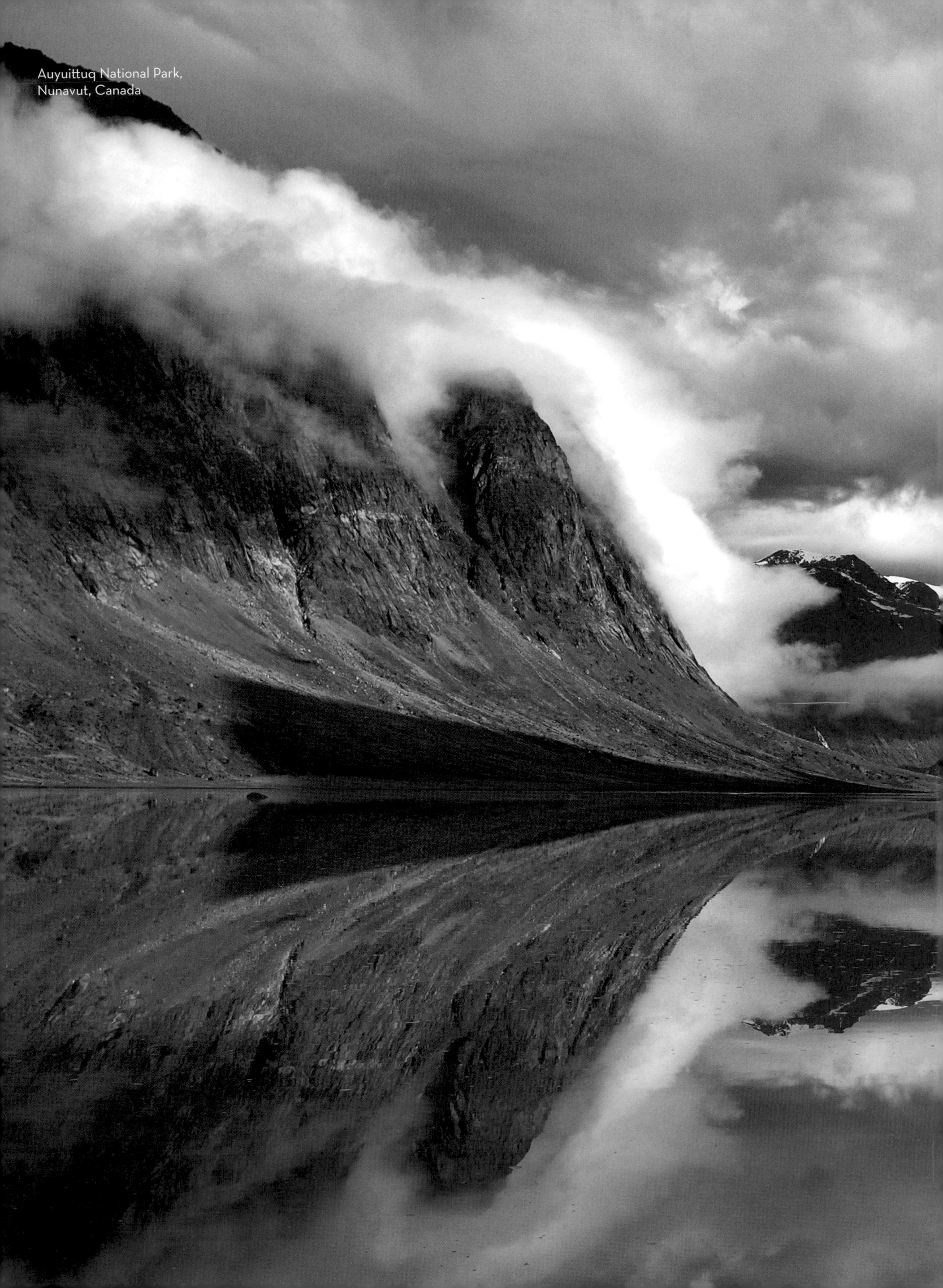

Auyuittuq National Park,
Nunavut, Canada

# World's Best Travel Experiences

## 400 EXTRAORDINARY PLACES

FOREWORD BY ANDREW MCCARTHY,
*NATIONAL GEOGRAPHIC TRAVELER* MAGAZINE EDITOR AT LARGE

NATIONAL GEOGRAPHIC

WASHINGTON, D.C.

Snorkeling at Virgin
Gorda in the British
Virgin Islands

# CONTENTS

Stockholm,
Sweden's
Gamla Stan
(Old Town)

# FOREWORD

BY ANDREW MCCARTHY, *NATIONAL GEOGRAPHIC TRAVELER* MAGAZINE EDITOR AT LARGE

The best place in the world? It's a big, brash, bold question. And the answer is easy—there are lots of them. For me, it's the crowded and chaotic suq in Marrakech, and that remote beach on the tiny atoll of Fakarava in the South Pacific. The rocky Burren in the rural west of Ireland, with the late day sun lingering over the Aran Islands, is the best place in the world. And so is my own backyard—New York City's Central Park.

What my best have in common is the ability to excite, to arouse big passions that allow—that demand—bold declarations: This is the best. My best is different from yours. Mine is different today than it was last year, and I bet it will be different next year. It's as subjective as a sunset, but we all know the feeling when a place, or a moment, takes our breath away and fills us with that feeling of connection, or that sense of discovery, or rediscovery; feelings of being lost, and then found—these are the experiences I search out while on the road.

Flipping the pages of this book I can't help but feel that excitement, that hope and sense of renewal. It makes me want to say, *Yes*—*yes* to possibility and adventure. *Yes* to places I've been, and to those I'm yearning to see—the pyramids of Egypt, the Galápagos, Petra, Nepal.

The best is a movable feast—the sweeping vistas of Patagonia to the back alleys of Barcelona; Costa Rica's wild Osa Peninsula to the canals of Venice; Vancouver's glass- and mountain-filled skyline to the gardens of Versailles. And the best is in the details—where to learn acupuncture in Beijing, or kayak the Cook Islands, or track down the best *macarons* in Paris. They're all here. From the Amazon to Zanzibar, the world's best have been assembled.

With some of the premier voices in writing—Mark Twain and Goethe, Paul Theroux and Jan Morris, Bill Bryson and Gore Vidal—and tapping into the finest of the National Geographic Society's legendary photography, the World's Best Travel Experiences are at your fingertips.

Say *yes*.

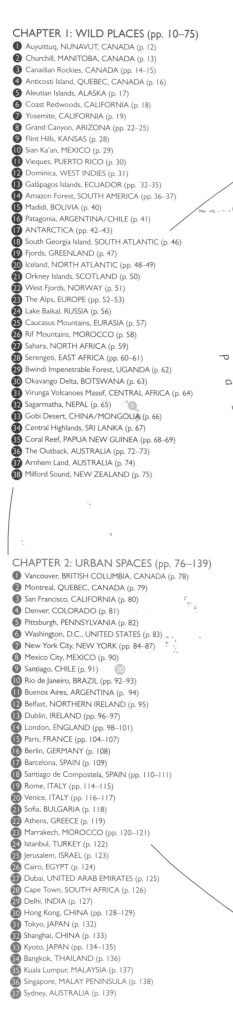

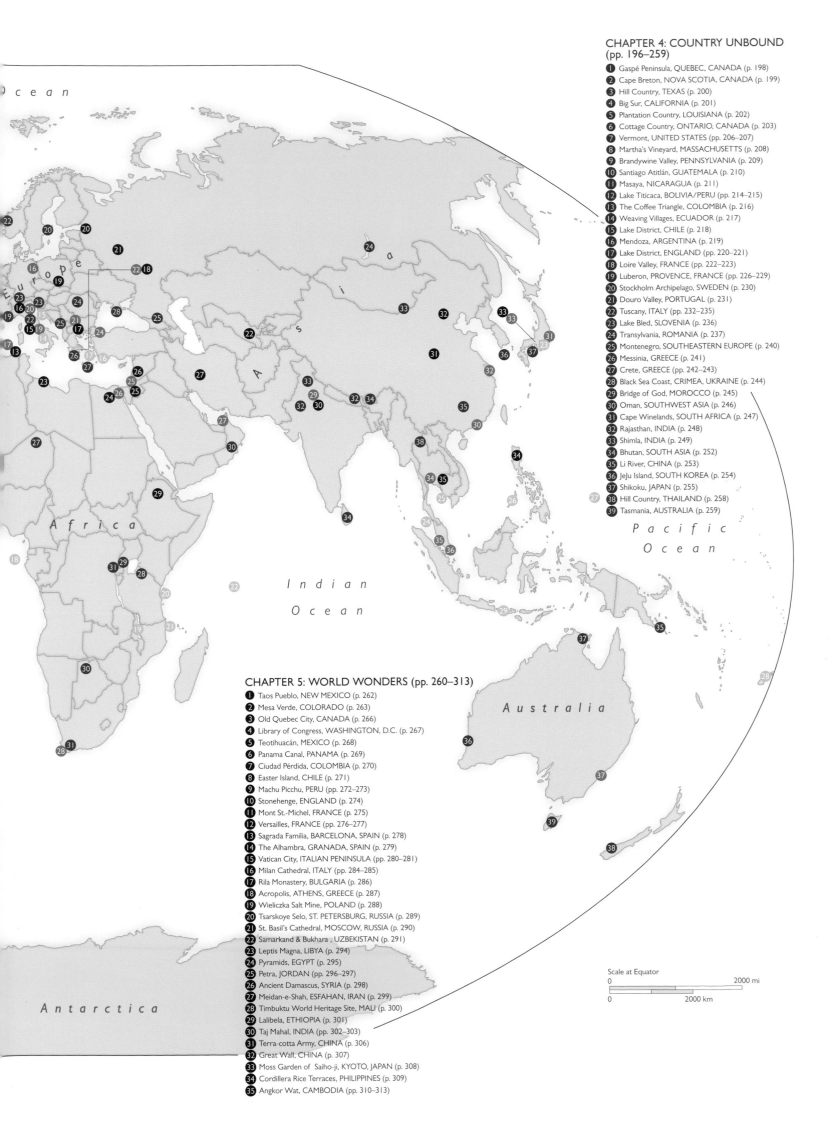

Scale at Equator
0          2000 mi
0          2000 km

# WILD PLACES

*Wildness Growing Ever More Precious*

Although our world seems to grow smaller with every year, vast, unspoiled wild places still exist. Protected by the extremes of geography and topography, many of these places demand time and effort from their visitors. Yet the reward they promise is great: the rejuvenation of the soul.

One of two active volcanoes in Zaire's Virunga Massif, Nyamula-gira spewed fire in 1989.

# AUYUITTUQ

Follow the midnight sun to the Arctic Circle.

Baffin Islanders like to joke that God didn't rest on the seventh day; he spent it throwing rocks at Baffin Island. Indeed, Auyuittuq National Park, jutting out toward Greenland from Baffin Island's Cumberland Peninsula, is an Arctic, glacial land of brutally high mountains. (God, evidently, had a good arm.) Another theory behind these rough, towering peaks: They are the handiwork of passing glaciers that dropped large, angular boulders known as erratics.

Auyuittuq, pronounced ow-YOU-ee-tuk and meaning "the land that never melts," is a redoubt of rock and glaciers, where fjords reach inland like crooked fingers. It is a place to savor soaring vistas of water, ice, and sky, inhabited only by the hardiest and most warmly dressed: sharp-hoofed caribou, arctic foxes, snowy owls, and lemmings. Polar bears like to den in the park's remote northeastern limits.

The Arctic Circle passes through the park and is most accessible in the near 24-hour daylight of early to mid-July (high water can lead to park closures in late July). Join a group that includes a boat trip and fjord hiking to explore this mystical land. The *inukshuk* (Inuit stone figure) marking the circle's location signifies what you'll most likely be thinking—"you are on the right path."

■ **PLANNING** **Auyuittuq National Park** www.parkscanada.gc.ca. Visit the park when the fjords are ice free, from mid-July–mid-Oct., but avoid the last week in July and first week in Aug. when water-related park closures are likely.

## ☙ BEST OF THE BEST ☙
### Akshayuk Pass

Ice-free Akshayuk Pass is one of the wildest and most dramatic valleys in this wild and dramatic place. Cutting across Baffin Island's Cumberland Peninsula from Pangnirtung Fjord in the south to Davis Strait in the north, the pass, which winds between upthrust mountains carved into otherworldly shapes, owes its deep, U-shaped profile to the glaciers that once filled it. When hiking, be prepared to cross frequent rubble mounds (the debris from glacial moraines) and several rivers. The best time for a crossing is between late July and mid-August.

Fierce weather rules all travel plans to—and through—Auyuittuq National Park.

The lights of the aurora dance over land that's best known for polar bears.

MANITOBA, CANADA

# CHURCHILL

Spot belugas from a boat or drop into the water for a closer look.

Accessible only by plane, train, or boat, and clinging to the bleak southwestern shore of Hudson Bay, Churchill has traded its historic status as a trading post, fort, and harbor for one as the Polar Bear Capital of the World. The best time for viewing polar bears is during October and November, when the animals—the largest land carnivores in the world—congregate along the shore of the bay and wait for the winter freeze. The ice provides a choice perch for hunting their favorite meal, the ringed seal.

But there are more than just bears to spot here. This remote corner of Manitoba is ideally situated for viewing beluga whales. Visit in the summertime, when the whales outnumber Churchill's human population of more than 1,000 by three to one. About 3,500 of the 25,000 belugas in Hudson Bay (a third of all belugas in the world) migrate to the Churchill River in June after wintering in the high Arctic.

Companies like family-owned Sea North Tours escort visitors via Zodiac boat, or custom-built 32-passenger tour boats, to encounter the toothed cetaceans, whose name comes from the Russian word *belukha,* the "white one." Those who favor more intimate encounters can snorkel or scuba dive in the (relatively) warm waters of the estuary—a limpid playground, a swimming pool, and a nursery for pale whales.

■ **PLANNING Churchill** www.churchill.ca. Churchill can be reached by air and rail only. Calm Air International and Kivalliq Air operate daily flights from Winnipeg. The VIA train departs from Winnipeg every Sun. and Tues. for the 48-hour trip. **Sea North Tours** www.seanorthtours.com.

### ✤ BEST OF THE BEST ✤
#### Polar Bear Tours

The best way to see polar bears in Churchill is through **Frontiers North** (*www.tundrabuggy.com*). This company's expert operators can arrange for visits to Cape Churchill, 18.5 miles (30 km) east of Polar Bear Point, which has the world's largest concentration of these big and beautiful creatures (a female weighs in at an average 660 pounds/299 kg, and a male at more than 1,300 pounds/590 kg). Guests stay at the Tundra Buggy Lodge, where they are pampered with around-the-clock bear viewing: In the morning, you can spot sleepy bears emerging from their Arctic snow quilts.

# CANADIAN ROCKIES

*Someone once said that the Canadian Rockies are 50 Switzerlands in one. They are as potent a landscape as you will find anywhere on the globe. Blues beyond belief. Peaks saddled with snow, oozing glaciers, and in summer drenched in wildflowers. Canada's Rockies are a northern paradise. Listen to the wind whisper the names that mark the map of this place: Jasper, Banff, Kootenay, Yoho, Takakkaw. It is a siren call hard to resist.*

*—*KEITH BELLOWS, EDITOR IN CHIEF, *NATIONAL GEOGRAPHIC TRAVELER* MAGAZINE

The jagged peaks of the
Canadian Rockies

Just 5,000 people get to explore the island each year.

# ANTICOSTI ISLAND

Hike through a mesmerizing canyon right to the foot of Vaureal Falls.

At the mouth of the St. Lawrence River, Anticosti Island, a wildlife sanctuary ten times the size of Manhattan, lures lucky visitors (only 5,000 allowed each season) with rare virtues: unadulterated wilderness and the virtual impossibility of crowds—that is, crowds of the human variety. There are 500 times more white-tailed deer than humans on the island. While

trucks with "deer bumpers" rocket down the Trans-Anticosti Expressway (the island's main drag), rivers serve as freeways for otters and beavers. The shore, meanwhile, is a thoroughfare for snowshoe hare, marten, moose, and ruffed grouse.

Discovered by Jacques Cartier in 1534, Anticosti was acquired by French chocolate magnate Henri Menier in 1895 and converted into an immense private hunting gallery. In 1975, the Quebec government turned about two-thirds of the island into a wildlife preserve.

Head into the wooded tangle, and thread your way through balsam fir, black spruce, white birch, and quaking aspen to Vaureal Falls. A 2-mile (3.2 km) hike through a canyon will lead you to a 250-foot (76 m) chute, loftier than Niagara Falls, where mist-thickened air is ribboned by rainbows and musky with the perfume of forest.

## ∽ IN THE KNOW ∽
### OFF-ROAD FOSSIL HUNTING

Rent a four-wheel-drive vehicle and head off down the only road leading east from Port-Menier to discover lonely beaches, the occasional shipwreck (more than 400 ships have gone down off Anticosti since the 1600s, earning it a reputation as the graveyard of the St. Lawrence), and sedimentary cliffs of Ordovician and Silurian limestone. Don a helmet and a headlamp and explore **Grotte à la Patate,** a cave system discovered in 1981 that is more than 1,969 feet (600 m) long. This is a choice spot for a fossil hunt: Fossils here are more than 370 million years old.

■ **PLANNING** Anticosti Island The island is accessible by air or car ferry only. For all-inclusive packages (including flight, accommodation, and car rental), consult Sépaq Anticosti (*www.sepaq .com*), which also manages all of the hotels, cabins, and campgrounds on the island.

ALASKA

# ALEUTIAN ISLANDS

Take in the extreme quiet and raw power of one of North America's most remote places.

Weather rules the world of this 1,100-mile (1,770 km) stretch of more than 200 islands and volcanoes hanging to the west off the Alaska Peninsula. More than in most any other place in the world, it is clear that the land here has been shaped by wind, water, ice, and time. This is where the North Pacific meets the Bering Sea. Although the landscape looks fragile and vulnerable when viewed on a map, the residents—including the Aleuts who first settled in the area around the second ice age—are some of the most steadfast in a state already known for its sturdy and determined people.

Though few venture there, the hardiest of travelers may opt to kayak near the dramatic Islands of Four Mountains, a starkly scenic group of volcanoes. This is one of the most remote pieces of this already remote chain. In three directions, snow-covered peaks can glisten pink as the light fades. "It takes so much to get out into a place this wild," photographer Barry Tessman told author Jon Bowermaster while they were paddling the area for a *National Geographic Traveler* magazine

piece, "that somehow it doesn't seem worth it. But now—right now—with all *this* around us, there's no place on the planet I'd rather be."

■ **PLANNING** Aleutian Islands www.travelalaska.com/Destinations/Regions/Southwest. **Alaska's Southwest Region** www.visitwildalaska.com/southwest_Alaska. **Alaska Marine Highway System** www.dot.state.ak.us/amhs.

## ❧ BEST OF THE BEST ❧
### Driving the Alaska Marine Highway

There are always flights down the chain, but a road trip is so much better—especially when that road trip is via the Alaska Marine Highway, the only marine route designated an All-American Road. The M/V *Tustumena* ferry makes the three-day trip down the chain, from Kodiak to Dutch Harbor (Unalaska), two times per month; book ahead if you want a cabin. You can also skip out on the cabin and do as a lot of locals do: Sleep on the comfy lounge chairs around the ship or set up a freestanding tent on the top deck (just remember to bring duct tape so the winds don't carry off the tent).

As the harsh winters subside, wild lupine signal the return of spring.

# COAST REDWOODS

Encounter Earth's tallest living things in the garden of the giants.

In the towering forests of northern California, years turn into centuries and then millennia, and the redwoods endure. Near the northern limit of the coast redwood's narrow range, Redwood National and State Parks—a composite of one national park and three state parks—preserve Earth's tallest living things, the remnants of a redwood forest that once covered two million acres (809,371 ha).

Beneath the redwood canopy, the sunlight is muted, a green-filtered radiance turning the redwoods into mysterious gray giants, some standing 350 feet (106 m) or more aboveground. Driving U.S. 101 through the park gives you a windshield-filled panorama of the redwood sentinels. But to appreciate the redwoods, you must walk among them.

Walk the 3.5-mile (5.6 km) Tall Trees Grove loop trail and stand amid the tallest of the tall. They're as ancient as they are soaring, estimated to be between 600 and 1,500 years old. Hyperion, the world's tallest tree at 379 feet (115 m), is in this watershed, but you won't find a sign to point it out and can't spot it reaching beyond the rest. From inside the grove, there is

no seeing to the top—about 50 feet (15 m) of the way up, each trunk disappears, like Jack's bean stalk, into the green clouds of its own foliage.

■ **PLANNING  Coast Redwoods** www.redwoods.info. **Redwood National and State Parks** www.nps.gov/redw. Free permits are required to access the Tall Trees Grove trailhead. Only 50 are issued daily (on a first-come, first-served basis) at the Thomas H. Kuchel Visitor Center.

## ~ IN THE KNOW ~
### REDWOOD RENAISSANCE

In 1978 Congress added 48,000 acres (19,425 ha) to the national park's 58,000 acres (23,472 ha), including about 36,000 acres (14,570 ha) that had been logged. The raw, clear-cut land, a park official wrote, had "the look of an active war zone." Today, in an epic earth-moving project, crews are beginning to reclaim vast stretches of logged-over lands. Hillsides, carved away for logging roads, are being restored. Most of the 400 miles (644 km) of roads are being erased. It will take at least 50 years for the scars of logging to disappear and another 250 or so years for the replanted redwood seedlings to grow to modest size.

California's redwoods can grow to heights of more than 350 feet (106 m).

Solid granite, El Capitan rises 3,000 feet (914 m) above Yosemite Valley.

## CALIFORNIA
# YOSEMITE

Explore the national park under the light of the full moon.

With granite mountains that hulk skyward and giant sequoias that have been alive since the Middle Ages, it's no wonder that Yosemite National Park's 1,200 square miles (3,100 sq km) attracts about four million people to California's Sierra Nevada every year. This land, dotted with meadows and waterfalls, is one of the first national parks in the United States, and, as John Muir wrote in the late 19th century, "No temple made with human hands can compare with Yosemite."

But to experience Yosemite at its dreamiest—indeed, in a way Muir once saw it—explore under the subtle light of the full moon. As the sun goes down, the crowds fade. A ghostly glow descends on the valley, and the waterfalls become brilliant streaks of white. The park offers moonlight tram rides several nights a month, but for a peaceful hike, Ranger Kari Cobb recommends the Sentinel Dome trail. "You get a 360-degree view of the entire park, and when it's a full moon you can see everything," she says, comparing the vista to a black-and-white photo. With less light, your other senses may heighten. Feel the contours of the granite under your feet, and savor the scent of the ponderosa pines—some say they make the entire park smell like vanilla and butterscotch.

■ **PLANNING** Yosemite www.nps.gov/yose. Moonlight tram tours are offered May through Oct. on the four nights leading up to the full moon and on the night of the full moon itself. Headlamps are recommended for night hiking.

### ～ IN THE KNOW ～
#### CLIMBING IN YOSEMITE

Big wall climbing evolved here in the 1960s, and today, climbers of all experience levels can find an appropriate challenge on the park's peaks. The Yosemite Mountaineering School teaches beginners and offers classes in self-rescue and ice climbing for the more advanced. If you'd still prefer to keep your feet on the ground, grab a pair of binoculars and head to El Capitan Meadow. There you can watch climbers scale and rappel on El Cap, the largest granite monolith in the world. Go at dusk to see the headlamps flicker on like fireflies. Visit www.yosemitepark.com to register for a guided climb or class.

# ADVENTURE TRIPS

Let the adrenaline race in some of the world's most beautiful places.

## 1 LAKE LOUISE
Banff, Canada

Surrounded by six glaciers, this icy blue lake in Banff National Park beckons ice-skaters in winter, paddlers in summer, and visitors year-round who stand on the pine-lined shore mesmerized by the Canadian Rockies' backdrop. See it all from 6,850 feet (2,088 m) by riding the Lake Louise Gondola (May–Sept.).
www.discoverlakelouise.com

## 2 MOAB
Utah

Biking slickrock brings great bragging rights among mountain bikers, while marathon runners take in the alpine mountains in the distance and the earthy tones of canyons along the Colorado River. The Old West is alive and well here, as cowboys still work the land and Native American influence is abundant.
www.discovermoab.com

## 3 WATER SPORTS
Southern West Virginia

Autumn colors swirl past in a roar when white-water rafting near Fayetteville on the Upper Gauley or New River in September and October. By contrast, just down the road a piece, on Summersville Lake, is silence broken only by the sound of an oar dipping into the placid water.
www.adventurewestvirginia.com

## 4 GRAND CAYMAN
Cayman Islands

With neon pink, yellow, and blue fish, green turtles, and dozens of species of coral, Grand Cayman offers up a con-stantly changing aquatic feast. The sandbar known as Stingray City is one of the world's few places to get intimate with stingrays in their natural habitat.
www.caymanislands.ky

## 5 RAIN FOREST
Costa Rica

Every turn in the road, every crest of a hill, every sunrise over a crocodile-infested river yields a new sight. Whether zip-lining high in the canopy and seeing toucans or the flamboyant scarlet macaw, or taking an aerial tram within inches of rare orchids and bromeliads, there isn't an inch from the Caribbean Sea on Costa Rica's east coast to the Pacific Ocean on the west coast that isn't a natural wonder.
www.rainforestadventure.com

## 6 RIO DE JANEIRO
Brazil

Hang gliding from atop Pedra Bonita for a soft landing on São Conrado Beach brings two landscapes together in a matter of minutes. While you are in the air, Sugar-loaf Mountain looms within reach, and Corcovado Mountain is in sight, with the iconic Christ the Redeemer statue.
www.riohanggliding.com

## 7 ISLE OF BUTE
Scotland

Take a hop, skip, and 90-minute jump from Glasgow to the heathered moors to the north. They offer rugged beauty, while the sandy beaches in Rothesay and the manicured gardens of Mount Stuart offer a completely different experience.
http://visitbute.com

## 8 AEOLIAN ISLANDS
Italy

Sailing through this chain of volcanic islands off the north coast of Sicily can be intoxicating. Pass by the largest island—Lipari—with its crumbling fortress, watch the sulfuric steam rising from the active craters of Stromboli and Vulcano, stare into the deep waters off the cliffs of Stromboli, or explore black-sand beaches.
www.bestofsicily.com

## 9 KRUGER NATIONAL PARK
South Africa

Not everyone gets a chance to witness the cycle of life from its unmerciful, violent side to its most breathtaking. Commune with majestic water buffalo, catch a glimpse of the menacing gaze of a hyena, and gain a deeper under-standing of the roles everyone plays in this cradle of mankind—from termites to vultures.
www.sanparks.org

## 10 QUEENSTOWN
New Zealand

Pick an extreme sport and imagine doing it on snowcapped mountains, in extreme weather, or with river spray in your face.you are likely to find it on the South Island of New Zealand. Just about anything goes, from heli-skiing to careening at high speeds near the rocky edge of a river in a jet boat to bungee jumping—in fact, bungee jumping was developed in Queenstown; the first trusting souls threw themselves off the town's Kawarau Bridge in 1988.
www.everythingqueenstown.com

Paragliding provides the ultimate view over Queenstown's Lake Wakatipu in New Zealand.

# GRAND CANYON

Worship at Earth's mile-deep temple.

If we want to feel huge, significant, and exalted, we go to one of America's last few remaining wild mountaintops and let the high winds press against us. But if we dare to realize who we are, we descend into temples of geology and time, and the greatest of these temples is arguably the Grand Canyon. In 1869 geologist John Wesley Powell, who led the first exploratory boat trip down the 1,450-mile (2,334 km) Colorado River, called the canyon the "most sublime spectacle on Earth."

Carving this chasm over the course of six million years, the Colorado created what may be the world's most comprehensive geological textbook. Stacked at the top are layers of ancient shale, sandstone, and limestone, telling stories

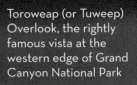

Toroweap (or Tuweep) Overlook, the rightly famous vista at the western edge of Grand Canyon National Park

of deserts, seas, and swamps that have covered the land over hundreds of millions of years.

## POSTCARDS FROM THE EDGE

Ever since the Santa Fe Railroad reached Grand Canyon Village in 1901, the South Rim has been a focal point for the park's five million visitors each year. About 90 percent of these wander to find their way to the overlooks and gaze down into the canyon, which is up to 18 miles (29 km) across and 4,800 feet (1,463 m) deep.

The classic place to start is Mather Point, with its panoramic view into the canyon, before striking out along

Located on Hualapai tribal land in Grand Canyon West, the Grand Canyon Skyway juts out 4,000 feet (1,220 m) above the canyon floor.

the historic, 7-mile (11.2 km) Hermit Road. Far below, a green cluster of Fremont cottonwood trees marks Phantom Ranch, a lodge and campground reached only by mule or by foot. At the observation station at Yavapai Point you can explore the geological history and identify major landmarks, and in poor weather it is an ideal spot to watch as the storm clouds roll in.

Many day hikers head for Indian Garden, 3,100 feet (945 m) below the trailhead at the top, which has a side trail that leads to Plateau Point, challenging even experienced hikers.

## Get Personal: Go North

The rugged isolation of the North Rim allows for a more intimate experience. Nearly 1,000 feet (305 m) higher in elevation than the South Rim, it is cooler, greener, and less crowded. Heavy snow closes the roads in winter, and spring runoff supports a forest of fir, spruce, aspen, and great stands of ponderosa pine. The focus is the historic Grand Canyon Lodge, built by the Union Pacific Railway in 1928 (and rebuilt after a disastrous fire). Made of rough-hewn logs and Kaibab limestone, the "Grand Canyon Lodge is one of the country's finest intact examples of railroad-constructed rustic architecture," says Stewart Fritts, one of the park's longest serving interpretive rangers.

From here, two scenic, short hikes await when you drive to the Cape Royal trailhead and take the paved trail to Angels Window, an opening eroded through the rock spur that frames the river below.

## Two Billion Years of Geology

Seeing the Grand Canyon from the river provides an adventurous perspective on the deep wilderness and chronology of the park. "Within a single vista you can experience two billion years of the earth's geological history," says Larry Stevens, a consulting ecologist at the Grand Canyon Wildlands Council.

Around almost every bend unfolds a new side canyon with ancient grottoes to explore. No roads reach the inner canyon; it's accessible only by boat or on strenuous trails. For about $250 per day, river runners tackle more than 160 world-class rapids and explore numerous side canyons. In spring you'll see colorful cactus blooms, while summer brings the monsoons that feed many side-canyon waterfalls. It's hard to look away from the fantastic display of the canyon itself, but also worth some attention is the amazing variety of wildlife, including elk, mountain lions, bighorn sheep, coyotes, and ringtails.

After the boat ride, walk the Trail of Time interpretative South Rim trail where a geologic time line leads backward in one-million-year increments toward the oldest rock in the canyon. Viewing tubes and interpretive markers help connect the rocks you saw from the river with specific spots on the time line.

■ **PLANNING Grand Canyon** www.nps.gov/grca. Check www.thecanyon.com/nps for information about fees, permits, and tours. **Grand Canyon Lodge** www.grandcanyonlodges.com.

## ☙ Best of the Best ❧
### Toroweap Overlook

Stand on the brink of the western canyon and experience what is often called the most inspiring view in Arizona. Accessible only by 61 miles (98 km) of primitive dirt road, Toroweap Overlook is also the perfect place to test your fear of heights: a 2,500-foot (762 m) rock face plummeting straight to the Colorado River. "Ancient lava flows topple over the bright orange canyon walls to the river like black frozen waterfalls," says Mike Anderson, a guide for the Grand Canyon Field Institute. Watch the river runners, far below, brave the rapids at Lava Falls, the largest white-water ride in the canyon, or just sit on the rim and take in the majestic charm.

Havasu Falls' 70°F (21°C) waters offer explorers a place to jump in after a long hike.

# IN TOUCH WITH NATURE

Interact with nature in some of the world's most dramatic—and most humble—settings.

## 1 TURTLES
### Holden Beach, North Carolina

The Holden Beach Turtle Watch Program, or Turtle Patrol, has been in operation for more than 20 years. Join forces with some 65 local volunteers to protect sea turtles by securing their nesting areas, tending to sick turtles, and helping baby turtles survive their epic journey to the ocean.
www.hbturtlewatch.org

## 2 RED-FOOTED BOOBIES
### Half Moon Caye, Belize

The crescent-shaped, white-sand island of Half Moon Caye is uninhabited by humans but home to more than 120 species of birds, including a colony of rare white red-footed boobies and a unique population of indigenous lizards and geckos. You can reach this UNESCO World Heritage site by boat.
www.ambergriscaye.com

## 3 GLACIERS
### Ilulissat, Greenland

*Ilulissat* means "icebergs" in Greenlandic, which is particularly apt given the town's location at the mouth of the 35-mile-long (56 km) Kangia Icefjord. Located 150 miles (250 km) north of the Arctic Circle, Ilulissat is ideally situated for contemplating the majestic scale and beauty of the ice fjord and Disko Bay.
www.ilulissaticefjord.com

## 4 GR20
### Corsica, France

One of Europe's toughest marked hiking trails, the GR20 (Grande Randonnée, or Great Walk) spans the length of Corsica and takes about 15 days to complete. The trail passes through dense forests and over dramatic mountain passes, skirts glacial lakes and pastures, and offers sweeping views of Corsica's dramatic coastline.
www.le-gr20.com

## 5 WETLANDS CANOE SAFARI
### Amsterdam, Netherlands

A peaceful Dutch landscape dominated by dense reed land, windmills, and 17th-century villages awaits just minutes from Amsterdam's busy canals and gabled houses. Surrounded by water plants, lush meadows, Frisian cows, and songbirds, you're plunged straight into the scenic world of Rembrandt and van Gogh.
www.wetlandssafari.nl

## 6 DE HOOP NATURE RESERVE
### South Africa

Some 40 percent of the world's population of southern right whales migrates to De Hoop to breed, providing visitors with unbeatable views of the females and their calves from its seemingly endless beaches.
www.dehoopcollection.co.za

## 7 OUR NATIVE VILLAGE ECO-RESORT
### Hessarghatta, India

Our Native Village is a 12-acre (5 ha) sustainable farm, 25 miles (40 km) north of Bangalore, operated as an eco-retreat where guests can reconnect with nature and the ancient ways of rural life. The resort boasts 24 comfortable rooms, a restaurant, and two spas.
www.ournativevillage.com

## 8 HONEY HUNTING
### Nepal

The ancient art of hunting honey is still practiced today in remote parts of Nepal. A "hunt" involves smoking the large Himalayan honeybees out of their hives, which cling to sheer cliffs, enabling a hunter to then clamber down a bamboo ladder to break off clumps of honeycomb. The unctuous booty offers an authentic taste of the Himalaya.
www.actual-adventure.com

## 9 CAMP LEAKEY
### Borneo

Established in 1971 by Dr. Biruté Mary Galdikas, Camp Leakey has remained a crucial point of primate research and conservation ever since. Located deep in the rain forests of Borneo, the camp enables visitors to walk with the inspirational Galdikas and watch the resident orangutans at play in their natural habitat.
www.orangutan.org

## 10 KAKAPO RECOVERY
### New Zealand

With just 127 living kakapo birds remaining in the world, New Zealand's indigenous parrot species needs all the help it can get. Join volunteers on the rugged Codfish and Anchor Islands, off the southern coast of South Island, two of the last bastions of the endangered kakapo, to assist with the preservation and recovery of what is probably the world's oldest living bird.
www.kakaporecovery.org.nz

Massive, mountain-like icebergs pack Greenland's Jakobshavn Fjord.

Tallgrass Prairie National Preserve glows gold in the fall and explodes with wildflower colors in early summer.

KANSAS

# FLINT HILLS

Wander the backcountry pathways of a rolling grassland sea.

Ribbons of unmarked roads crisscross the undulating Kansas Flint Hills—the last big remnant of the tallgrass prairie that once covered 170 million acres (69 million ha) of North America. Stretching from north to south, the 50-mile-wide (80 km) grassland sea upholsters the gentle, treeless slopes in layer upon layer of deep-rooted grasses. From midsummer to fall, velvety green, brown, and purple Indian grass, bluestem, and switchgrass can reach 3 to 8 feet (1 to 2.4 m) up into the brilliant blue midwestern sky.

Limestone and steely chert, or flint, hide just beneath the soil. Since farmers couldn't easily till the unforgiving soil, they switched to ranching, thus preserving the rolling and seemingly endless hills from agricultural and residential development.

It's possible to drive through the florid grassland in a few hours, but that would be missing the point. Instead, plan an early summer visit to explore the backcountry trails at Tallgrass Prairie National Preserve. Try hiking in silence to hear the gentle wind whispering through more than 300 species of wildflowers. Pause to watch monarch butterflies dancing amid the milkweed and bison grazing in a distant pasture. Sit a spell on any hill to soak it all in. Standing here is like stepping into a children's storybook illustration: big, round, Technicolor mounds rising like bread dough for as far as the eye can see.

## ∼ IN THE KNOW ∼
### WESTWARD HO

The Santa Fe Trail, the famed wagon route to the West, once cut through the Flint Hills but has virtually disappeared. The area's remaining local working ranches provide a living link to the tall-grass prairie's pioneer past and cowboy culture. Some, like the **Flying W** (*www.flinthillsflyingw.com*), an 1890s Cottonwood River Valley homestead in Cedar Point, welcome guests to bunk in rustic lodging, to ride horseback in pastures and on trails, and to lend a hand with daily cowboy chores. To appreciate why westward pioneers often walked when they could have ridden, take a bone-rattling ranch tour in a horse-drawn wagon.

■ **PLANNING** Flint Hills www.kansasflinthills.travel. **Tallgrass Prairie National Preserve** www.nps.gov/tapr. The preserve is located in northern Chase County, about 85 miles (136 km) northeast of Wichita. There's no entrance fee, and hiking trails are open 24 hours a day, year-round.

# MEXICO
# SIAN KA'AN

Venture beyond beaches and ruins to mysterious rain forests, cenotes, and ancient canals.

This living quilt of lowland rain forest, grassy savannas, and coastal barrier reefs blankets 1.3 million acres (526,000 ha) of Quintana Roo on the eastern Yucatán Peninsula. While technically part of Riviera Maya (Mexico's tourist playground), Sian Ka'an Biosphere Reserve is light-years removed from the region's all-inclusive megaresorts.

Set against the ivory shores of the Caribbean, the UNESCO World Heritage site offers visitors a glimpse of a peninsula untouched. Elusive jaguars, ocelots, Morelet's crocodiles, and howler monkeys still roam freely. Rare trees like mahogany and red and white cedar grow here. More than 300 species of birds, including the keel-billed toucan and the flamboyantly iridescent trogon, flit through the trees. Among the endemic species is the resplendent quetzal, sacred to the Aztec and the Maya.

Explore the reserve on a low-impact tour along the inland, freshwater canal built by Maya traders more than 1,200 years ago. Centro Ecologico Sian Ka'an (CESiaK), which oversees the visitor's center and uses its revenue to fund regional conservation efforts, leads guided treks to the partially excavated Muyil (Chunyaxché) archaeological site. For a treetop view of the surrounding ruins and jungle, climb the 50-foot-high (15 m) El Castillo pyramid, Muyil's tallest and best preserved structure.

■ PLANNING Sian Ka'an www.cesiak.org. Guests must follow the 1,200-year-old trade routes on foot and by boat with trained volunteers, marine biologists, and other scientists.

## ᘯ BEST OF THE BEST ᘰ
### Nearby Cenotes

One of the peninsula's deepest cenotes (sinkholes) is **Dos Ojos** (*www.cenotedosojos.com*), an exceptionally clear and long underwater cave system, with depths up to 387 feet (118 m), located 10.5 miles (17 km) north of Tulum. Family-friendly **Gran Cenote** (*www.grancenote.com*), 2.5 miles (4 km) from Tulum on the road to Cobá, boasts water so clear you won't need goggles to see the dramatic underwater stalagmites, stalactites, and columns. Zip-lining, dry caving, and snorkeling are available at **Cenote Labnaha** (*www.labnaha.com*), an ecopark 5 miles (8 km) north of Tulum that features cenotes connected by ecotrails.

Flamingos and more than 300 species of other birds put on an ever changing colorful show.

## PUERTO RICO
# VIEQUES

View a glow-in-the-dark undersea world through a clear-bottom canoe.

Neon turquoise waters bring a magical evening glow to this 21-mile-long (34 km), 3.7-mile-wide (6 km) island 8 miles (13 km) off Puerto Rico's eastern coast. Off the tourist grid until 2004 (when the U.S. military closed its bomb-testing naval base), Vieques's treasures—pristine beaches, mangrove-lined lagoons, and Vieques National Wildlife Refuge, home to sea turtles and manatees—now draw adventure seekers searching for uncharted Caribbean experiences.

The island has warded off most megaresorts and retains a gentle pace not easily found in Caribbean beach towns. Wild horses and free-range chickens roam parts of the island. The nightlife hot spot is wet and wild Bioluminescent Bay (Puerto Mosquito), where millions of microscopic dinoflagellates illuminate when agitated, sparking an undersea light show.

The glowing bio-bay is best viewed during new moons, particularly on clear nights when the sky is indigo-black and dotted with stars. Hop aboard a clear-bottom canoe and head out into the bay. The guides explain the biology behind the bioluminescent sparkle, but chances are you'll be more focused on the living art exhibit below. Wiggle your fingers in the water to add your own swirl of vibrant color to the magical scene.

◢ **PLANNING** **Vieques** www.viequestourism.com. **Biolumines-cent Bay** www.biobay.com. **Vieques Adventure Company** www.viequesadventures.com. Canoe excursions offered.

## ∼ IN THE KNOW ∼
### WHY DOES THE WATER GLOW?

Bioluminescence is the production and emission of light, often in the violet to green spectrum, by living organisms like fire-flies, glowworms, jellyfish, squid, and even mushrooms. In the case of Vieques, microorganisms called dinoflagellates, the same marine plankton that cause red tide, are responsible. The plankton feed on the dead leaves of the endemic red mangrove trees that surround the water. Much about the process of bioluminescence is still being discovered today, and the 18 bioluminescent genera of dinoflagellates continue to perplex zoologists and botanists who, until recently, had classified them separately.

# DOMINICA

Rappel into volcanic bedrock canyons on an exhilarating canyoneering tour.

Wild, rugged, and waiting to be explored, Dominica—the Nature Island—is the Caribbean beyond the white sandy beach. Perpetual geothermal and volcanic activity (there are seven active volcanoes) and rare oceanic rain forests create a Hawaiian-like landscape on this lush paradise located between Guadeloupe and Martinique.

Survey your surroundings on a strenuous 7-mile (11 km) round-trip hike from Titou Gorge to Boiling Lake (a vapor-covered cauldron billed as the world's second largest hot springs). The payoffs are plentiful: panoramic ocean views from atop 3,000-foot (914 m) Morne Nicholls and brightly colored sulfur springs, mini-geysers, and bubbling mud pools in the Valley of Desolation. Hire a guide to take you there.

If hiking is too tame for you, plunge into the backdrop on a guided canyoneering tour. After a short training session (and with helmet and life vest secured), you'll rappel down pristine waterfalls, deep gorges, and volcanic bedrock canyons. The payoff for each exhilarating descent is the dramatic view back up the towering walls. Recharge at Secret Bay, a bungalow and villa retreat perched on the northwest coastal cliffs. Floor-to-ceiling windows and sustainably sourced Guyanese greenheart hardwood produce a tree-house feel, albeit one with a Jacuzzi for soaking your sore muscles.

■ **PLANNING Dominica** www.dominica.dm. **Extreme Dominica** www.extremedominica.com. One of many operators offering canyoneering. **Secret Bay** www.secretbay.dm.

## ❦ BEST OF THE BEST ❧
### The Parrots of Morne Diablotin

Morne Diablotin dominates the 22,000-acre (8,903 ha) Northern Forest Reserve in the island's northern interior. At 4,747 feet (1,447 m), it's the island's highest peak and the main residence for two endangered parrot species unique to the island: the jaco (green, red, and yellow) and the magnificent purple and green imperial sisserou. The Syndicate Parrot Preserve has designated lookout stations. Dawn and dusk are the best times to catch a glimpse of the parrots, or at least flashes of winged color in the foliage. Bring binoculars and follow the 0.75-mile (1.2 km) Syndicate loop trail, stopping at each overlook to scan the forest for birds.

Seemingly endless, the green canopy harbors colorful parrots that pass just overhead.

# GALÁPAGOS ISLANDS

Commune with the unique species that helped inspire Darwin's theory.

A re the Galápagos Islands enchanted? Mariners once thought so. In the early days of global exploration, seafarers had trouble locating the caldera-pocked archipelago, and thus arose the legend that the islands were drifting randomly around the Pacific Ocean. Spanish sailors originally named them Islas Encantadas, or the Enchanted Isles.

Today the Galápagos Islands cast a spell that's part Peter Pan, part *Jurassic Park*—a glorious blend of arrested development and creatures from our primeval past. Ninety-seven percent of the archipelago's 21 islands is a park, fiercely protected by Ecuador and a phalanx of international agencies. Straying from the marked trails is verboten, lest one stumble into a field of turtle nests or the private domain of some rare creature.

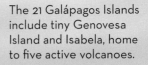

The 21 Galápagos Islands include tiny Genovesa Island and Isabela, home to five active volcanoes.

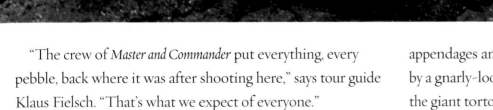

"The crew of *Master and Commander* put everything, every pebble, back where it was after shooting here," says tour guide Klaus Fielsch. "That's what we expect of everyone."

## WORLDS OF WONDER

There's no more wondrous place on Earth to amuse (and educate) kids. Suddenly they're willing to drop their electronic appendages and walk miles over baking lava to stand transfixed by a gnarly-looking iguana, a scuttling Sally Lightfoot crab, or the giant tortoises that gave the islands their name.

Leapfrogging by boat from Santa Cruz, home to Galápagos National Park headquarters and the Charles Darwin Research Station, you'll appreciate how each island features animals and plants that have adapted to their particular remote

The blue-footed booby may be the islands' most famous avian resident, but it's not alone. Here is a red-footed booby.

environment. After his visit in 1835, Darwin referred to the effect of geographic isolation and natural selection on genes.

## ISLAND-HOPPING BY *PANGA*

Each day brings a new island, a glimpse of a very old new world, and never-again adventures. Through thick fog, huge green turtles give the beady eye to visitors arriving on a *panga*, a motorized rubber boat, at the western isle of Fernandina. The animals are curiously unfazed by these two-legged visitors, partly because there are no natural land predators larger than a hawk. Don't be surprised if a sea lion or a refugee from tuxedo junction (yes, there are penguins at the Equator) waddles over to check you out.

On tiny Genovesa Island, the bushes are thick with male frigatebirds, wings extended to 6.5 feet (2 m). Everywhere red-footed boobies perch like lawn ornaments. Carpets of black, gargoyle-faced marine iguanas, squashed atop one another in easy camaraderie, molt in the baking sun. If snorkeling is on your agenda, first consider the unsettlingly clear waters revealing 4-foot (1.2 m) moray eels, 6-foot (1.8 m) Galápagos sharks, and 9-foot (2.7 m) manta rays. Don't worry: All these bellies are most likely already fat with more suitable and abundant prey.

## UPSETTING THE APPLECART

We all think that Darwin's island laboratory was a place where nature emerged at a remove from the outside world. On the island of Santiago we learn something different. Early visitors to the Galápagos, many of them pirates, introduced cats, dogs, donkeys, goats, pigs, and other species that upset the evolutionary applecart.

"The single biggest challenge to the Galápagos Islands today is the introduction of invasive species," says Johannah Barry, president of the Galápagos Conservancy. "This is an ongoing, critical battle for the long-term health of this iconic world treasure." The national park enforces strong quarantine and containment measures on the islands and the mainland and it is working on control and eradication with the Charles Darwin Foundation and other institutions. On Bartolomé, a small, fish-shaped island, a thin neck of land at the western end separates two white-sandy beaches, and on the other side a trail leads steeply to a volcanic summit. The beach is an ordinary-looking place where extraordinary things happen. Snorkelers cruise the shallow bay as brown pelicans drop into the water like brown bombs, competing for fish with those black-and-white charmers, the penguins. Overhead, a booby folds its wings and knifes bill-first into the water, narrowly missing a snorkeler and a penguin.

Are the Galápagos enchanted? Perhaps not. But enchanting? No question about it.

■ **PLANNING** **Galápagos Islands** www.galapagospark.org. **Galápagos Conservancy** www.galapagos.org. **Charles Darwin Foundation** www.darwinfoundation.org.

## PLACES THAT CHANGED ME
*Charles Darwin, excerpt from* **The Voyage of the Beagle**

Considering the small size of the islands, we feel the more astonished at the number of their aboriginal beings, and at their confined range. Seeing every height crowned with its crater, and the boundaries of most of the lava-streams still distinct, we are led to believe that within a period geologically recent the unbroken ocean was here spread out. Hence, both in space and time, we seem to be brought somewhat near to that great fact—the mystery of mysteries—the first appearance of new beings on this earth.

Impress guides by calling out the scientific name of the Sally Lightfoot crabs: *Grapsus grapsus.*

# AMAZON FOREST

Slow time down by disappearing—at least temporarily—into the thick of the Amazon forest.

Amazon river dolphins forage for food.

The Amazon by day is a place of plants, water, and silence. The overwhelming grandeur of the tropical rain forest lies in its subtlety. There are no herds of ungulates as on the Serengeti Plain, and there are few cascades of orchids. Just a thousand shades of green, an infinitude of shape, form, and texture that mocks the terminology of temperate botany. It is almost as if you could close your eyes and hear the constant hum of biological activity, of evolution working in overdrive.

Creepers lash themselves to tree trunks, and herbaceous heliconias and calatheas give way to broad-leafed aroids, such as philodendrons, that climb into the shadows. Overhead,

lianas drape from immense trees, the vines blinding the canopy of the forest into a single interwoven fabric of life. As British writer and adventurer Peter Fleming wrote in 1934, "You can believe what you like about those regions: no one has authority to contradict you. You can postulate the existence . . . of prehistoric monsters, of white Indians, of ruined cities, of enormous lakes."

## IQUITOS, PERU

Peru's main Amazon outpost, Iquitos, is 2,300 weaving miles (3,700 km) from the river's mouth by the Atlantic Ocean and accessible only by boat or airplane. It is hot and steamy, smelling of smoke and fish and rain on concrete. When *National Geographic Traveler* magazine contributing editor Carl Hoffman visited, he found "a humid circus" of "jugglers and a transvestite clown; couples holding hands; sellers of balloons and chicle gum and earrings; beggars and shoe-shine boys. But this is the Amazon, and hints of the romantic primitive are all around."

## WILDLIFE

Pygmy marmosets. Scarlet macaws. Jaguars. Butterflies in color combinations so bright they would make the works of

## PLACES THAT CHANGED ME

Jenna Schnuer, National Geographic Traveler *magazine writer*

Halfway into a four-hour trip down the river in a barely motor-ized wooden boat, the engine sputtered and stopped. The guide pulled the cord once, twice, and again, and the engine agreed to one last go, enough to get us to an oil-drilling station so the guide could borrow the necessary replacement parts. During the first while of the extra two hours on Río Napo, we all went quiet. I imagined—as I'm sure everybody else in the boat did—days spent at the drilling station instead of at Sani Lodge (www .sanilodge.com) on Challuacocha Lake. Then, one by one, we all relaxed back into the robin's-egg blue and white wooden boat seats. We would get there when we got there. This was already unlike anything else we had experienced before.

Andy Warhol or Roy Lichtenstein look gray in comparison. The Amazon's 2.6 million square miles (7 million sq km) is home to one-tenth of Earth's known species (including some of the largest bugs you'll ever care to meet). But no matter the marvels of the animals you expect to see in the wild, there is something beyond thrilling about the first time a wild parrot flies overhead. Right at that moment, the world feels like a much more intimate place.

■ **PLANNING** **Amazon Forest** www.amazon-rainforest.org. **Peru** www.visitperu.com. **Iquitos** www.go2peru.com/Iquitos_travel_guide.htm. The major international airport for Iquitos is Lima's Aeropuerto Internacional Jorge Chávez. **Amazonian Wildlife** www.worldwildlife.org.

The San Rafael waterfall thunders down in Ecuador's Amazonian zone.

# VOLUNTEER ANIMAL RESCUE

Reconnect with your own humanity by helping to rehabilitate at-risk animals.

## 1 THE OASIS SANCTUARY
Cascabel, Arizona

Oasis offers a lifetime home in natural habitats to unadoptable psittacines (parrots, cockatoos, and macaws). Psittacines can live as long as humans, and their care is complex and demanding; casually purchased birds often end up unwanted. Volunteers help with care and habitat enrichment.
http://the-oasis.org

## 2 BEST FRIENDS ANIMAL SANCTUARY
Kanab, Utah

Founded in the 1980s, the largest no-kill sanctuary in the United States, set on 33,000 acres (13,355 ha) in Utah canyon land, shelters, rehabs, and re-homes dogs, cats, horses, potbellied pigs, birds, and wildlife. If an animal cannot be re-homed, it lives out its life in the loving shelter environment.
www.bestfriends.org

## 3 THE WILD ANIMAL SANCTUARY
Keenesburg, Colorado

This 720-acre (291 ha) sanctuary shelters large carnivores (lions, tigers, wolves, coyotes, leopards) rescued from circuses, carnival shows, and "collectors." Visitors observe the animals living in free-roaming habitats from elevated walkways.
www.wildanimalsanctuary.org

## 4 WOODSTOCK FARM ANIMAL SANCTUARY
Willow, New York

The Woodstock Farm Animal Sanctuary offers a true home in the country to chickens, cows, goats, pigs, turkeys, and other animals rescued from factory farms. Besides sheltering animals, the sanctuary educates the public about the living conditions of food animals on commercial farms.
http://woodstocksanctuary.org

## 5 SAVE A SATO
San Juan, Puerto Rico

Puerto Rico is overrun with thousands of *satos,* homeless street dogs, scrounging for survival. This shelter takes in, feeds, and medicates the abandoned canines, then partners with shelters in the U.S. to find happy homes for them. Visitors leaving Puerto Rico via American Airlines to select U.S. cities are needed to escort dogs on flights.
http://saveasato.org

## 6 THE DONKEY SANCTUARY
Sidmouth, Devon, England

The poor man's horse or car, donkeys are worked relentlessly all over the world but often abandoned after their working days are over. This sanctuary, which has cared for hundreds of donkeys and mules, encompasses several farms. Slade Hill Farm located at the main headquarters is the only farm open to the public.
www.thedonkeysanctuary.org.uk

## 7 ENKOSINI WILDLIFE RESERVE
Outside Lydenburg, South Africa

Enkosini Wildlife Reserve ("place of kings" in Zulu), founded in 2001, was created from former South African farms. Volunteer opportunities are available in projects including baboon and vervet monkey rescue and at the Noah's Ark Wildlife Centre.
www.enkosinicoexperience.com

## 8 KARUNA SOCIETY FOR ANIMALS & NATURE
Puttaparthi, Andhra Pradesh, India

Established in 2000, Karuna ("compassion" in Sanskrit) treats and shelters sick, abused, or injured animals in Puttaparthi and surrounding areas. Volunteers are asked to commit a month to projects that include animal birth control, vaccination initiatives, and a center that rescues sloth bears, sambar deer, and monkeys.
www.karunasociety.org

## 9 BOON LOTT'S ELEPHANT SANCTUARY
Thailand

This sanctuary is home to "elephants being elephants"—no performances or exploitation. Guests stay at huts on 400 forested acres (162 ha) and may volunteer to help the Thai mahouts bathe and care for the elephants.
www.blesele.org

## 10 CHENGDU MOONBEAR RESCUE CENTER
Chengdu, China

This center, associated with the Animals Asia Foundation, is home to Asian black bears rescued from the horrific life of "bile bears," kept in small, crushing cages and "milked" for bile used in traditional Chinese medicine. During two days each month, staff members lead small groups on sanctuary tours.
www.animalsasia.org

Get up close and personal with cockatoos and other animals at Best Friends Animal Sanctuary in Kanab, Utah.

## BOLIVIA
# MADIDI
See more wildlife than you ever thought possible.

Glacier-clad mountains in the west drop down to cloud forests in the east. Then come the vast grasslands and lowland forests. This is Bolivia's Madidi National Park, opened by supreme decree in 1995, a 4.7-million-acre (1.9 million ha)

park of dramatically varying altitudes spread across Chalalán and San José in the northwest of the country. No other place in Bolivia—or, for that matter, most of the world—teems with as much wildlife.

Guides are a must. They'll lure out the peccaries—wild pigs that, quite simply, you don't want to go head-to-head with on your own. The guides snap their fingers against their cheeks to imitate the sounds of the animals cracking palm nuts with their teeth.

By the time author Tim Cahill visited Madidi, he'd already spent a good deal of time in the Amazon and other tropical forests. In most areas, Cahill wrote, "you almost never see living creatures. But here in Madidi, I was seeing more wildlife than I'd ever seen before"—including, while on a boat, "bats hanging in a dank cave."

■ **PLANNING Chalalán Ecolodge** www.chalalan.com. Run by the local indigenous community, Chalalán Ecolodge is your best source for information about Madidi National Park and available tours. With room for up to 28 guests, Chalalán can be reached by boat from the city of Rurrenabaque.

---

### ❧ BEST OF THE BEST ❧
#### Must-See Wildlife

With the possibility of so much wildlife at hand, it's worth putting in requests to your guides if one or another animal ranks high on your must-see list. Here are five you'll remember forever: **Caimans** are best viewed at night, when flashlights shined into the grasses along the water make their eyes glow bright. **Jaguars,** the largest of South America's big cats, are strong swimmers and can climb trees to ambush prey. Once almost hunted out of existence in the area, **squirrel monkeys** have been making a comeback. An omnivore, the **white-lipped peccary** lives in herds of up to hundreds of animals. The **capybara,** the world's largest rodent, can swim underwater for up to five minutes.

## ARGENTINA, CHILE
# PATAGONIA

Explore granite spires and glacial waterfalls beneath dramatic snowcapped peaks.

Carved by pristine fjords and capped by glistening glaciers, Patagonia is a vast wonderland. "Patagonia is a land encompassing almost all of nature," says Argentine native Sandra Borello. "You have whale-watching in Península Valdés from its high cliffs, to skiing in Bariloche, which feels like being in Switzerland, to dramatic glaciers like Perito Moreno, and the Andes Mountains hovering over it all."

From the east, the region begins as wave-washed cliffs hugging the Atlantic. West against the Andes rise the Torres del Paine, a dramatic triplet of mountain summits, with Chile's Lake District spilling out below. The region's roads have been traversed and put into words by legends as diverse as Che Guevara and Bruce Chatwin.

Patagonia's crown jewel is Torres del Paine National Park in southern Chile. Base yourself at the park's Explora Lodge, located on the shores of Lago Pehoé, for a week of hiking and horseback riding amid granite spires, glacial lakes, and waterfalls. Discover Grey Lake and its incredibly blue ice sculptures, trek through southern beech forests along the shore of Laguna Azul, and encounter one of Patagonia's most beloved residents—the once endangered guanaco (wild counterpart of the domesticated llama).

■ **PLANNING** Patagonia www.argentina.travel. **Torres del Paine National Park** www.parquetorresdelpaine.cl. **Explora Lodge** www.explora.com.

## PLACES THAT CHANGED ME
*Michael Luongo*, National Geographic Traveler *magazine writer*

———◆⟫⟫⟫⟫⟫⟩⟨⟨⟨⟨⟨⟨◆———

We had just come down the path leading toward the Perito Moreno glacier when we heard it: the strange, deafening crunching sound of ice grinding on itself. We heard it long before we saw it. As we came around the bend, the glacier's awesome sky-blue wall of ice, more than 200 feet (60 m) high, suddenly revealed itself. For me, the Perito Moreno glacier was the one part of Patagonia no one should miss, and it changed my view of Argentina altogether. Until that moment, most of what I knew of the country was the city of Buenos Aires. Now I had a better understanding of the country's rugged, powerful, natural beauty.

With boosts from a nearby ice field, Perito Moreno Glacier keeps growing.

# ANTARCTICA

*Nature's color-schemes in the Antarctic are remarkably crude, though often wondrously beautiful. Bright blues and greens are seen in violent contrast with brilliant reds, and an accurate record of the colours displayed in a sunset, as seen over broken ice, would suggest to many people an impressionistic poster of the kind seen in the London streets.*

— ERNEST SHACKLETON, *THE HEART OF THE ANTARCTIC*, 1909

Though many climbers only have eyes for the area's highest peak, Vinson Massif, nonclimbers will find its shorter cousins just as memorable.

# EXTREME ENVIRONMENTS

Be inspired anew at the world's most intense places—and at your own strength in discovering them.

**1 TUCSON, ARIZONA**
A seeming paradise that claims to have 350 sunny days a year, Tucson boasts geological beauty and hiking so fantastic that visitors can be lulled into a false sense of security. Be warned: It isn't unusual for temperatures to soar higher than 110°F (43°C) in summer months, when the rocks and cement can hold that heat well into the evening hours.
www.visittucson.org

**2 KILLINGTON, VERMONT**
This popular skiing area, which has some of New England's highest mountain terrain, goes from extreme icy, nor'easter conditions in winter to warm summer days to perfectly crisp and golden autumns.
www.killingtonchamber.com

**3 GRENADA**
Known as the Isle of Spice for its abundance of nutmeg, cinnamon, and cloves, Grenada is one of the southern-most Windward Islands in the Caribbean Sea. Its spices have been devastated by hurricanes in the last decade. The central mountainous terrain's cooler air and waterfalls produce a near-constant cloud cover of condensation.
www.grenadagrenadines.com

**4 SOUTHERN BELIZE**
With flash rainstorms that instantly fill the dirt roads and humidity that makes it one of the greenest places on Earth, this Maya wonderland is home to the longest barrier reef in the Western Hemisphere and the deepest diving—the Blue Hole. But it is the back roads of the Toledo district, where rain forest meets jungle safari, that truly inspire awe.
www.travelbelize.org

**5 NEWFOUNDLAND & LABRADOR, CANADA**
This Canadian province, which sits at the eastern edge of North America, encroaches on the home of 22 whale species and dozens of seabirds that play among the icebergs. While the capital city of St. John's can be quite mild, the actual island of Newfoundland has more extreme and unpredictable weather moods.
www.newfoundlandandlabrador.com

**6 GRÍMSEY, ICELAND**
This island straddling the Arctic Circle is the northernmost point of inhabitable space in Iceland. It is a small, rocky island with little vegetation, only a few hundred permanent residents, and cliffs teeming with arctic birds known as puffins, which seem oblivious to the chill as they dive-bomb from high on the rocks into the Arctic Ocean for food.
www.visiticeland.com

**7 CUENCA, SPAIN**
Known as the walled city because of its "hanging houses" atop (or actually part of) walls carved out of a rocky hillside in the 15th century, Cuenca's fortress-like facade sits imposingly above the Jucar River gorge. The houses, which bake in the high summer temperatures, are now home to an abstract art museum reached by crossing a wooden pedestrian swinging bridge.
www.spain.info

**8 MONT BLANC**
The highest mountain in the Alps lies between Italy and France, and you'll feel the altitude—15,782 feet (4,810 m) above sea level—if you are not accustomed to it. Its location lends itself to prime skiing and snowboarding, and the blaze of ice and snow at the top is a sharp contrast to the warmth and glow coming from the shops and cafés in Chamonix, France, at its base.
www.mountblanc.net

**9 NORTHERN NORWAY**
From the world's strongest tidal current at Saltstraumen to the city of Bodø, this area is especially bewitching during the winter's northern lights (aurora borealis), which may keep you up late into the cold night. Nothing feels as warm as a hearty lunch of reindeer stew outside on benches covered in reindeer skins after hiking the peaks and valleys of the Svartisen Glacier—actually a 143-square-mile (370 sq km) multiple glacier system—renowned for its deep blue ice and relatively easy accessibility.
www.visitnorway.com

**10 SOUTH CHINA SEA**
Taking a day trip by boat from Hong Kong to one of the 235 outlying islands can quickly turn into a battle against the chop—and seasickness. But the sparsely inhabited destination will prove nothing short of surreal, with little to distract from the beauty of its ornate ancestor shrines and the movements of fishermen at work.
www.discoverhongkong.com

Nearly 1,000 feet (300 m) deep, Belize's aptly named Blue Hole is a 410-foot (125-m) underwater playground for divers.

# SOUTH GEORGIA ISLAND

Flock to this island to see thousands of penguins.

Like a stone accidentally dropped in the Southern Ocean, South Georgia Island lies about 800 miles (1,300 km) east of the Falkland Islands and at the edge of mankind's inhabitable world. The island is rugged and treeless, and its mosses, lichens, and grasses hug the ground, as if deliberately ducking from the high winds and cold air. Yet the surrounding Antarctic Ocean brims with life. Phytoplankton thrive in these waters and draw krill, squid, fur seals, and various species of whale: fin, humpback, southern right, and minke. But more than anything, this island attracts penguins—hundreds of thousands of them.

Arrive by boat—the only way to get here—in the Antarctic summer to see the king penguins populate the vast glacial plain, their white bellies and dark backs roaming the 1,450-square-mile (3,800 sq km) island purposefully. During their brief breeding season they eat heartily, getting into top form to court, to display, to mate, and to raise their chicks. Some call it the greatest wildlife spectacle of all. Naturalist Brent Houston puts it this way: "If the doctors told me I had only two weeks to live, I'd spend one week on South Georgia and the other week getting there."

■ **PLANNING** South Georgia Island www.sgisland.gs. Most people visit South Georgia Island by cruise ship. For a directory of companies that offer tours in the Antarctic region, go to http://apps.iaato.org/iaato/directory/list.jsf.

---

### ∽ IN THE KNOW ∽
#### ERNEST HENRY SHACKLETON

Great Antarctic explorer Sir Ernest Henry Shackleton died on South Georgia Island during his last expedition. He never met his goal of reaching the South Pole, but he's known for saving his crew after ice crushed and eventually sank their ship, *Endurance*. About 500 days after setting foot on land, the crew escaped in lifeboats to the South Shetland Islands. Shackleton then sailed about 800 miles (1,300 km) in a whaleboat to South Georgia to seek aid. He eventually rescued his men. On a later trip, in 1922, Shackleton had a heart attack on South Georgia. His grave symbolizes his deep connection to the hostile, beautiful landscapes of the polar regions.

---

The island's permanent residents relax on a sunny day.

# FJORDS

Feel the chill of one of the world's most active glaciers.

Glacial melt-
water flows into
Tasermiut fjord.

With temperatures dipping to minus 20°F (-29°C) even in early spring, it would take a very special event to pry people from the warmth of their beds in the middle of the night. But from September to early April in Greenland, the dark night sky often starts to pulse and swirl from the north with the mysterious and haunting colors of the aurora borealis.

## ∽ IN THE KNOW ∽
### DOGSLEDDING

Dogsleds are often the most efficient way to get from place to place in Greenland—provided you don't bump into a polar bear along the way, a rare but not unprecedented event. For an island nation of slightly more than 56,000 people, Greenland has a sizable sled-dog population of 25,000. If, after a sled ride or two, you're anxious for more, visit the east coast fjord town of Tasiilaq; after a two-day course, you'll walk away with a license to drive your own team of eight dogs. For information about tour providers and accommodation, consult www .eastgreenland.com.

Light plays a big part in Greenland adventures; there's very little of it during the winter, and nothing but it during the summer months. Either way, the dramatic landscape of Greenland's fjords delivers. On the west coast, the town of Ilulissat sits at the mouth of an ice fjord thick with icebergs that calved from the Sermeq Kujalleq glacier, the accompanying sound alerting people miles away to the activity. One of the world's most active glaciers, Sermeq Kujalleq has no rivals outside of Antarctica. You'll do well to experience the area from several perspectives: on foot, by boat, and, in the ultimate flyover, by helicopter. Just remain flexible in your plans: Greenland's weather is the ultimate decider.

The natural sculptures of icebergs and glaciers play with light, some areas translucent, others a robin's-egg blue. Icebergs shift ever so slightly, some bobbing in the water, looking deceptively smaller and lighter than their true bulk. But then just like that, they shift, roll, or shed thousands of pounds of ice.

■ **PLANNING** Greenland Fjords www.greenland.com. **Ilulissat Icefjord** www.ilulissaticefjord.com.

# ICELAND

Discover a haunting land of fire and ice.

Vestmannaeyjar is home to the world's largest puffin colony.

I celand has always been a loner, both culturally and geologically. The young Arctic-adjacent island is born of the subterranean fires deep below the Mid-Atlantic Ridge and roils aboveground with volcanoes, geysers, bubbling mud, and thermal lagoons. What's left behind—lava-tube caves, vertical cliffs gushing with shimmering waterfalls, and more than a dozen glacier-capped calderas—has become part of the island's physiographic makeup and provides ideal spots to witness the aurora borealis.

Culturally, this mountainous island nation has a muddled early history that includes fierce Norsemen, banished Vikings, Celtic monks, and Scottish hermits, creating a heritage laced with an independent streak that dates from the ninth century A.D. Today the welcoming people are known for their quirkiness as much as for their hospitality and sense of humor.

## MUSIC IN REYKJAVÍK

In the 1990s, music phenomenon Bjork helped usher in Iceland's contemporary music scene. Today rising artists like Jónsi of Sigur Rós, GusGus, and múm continue to keep Reykjavík relevant. You can find the sounds of Iceland just about everywhere in the city, from the ultramodern Harpa, a glittering concert hall completed in 2011, to the city's pulsing clutch of bars and clubs. Iceland Airwaves, a five-day festival held every October, showcases new music from Icelandic and international artists, while Iceland Music Export (IMX) is an organization devoted to promoting Icelandic music in all its forms around the world.

## RING ROAD & OFF-ROAD

For unmatched adventure set your course for the excellent 832-mile (1,339 km) Ring Road. Filled with spectacular primordial views, it offers encounters with seals, whales, and puffins. It also gives views of Eyjafjallajökull, the volcano that shut down airports across Europe in 2010. Other sites along the route include the 0.6-mile-deep (1 km) Raufarhólshellir lava-tube caves, the dramatic sea cliffs of Látrabjarg, and the cobalt-tinged Jökulsárlón icebergs. Whether you choose to spend a weekend on the road or two weeks, the otherworldly opportunities are seemingly endless.

You can also head off the Ring Road into Iceland's rugged interior, accessible by four-wheel-drive vehicle only in summer months, when the midnight sun breaks up the icy passes. Or explore Iceland's 30 or so islands, including the Vestmannaeyjar archipelago in the southwest, where new volcanic islands were born as recently as 1973 and continue to draw biologists and botanists studying the island's newest forms of plant life and birdlife.

■ **PLANNING** Music In Reykjavík www.visitreykjavik.is. **Harpa** http://en.harpa.is. **Iceland Airwaves** www.icelandairwaves.is. **Iceland Music Export** www.icelandmusic.is. **Ring Road & Off-Road** www.extremeiceland.is.

## ⚘ BEST OF THE BEST ⚘
### Thermal Baths

A byproduct of man and nature working in harmony, **Nauthólsvík** *(www.nautholsvik.is)*, a geothermally heated beach in Reykjavik, is open from May through August. The naturally frigid waters offshore are regulated with hot water piped in to create swimmable temperatures of 64 to 68°F (18 to 20°C), while the beach's individual hot-tub temperatures soar to 95°F (35°C). Known for its pools, which feature a seemingly infinite variety of blues, **Hveravellir** *(www.hveravellir.is)* is said to have been discovered by Iceland's most notorious outlaw, Eyvindur, who hid here among the otherworldly smoking fumaroles and presumably admired the fantastic views of Kjalhraun lava field and Langjökull glacier.

There is but one breed of horse in all the country (and it's quite a sturdy specimen): the Icelandic horse.

Fewer than half of the Ring of Brodgar's original standing stones remain upright.

SCOTLAND

# ORKNEY ISLANDS

Learn the stone secrets of an ancient North Atlantic colony.

Nearer to Oslo than they are to London, the 70 rocky islands collectively called Orkney pull a visitor far from crowds, congestion, and contemporary urban life. Roaring winds and waves provide the soundtrack in this northern archipelago, home to more birds than people.

## ~ IN THE KNOW ~
### SCAPA FLOW

During both world wars, Orkney's Scapa Flow (*www.scapaflow.co.uk*) was a major British naval base. It was also a graveyard for 74 German ships, scuttled in this vast natural harbor by their commanders at the end of World War I, and the mighty *Royal Oak*, whose sinking by a German U-boat in 1939 cost more than 700 lives. Long popular with scuba divers, the anchorage is proud of its marine history, interpreted at the Scapa Flow Visitor Centre and Museum in Lyness, on the island of Hoy.

Humans have farmed these gentle hills for more than 5,000 years, from the Neolithic era to the Vikings to the present-day Scots. The burial cairns and standing stones of the dramatic Ring of Brodgar, built by a people who had a living relationship with the sky, pre-date Stonehenge. When a wild 1850 storm swept a sandy beach out to sea, it revealed another ancient marvel: the astonishing fishing village of Skara Brae. Europe's most complete and best-preserved prehistoric site, the UNESCO-protected village dates as far back as 5000 B.C., making its remains even older than the Egyptian pyramids. Walk through the site to find prehistoric homes with shelves and beds carved from stone. Connected by sheltered passageways, the homes suggest a close-knit community whose peaceful life may not be as different from your own as you might have imagined.

■ **PLANNING** Orkney Islands www.visitorkney.com. **Ring of Brodgar/Skara Brae** www.historic-scotland.gov.uk.

# WEST FJORDS

Sail past glaciers and mountains on a classic voyage.

Threading through a fringe of glacial mountains and forested islands, the classic voyage along Norway's western coast is a journey into the light. From the Hanseatic wharf at Bergen to Kirkenes, a tiny mining town above the Arctic Circle, the 1,500-mile (2,414 km) route dazzles, lit by the aurora borealis and summer's midnight sun.

Steamers have plied Norway's fjord-slashed shoreline for nearly a century. The Hurtigruten, or Quick Route, carries cargo, mail, and people from one brightly painted port to the next. Between towns, the ships navigate a landscape studded with glaciers and islands that emerge from fast-moving clouds.

Hurtigruten passengers debark to explore tiny villages and desolate channels like Trollfjord, named for the mythical Scandinavian gremlins. A memorable excursion is climbing the Lofoten Wall, a 60-mile-long (97 km) range of granite.

"I love hiking in the Lofotens for the tremendous variation in such a small area: mountains, tiny fishing villages, cities, white-sand beaches, evergreen forests, archipelagoes," says Geir Lundestad, secretary of the Norwegian Nobel Committee. "From a distance even the mountains look blue, but when you get closer the lush vegetation is revealed, exploding into a deep, deep green."

■ **PLANNING** **West Fjords** www.fjordnorway.com, www.gonorway .no. **Hurtigruten** Visit www.hurtigruten.com for cruise itineraries and online bookings.

## PLACES THAT CHANGED ME
### *Eric Andersen, singer-songwriter*

Summer in Norway is a season of enchantment, a time to move through hours of almost endless light, to sit in a garden or on a sea rock, reading or watching a lone fisherman calmly cast his line into the still waters of a fjord . . . On the night of the longest day, before midnight, families in our village walk to the beach at Lundevannet, a four-mile-wide lake. We spread blankets and build a fire . . . We watch the drama of the immense fires flaring up and illuminating the faintly visible shoreline across the water. And feel for a long moment the peace and contentment that comes from being together on another midsummer night.

The aurora borealis swirls from October through March.

# THE ALPS

*At the head of a smiling valley, itself 5,315 feet above sea level, towers the mighty Matterhorn, its isolated grandeur dominating the scene from every point. By means of a funiculaire, even those who do not climb may here behold the "panorama grandiose" of these finest peaks of the Alps, and as they gaze . . . even the least imaginative traveler feels the inspiration of the scene.*

—DORA KEEN, *NATIONAL GEOGRAPHIC* MAGAZINE, JULY 1911

Standing tall—very tall—over the town of Zermatt, the Matterhorn challenges climbers and photographers alike.

# MOUNTAINS TO CLIMB

Escape the fast-paced life with a slow ascent to the top of the world.

## 1 MOUNT LOGAN
### Canada

At 19,551 feet (5,959 m), Canada's highest mountain towers above Kluane National Park and Reserve in the rugged Yukon Territory. Mount Logan provides budding mountaineers with an inspiring introduction to high-altitude expeditions in a largely untouched corner of the world.
www.pc.gc.ca

## 2 MOUNT WHITNEY
### California

The highest point in the contiguous U.S., Mount Whitney is an imposing mass of granite thrusting up to a peak at 14,505 feet (4,421 m). The summit is reached by routes of varying difficulty, from a rocky hiking trail to technical climbs, and affords views over Sequoia and Kings Canyon, Death Valley, and Yosemite National Parks.
www.nps.gov

## 3 ACONCAGUA
### Argentina

Aconcagua is the highest mountain in the Andes and the highest peak outside of Asia, at a lofty 22,841 feet (6,962 m). However, it's a surprisingly nontechnical climb, lending it the name of "everyman's Everest." The greatest threats to climbers are altitude and underestimation.
www.aconcaguaexpeditions.com

## 4 BEN NEVIS
### Scotland

Ben Nevis, Britain's highest mountain at 4,406 feet (1,344 m), welcomes some 100,000 visitors to its summit each year. Up the ante by climbing Ben Nevis, Scafell (3,209 feet/978 m), and Snowdon (3,560 feet/1,085 m) in 24 hours, thus completing the Three Peaks Challenge to summit the highest mountains in the United Kingdom in a day.
www.lochabergeopark.org.uk

## 5 MATTERHORN
### Switzerland

Rearing up 14,690 feet (4,478 m), the dramatic Matterhorn dwarfs the village of Zermatt, whose cemetery is home to several climbers who lost their lives to its allure. Avoid joining them by building up some rock-climbing and crampon experience before attempting to conquer the peak.
www.zermatt.ch

## 6 MOUNT ELBRUS
### Russia

The glaciated twin summit of Europe's highest mountain, Mount Elbrus, at 18,510 feet (5,640 m), dominates the surrounding Caucasus Ridge. A chairlift whisks climbers up to 12,467 feet (3,800 m) for a relatively straightforward ascent, and helicopters drop skiers on its flanks, but Mount Elbrus remains a strenuous venture.
www.elbrus.org

## 7 MOUNT KENYA
### Kenya

The snowcapped peaks of Mount Kenya, Africa's second highest mountain, provide a less frequented and arguably more dramatic climb than Kilimanjaro. Batian (17,057 feet/5,199 m) and Nelion (17,021 feet/5,188 m) are accessible by experienced climbers, while a trekking trail ushers walkers to Point Lenana (16,355 feet/4,985 m).
www.mountkenyatrust.org

## 8 MOUNT KAILASH
### Tibet

So sacred is Tibet's Holy Mountain that it has never been climbed, although thousands may circumambulate, an ancient ritual known as the *kora*. Prayer wheels and stupas pepper the 32-mile (52 km) path, which typically takes three days to walk.
www.kailashtrekking.com

## 9 MOUNT COOK
### South Island, New Zealand

Standing at 12,316 feet (3,754 m), Mount Cook is New Zealand's highest mountain. Tackling Aoraki ("cloud piercer" in Maori) is a serious undertaking, but the views across Aoraki/Mount Cook National Park, with jagged peaks, glaciers, countless lakes, and dense rain forest, warrant the effort.
www.doc.govt.nz

## 10 MOUNT FUJI
### Japan

While the conical summit of Mount Fuji is often veiled in cloud, it's said to be the world's most climbed mountain, with well-trodden paths leading thousands of visitors to its 12,389-foot (3,776 m) summit each year. Tackle Fuji-san out of peak season to avoid the crowds, and watch the sunrise over Tokyo in relative peace.
www.insidejapantours.com

New Zealand's Aoraki—the "Cloud Piercer"—rewards climbers who make it to the top with a view of glaciers, rain forest, and 140 other peaks.

# LAKE BAIKAL

Marvel at Russia's seductive blue jewel in a Siberian setting.

Impassively deep and ancient, like the Russian collective unconscious, Lake Baikal humbles even in the 21st century. The scimitar-shaped southern Siberian lake, formed from the pulling apart of the Eurasian and Amur plates, is 25 million years old and 5,371 feet (1,637 m) deep—the oldest, deepest lake on Earth. Since the 17th century, when Cossack explorers first alerted Russia to the existence of Baikal, civilization has attempted inroads on the lake and the mountainous taiga that encircles it. With magnificent disdain, however, Baikal has—thus far—deflected man's worst depredations.

Baikal is Russia's precious genetic wellspring, with its forests of larch, birch, and pine; its necklace of five separate mountain ranges; and its singular ecosystem, which boasts 1,200 animal species, including wolf, bear, reindeer, more than 250 varieties of shrimp, nerpa (a freshwater seal), golomyanka (a type of viviparous sculpin), and the noble *Epischura baicalensis* (a minute copepod that filters Baikal's oxygen-saturated, famously clear water). The lake's charisma has galvanized Russians, who are fighting to preserve it from industrialization by any means

necessary. Hoping to foster ecotourism in the region, the Great Baikal Trail Association recruits volunteers from around the world to build trails that will help prevent more damaging development from engulfing the region.

■ **PLANNING** Lake Baikal www.russia-travel.com. **Great Baikal Trail Association** www.greatbaikaltrail.org. **Lake Baikal Tours** www.baikalex.com. Lake tours, including ice-diving excursions.

## ∼ IN THE KNOW ∼
### CONSERVING A NATURAL & NATIONAL TREASURE

In 2006, Vladimir Putin rejected a proposal for an oil pipeline routed along the shores of Lake Baikal, but only after concerted opposition. Now, a uranium-enrichment facility has been proposed, and the lake is already suffering the effects of a paper and pulp mill constructed directly on its shoreline in 1966. The Great Baikal Trail Association understands the realities of development in an enormous country with pressing economic needs. Its volunteers design trails to minimize impact and erosion, with the hope that eco-friendly development will save the sacred sea, as Lake Baikal is known in Russia.

The world's deepest lake, Baikal first formed 25 million years ago.

A craggy natural border, the mountains separate Russia from Georgia, Turkey, Iran, Armenia, and Azerbaijan.

# CAUCASUS MOUNTAINS

Visit the ancient mountain hamlets of a Georgian Shangri-La.

Many places in Eurasia claim to be the meeting spot of East and West, the precise point where Old World Europe melts into Asia's vast and wild expanse. But the ancient, craggy Caucasus Mountains—located on a geologically dynamic 746-mile (1,200 km) cutlet of land separating the Black and Caspian Seas—live up to the claim.

Twenty million years old, the mountains soar up to

18,510 feet (5,640 m) at Mount Elbrus and plunge 5,577 feet (1,700 m) in Abkhaziya, Georgia's breakaway republic and home to the deepest known cave on Earth. The mountain range creates a spine that separates Russia from Georgia, Turkey, Iran, ancient Armenia, and oil-rich Azerbaijan.

Emerging capital cities like Baku, Yerevan, and Tbilisi have begun to beckon tourists, but the Caucasus region's unfettered wilderness remains its primary attraction. California-based Explorers' Corner collaborated with the United Nations and the Georgian government to help establish Tusheti National Park in Georgia's northeastern Caucasus Mountains. Follow local guides on a challenging, multiday trek high into the park and surrounding nature reserve. Retire to ancient mountain hamlets each evening where local villagers heartily welcome visitors into their homes.

■ PLANNING **Caucasus Mountains** Diversity has also made the region an explosive center of geopolitical border rivalries, which include disputed regions of South Ossetia and Abkhaziya and the Nagorno-Karabakh Republic, making border crossing a hassle and potentially dangerous. Consult the U.S. Department of State (www.travel.state.gov) for current travel conditions. **Explorers' Corner** www.explorerscorner.com. Multiday hikes.

## ～ IN THE KNOW ～
### THE ORIGINS OF WINE PRODUCTION

Contrary to popular belief, the Greeks did not invent wine. Nor did the Romans, the Egyptians, or the Chinese. Recent archaeological findings suggest that wine production began in Georgia in 6000 B.C. and flourished in adjacent Iran and Armenia. In January 2011, archaeologists discovered the world's oldest known winery in Armenia's Vayots' Dzor province. The 6,000-year-old winery contained a wine press, fermentation containers, jugs, cups, and grape seeds from the species *Vitis vinifera*, suggesting that the drink's history is much longer than scholars originally thought.

Bright sunflowers dot a country road near the city of Chefchaouene.

MOROCCO
# RIF MOUNTAINS
Embark on a nomadic spring trek through the blooming Berber heartland.

Running west to east a short distance from the African Mediterranean coast, the wild, untamed Rif Mountains rise from northern Morocco's Berber heartland in Talassemtane National Park. Their craggy limestone peaks; forests of fir, cedar, and oak; and fast-flowing highland streams offer opportunities for relaxed trekking and good views of the Mediterranean.

Plan a springtime visit when hillsides near Chefchaouene turn into sprawling bedspreads of wildflowers; when almond trees pop into cottony bloom; and when you'll be joined by fresh and fragrant breezes, grazing donkeys, and Berber women singing softly and collecting poppies. There is a stark beauty in the Rifs' patchwork fields, an absolute serenity, as if the people who cultivate the nut brown land walk softly because they understand their good fortune.

Experienced outfitters lead overnight walking and hiking excursions up and around 4,921-foot (1,500 m) Mount Bouhachem, 5,249-foot (1,600 m) Mount Soukna, and 4,291-foot (1,500 m) Mount Mejbarra. Multinight treks include a dramatic sunset view of the red-rock God's Bridge formation. The lower altitudes and helpful pack mules make for a moderate meander through pastures, forests, rolling hills and the surrounding Berber villages. At day's end, bunk down in a nomadic-style tent under the starlit sky.

■ **PLANNING** Rif Mountains www.visitmorocco.com. **Journey Beyond Travel** www.journeybeyondtravel.com. Experienced outfitters. Treks are available year-round and last from two to five days.

## ❧ BEST OF THE BEST ❧
### Al Hoceima National Park

Al Hoceima National Park is a remote, ragged, and seldom discovered treasure of the region. At 185 square miles (485 sq km), this park along Morocco's Mediterranean coast is home to the Bokkoya people and boasts astonishing biodiversity, as well as a winsome (and rare) assortment of trees: pomegranate, wild olive, ilex, wild carob, and the endangered thuya, precious for its wood. Here, hiking boots and four-wheel-drive vehicles prove the best modes of transport. Visit www.marocecotourisme.com for information about the park, lodging, and tour operators.

## NORTH AFRICA
# SAHARA
Ride a camel amid golden dunes.

The great Sahara is a desert of extremes—of mountains, plains, and sand seas so hot and dry and trackless that people here still die of thirst. Its surface can reach 130°F (54°C), and at its heart, temperatures can swing as much as 70 degrees in a single day. The largest desert in the world and one of the wildest places on Earth, the Sahara stretches 3.5 million square miles (more than 9 million sq km) from the Atlantic Ocean in the west to the Red Sea in the east, and from the Mediterranean Sea south to the Sudan. Its beauty seems as vast as its sand dunes.

Start your adventure in the small Saharan oasis of Merzouga, in Morocco, at the foot of photogenic Erg Chebbi, an 18.6-mile (30 km) stretch of golden, wind-sculpted dunes, some reaching 820 feet (250 m) in height. Whether you'd like to spend an hour or several days among the dunes, camel drivers in Merzouga will happily escort you into the sandscape. The best times for a visit are at sunrise and sunset, when a tender, bruised light transforms the Sahara into an ever shifting fantasia of bronze, copper, and gold.

■ **PLANNING  Sahara** www.morocco-excursions.com. One- and two-night camel treks into the Sahara from Merzouga. **Auberge du Sud** www.aubergedusud.com. Auberge du Sud operates a luxurious hotel in the dunes near Erg Chebbi. Visit the website for information about desert camping, camel treks, and four-wheel-drive tours.

### ❧ BEST OF THE BEST ❧
#### Ténéré Desert

The most beautiful area in the Sahara may just be the Ténéré desert of Niger, in the Sahara's lower reaches. Roughly the size of Germany, the Ténéré is a 154,440-square-mile (400,000 sq km) sea of towering dunes, black volcanic peaks, dinosaur fossils, and Neolithic petroglyphs. In Gadafoua, you may even come upon the enormous, 100-million-year-old bones of the Jobaria ("monster"). Once the site of the trans-Sahara caravan route, the Ténéré remains a vast freeway of camel caravans helmed by Tuareg nomads who trade household supplies and herds of sheep and goats for huge pillars of salt. Dunes-Voyages (*www.dunes-voyages.com*) offers 12- to 14-day tours of the Ténéré that follow the path of the caravans.

The Sahara glows warm with color at sunrise and sunset.

# SERENGETI

*The great migrating herds of wildebeests and zebras are probably the single most impressive sight, although the endless plains, fantastic clouds, and kaleidoscope of natural colors are pretty hard to best . . . Sound and activity are everywhere. The ground seems to be alive. It invigorates and recharges the spirit of our humanity right at its roots.*

—RICHARD LEAKEY, PALEOANTHROPOLOGIST & AUTHOR OF *WILDLIFE WARS*

The Serengeti's wilde-
beests migrate up to
1,000 miles (1,610 km)
each year.

# BWINDI

Track the planet's gentle giants in a mist-shrouded African forest.

Deep in the Albertine Rift Valley of southwestern Uganda, about half of the world's estimated 700 mountain gorillas have found refuge in the fragile and foreboding Bwindi Impenetrable Forest. The rugged topography of the 123-square-mile (327 sq km) UNESCO World Heritage site alternates between steep, mist-shrouded slopes and narrow, lush valleys.

Tropical Bwindi is home to chimpanzees, L'Hoest's monkeys, and eight other primates, plus African elephants and 78 other mammal species; 23 endemic bird species, several classified as threatened; and two endangered butterflies: African giant swallowtails and cream-banded swallowtails. But it is the rare opportunity to glimpse the magnificent mountain gorillas in the wild that inspires visitors from around the world to trek on foot along jungle trails through the ancestral lands of the indigenous Batwa Pygmy tribe.

An intellectual understanding of the genetic connection to our critically endangered, charismatic cousins rarely prepares people for face-to-face, wild encounters with the planet's gentle giants. The poignant sight of a young silverback calmly feeding or a baby gorilla snuggling safely in its mother's arms has been known to move some visitors to tears.

■ **PLANNING** Bwindi Impenetrable Forest www.bwindiforest nationalpark.com. **The Gorilla Resort** www.gorillaresort.com. Ranger-guided tracking excursions with lodging in elevated tents or luxurious cottages. Tracking groups are limited to eight people.

## ⁓ IN THE KNOW ⁓
### FLYING GEMS

The "Impenetrable" part of the forest's name is due to the dense flora supporting one of the richest fauna communities in East Africa, including at least 310 species of butterflies. Bwindi researchers estimate that a day hike through the forest, considered one of the most important in Africa for montane forest butterflies, would reveal at least 50 different species of these "flying jewels." Three butterflies endemic to the Albertine Rift—*Papilio leucotaenia*, *Graphium gudenusi*, and *Charaxes fournierae*—have been spotted only in Bwindi or in the nearby Congolese forest.

Guided trips often result in close encounters with our hairier cousins.

# OKAVANGO DELTA

Meander through the jewel in Africa's crown.

The Okavango Delta offers visitors the opportunity to "live with elephants."

Most rivers run to the sea, but the Okavango runs to a desert and disappears into the hot sands. On that spectacular journey, it waters an Eden that has been called the "last of Old Africa," a wild oasis in the Kalahari Desert.

The land around the Okavango Delta has its own rainy season, which greens up the Kalahari so that animals can graze and wander in its vastness. But the water holes soon dry up, leaving animals desperate for food and drink. A second life-giving deluge arrives from the highlands of Angola after a 1,000-mile (1,609 km) trek—a cause for celebration.

Hippos by the hundreds lounge in deep pools, while crocodiles feed on fish, waterbirds, and any careless mammals they can snatch from the banks. Tens of thousands of elephants, zebras, wildebeests, and Cape buffalo appear in herds of rumbling thunder. Feeding off the game are legions of predators, among them lions, leopards, cheetahs, and hyenas.

Dedicated visitors may take a *mokoro* (dugout canoe) into the interior for a few days. "Most of the people who visit Botswana are what I would call game connoisseurs," explains Dave van Smeerdijk, a guide at Wilderness Safaris. "Folks come here to go a bit deeper."

■ **PLANNING** Okavango Delta www.botswanatourism.co.bw. For lists of safari tour operators, consult www.okavangodelta.com. **Wilderness Wildlife Trust** www.wildernesstrust.com.

## PLACES THAT CHANGED ME

*Frans Lanting, nature photographer*

I've been in the Okavango in all seasons, during wildfires, torrential downpours, and when it's bone-dry. I've walked there, camped there, photographed it extensively from the air. I'm pleased to report that the delta is still truly wild . . . The Okavango Delta, however, will only survive if it's kept whole. As long as the rivers stay wild—with no dams—and as long as no fences are put in the way of animal migrations, I'm very optimistic that the Okavango Delta will remain one of the world's greatest wild places.

Two-fifths of Africa's volcanic eruptions blast out of this chain.

## CENTRAL AFRICA
# VIRUNGA VOLCANOES

Make a Kilimanjaro-like climb in half the time—and connect with a more primal you.

Perhaps nowhere on Earth is the dual creative and destructive nature of volcanoes more evident than in central Africa's Virunga Volcanoes Massif. Straddling the borders of Rwanda, Uganda, and the Democratic Republic of the Congo, the eight-volcano chain is one of Earth's most active volcanic regions—two-fifths of all of Africa's eruptions blast out of the very active Nyiragongo and Nyamulagira Volcanoes, which form a veritable salad bowl for mountain gorillas, chimpanzees, elephants, and other wildlife.

One of the chain's dormant volcanoes, the 14,787-foot (4,507 m) Mount Karisimbi—named after the local word for "white shell" because of the rippling pattern of snow on its top—provides trekkers with an experience similar to climbing Kilimanjaro but with a hike that takes only two days instead of five or more. You can begin your climb up the volcano in Rwanda's Volcanoes National Park—and head through the same rain forest where Dian Fossey lived and worked while studying mountain gorillas—or in Virunga National Park in the Congo. Just make sure you check on the region's security situation before you go.

■ **PLANNING Volcanoes Massif** www.rwandatourism.com, www.visituganda.com. The U.S. Department of State (*www.travel.state.gov*) publishes valuable information about travel conditions in the Democratic Republic of the Congo, Rwanda, and Uganda. **Virunga National Park** www.visitvirunga.org.

### ⁂ BEST OF THE BEST ⁂
#### Support & Celebrate Local Heritage

After roughing it on Mount Karisimbi for a night or two, dry your boots at more luxurious digs. The high-end **Sabyinyo Silverback Lodge** is located just outside the Volcanoes National Park boundary in the foothills of the Virungas. The upscale property, one of eight luxury **Governors' Camp** safari lodges (*www.governorscamp.com*) in East Africa, is representative of Rwanda's drive toward niche tourism. The lodge is owned by a Community Trust (SACOLA), which supports sustainable economic development and conservation initiatives in neighboring communities. See SACOLA's efforts in action at the **Iby'iwacu Cultural Village** (*http://cbtrwanda.org/*), where former poachers now work to celebrate local Rwandese culture.

# NEPAL
# SAGARMATHA PARK

Stand at the foot of the "mother of the universe."

Howling winter winds strip the mountain's snows to reveal immense black granite walls, sending eastward a telltale streamer of white from the summit, highest point of the world's highest national park. Mount Everest, known to the Nepali as Sagarmatha, "mother of the universe," stands as the centerpiece of Sagarmatha National Park, a 480-square-mile (1,243 sq km) wonderland located in northeast Nepal along the border with Tibet.

The park's boundaries embrace more than 25 mammal species. Larger animals, higher up, have adapted to thin air and freezing temperatures—the noble snow leopard with a thick coat and great stealth, the black bear with fur and large lungs. And the mother of the universe also watches over bird species including the national bird of Nepal, the impeyan pheasant, known locally as the *danphe,* meaning "nine colors."

A UNESCO World Heritage site since 1979, the park is best experienced on foot. Join a challenging, Sherpa-led trek into the park via the Dudh Kosi (River of Milk) valley. Catch a first glimpse of Everest during a steep climb to the Sherpa market town of Namche Bazaar. Short hikes from here deliver dual rewards: multiple Everest views and ample time to gradually acclimatize to the altitude.

■ **PLANNING** **Sagarmatha National Park** http://nepal.saarc tourism.org. **National Geographic Expeditions** www.national geographicexpeditions.com. Multiday treks available.

## PLACES THAT CHANGED ME
*Peter Hillary, author & son of Edmund Hillary, first to summit Everest*

The first time I saw Everest I was seven years old. I was on the Singalila Ridge near Darjeeling . . . We stared across to what is now Sagarmatha National Park at these beautiful views, sparkling and clear. I remember thinking: These are the greatest mountains on Earth; they are just bigger than anything else.

I wasn't quite sure which one of those huge mountains was Everest. I looked at my father as he stood there pointing from the ridge. There was this intensity as he stared out toward his mountain, saying, "There it is. There it is." There was something magical about that to a little boy.

Trekkers explore under the watch of Mount Everest.

# GOBI DESERT

Walk and ride through the teeming life and history of the world's third largest desert.

Travelers who bemoan the lack of unexplored destinations haven't been to Mongolia's Gobi desert. This vast expanse of desert counts among its "locals" soaring peaks, broad steppe lands, snow leopards, and Gobi bears. The site of prehistoric inland seas, it was once a land of dinosaurs, as revealed through a treasure trove of fossilized bones and eggs.

Uniting the plains of Europe with the mountain ranges of Asia and the sand dunes of Africa, Mongolia is a land of three continents. It's also a country of nomads, unique in that the majority of its population live in tents as they follow their camels and live on their milk and cheese. Thanks to the pioneering Mongolia-based tour operator Nomadic Expeditions, it's possible to scratch the surface of the mighty Gobi desert and to meet some if its extraordinary locals.

A 14-day trek on foot and camel through this mysterious landscape will bring you to the desert's hidden mountain springs—to Kharakhorum, the 13th-century capital of the Mongol Empire, and the Gorkhi-Terelj National Park, where ibex roam among prehistoric rock paintings. You'll also have the rare opportunity to experience traditional nomadic hospitality: Witnessing firsthand the nomads' tenacity and personal warmth, you will take milk tea and cheese with a Mongolian family.

■ **PLANNING Gobi** www.mongoliatourism.gov.mn. For more detailed information about the 14-day Gobi Trek offered by Nomadic Expeditions, visit www.nomadicexpeditions.com.

## ∼ IN THE KNOW ∼
### EAGLE FESTIVAL

Travel to the Altai Mountains in western Mongolia in October to experience the Eagle Festival in Bayan-Ölgiy, an annual event where Kazakh hunters from across Mongolia demonstrate the dramatic tradition of hunting small prey on horseback with eagles. The trained eagles swoop down from the peak of a 1,000-foot-high (305 m) mountain to land on the arms of the galloping hunters or on fox skins dragged behind the hunters' horses. While these displays are the highlight of the event, there are also horse races, archery, music, dancing, a parade, and a play in honor of the hunters and their eagles.

Dinosaurs once roamed the otherworldly Junggar Basin.

Some of the world's most highly prized teas grow on the hills of Sri Lanka.

## SRI LANKA
# CENTRAL HIGHLANDS
Greet the day atop a sacred mountain.

Sri Lanka's stunning hill country is a mountainous, mist-draped realm. Long popular with backpackers and other adventurers, this super biodiversity hot spot is known for its tea plantations and rain forest preserves: the Central Highlands, a UNESCO World Heritage site.

In this region there's a mystical energy fueled by legend, lore, and spirituality. In January through April, two million pilgrims visit the Central Highlands to climb 5,000 narrow steps up 7,362-foot (2,243 m) Adam's Peak or Sri Pada (Sacred Footprint). Here, according to the Mahavamsa, the Great Chronicle of Sri Lanka, the projection of Buddha's image is believed to have visited and left a footprint. In Hindu tradition, the ancient rock formation is Shiva's imprint. For Muslims and Christians, it's Adam's.

Long lines of lights illuminate the winding path to the summit during Poya Festivals, monthly Buddhist observances held on the full moon. On these religious holidays and weekends, trails are overrun with pilgrims, so plan a midweek guided trek, heading out around 2 a.m. to reach the peak before sunrise. Sip a cup of steaming white tea to stay warm as you wait for the dramatic emergence of the new day: the exhilarating moment when a giant shadow cast by the peak falls across the dense layer of morning mist blanketing the lush valleys below.

■ **PLANNING** **Central Highlands** www.srilankatourism.org. **Adam's Peak** The easiest route is from Dalhousie and takes about four hours one way. Check the weather before going to ensure a fairly clear day.

## ⚜ BEST OF THE BEST ⚜
### Ceylon Tea Trails

No wonder the British liked the damp and bracingly cool Central Highlands. It feels like home here, particularly in the Bogawantalawa Valley, the Golden Valley of Tea, 30 miles (48 km) south of the colonial-era resort town of Nuwara Eliya. The valley's Ceylon Tea Trails (*www.teatrails.com*), the world's first integrated tea bungalow resort, features four authentically restored tea planters' villas, as well as tea garden walking and mountain biking trails. A "Tea Experience" tour with the resident planter sends guests in search of the perfect artisanal black brew—from planting and plucking to processing and tasting.

# CORAL REEF

*Generally speaking, the number of reef species — biodiversity — increases as you move southwestward across the Pacific from Hawaii. Papua New Guinea is one of the least damaged regions of the Indo-Pacific. You can observe in a single reef there twice as many coral and fish species as live in the entire Caribbean.*

—JEAN-MICHEL COUSTEAU, ENVIRONMENTALIST &
FOUNDER OF OCEAN FUTURES SOCIETY

A rainbow of reef fish, including orange basslets, turn Papua New Guinea's coral reef into a living kaleidoscope.

# UNUSUAL SCUBA-DIVING SITES

From brilliantly colored coral reefs to a hotel beneath the waves, dive into the world's least visited places.

**1 LOST VILLAGES OF CANADA**
Cornwall, Ontario, Canada

The construction of the Moses-Saunders Power Dam on the St. Lawrence Seaway forced the relocation of residents in ten communities between 1955 and 1958. An abandoned powerhouse, a paper mill, a bridge, and even a canal system can still be seen below the water's surface.
www2.canada.com/ottawacitizen/features/lostvillages/

**2 JULES' UNDERSEA LODGE**
Key Largo, Florida

This chic 1970s-era aquanaut habitat and former marine research station rests 21 feet (6.4 m) below the surface in the tropical mangrove habitat of Emerald Lagoon. Up to six people sleep comfortably in this hotel accessible only by scuba.
www.jul.com

**3 SUNKEN PIRATE CITY**
Port Royal, Jamaica

Port Royal was the largest port city in the New World before a catastrophic earthquake and tidal wave in 1692 sent two-thirds of it below the sea. The only authentic sunken city in the Western Hemisphere, this archaeological site features warehouses, taverns, ships, and houses frozen in time.
http://whc.unesco.org/en/tentativelists/5430

**4 UNDERWATER MUSEUM**
Punta Cancún & Punta Nizuc, Mexico

Spread across 4,520 square feet (420 sq m) of barren seabed, Jason deCaires Taylor's life-size, human-shaped sculptures in the Isla Mujeres National Marine Park seed the foundation for coral growth and encourage marine life in an area where native coral has suffered.
www.underwatersculpture.com

**5 PENÍNSULA VALDÉS MARINE WILDLIFE RESERVE**
Argentina

This UNESCO World Heritage site off the coast of Patagonia is home to endangered southern right whales, orcas, dolphins, elephant seals, sea lions, and even penguins. Explore sunken ships to the ethereal sounds of calling whales echoing from the deep.
http://whc.unesco.org/en/list/937

**6 CLEOPATRA'S PALACE**
Alexandria Harbor, Egypt

Large swaths of the city, including Cleopatra's Palace, were reclaimed by the sea following earthquakes in the fourth and eighth centuries. Swim through toppled buildings, statues, columns, and ornate carvings from the pre-Roman conquest of Alexandria. Also dive to limestone blocks believed to be the base of the famed lighthouse Pharos of Alexandria, one of the seven ancient wonders of the world.
www.touregypt.net

**7 KANDE BEACH**
Malawi

The warm, blue waters of Lake Malawi teem with a thousand different species of colorful cichlids. Look for tiny fish seeking refuge in their mothers' mouths, or try a night dive to see the dolphin fish hunt.

The dive shop's research center educates local villagers about the importance of conserving this unique natural resource.
www.aquanutsdivers.com

**8 SARDINE RUN**
Eastern Cape, South Africa

The largest annual oceanic migration on Earth occurs in May and June off the shores of Cape Point as sardines make their way from the cold waters off the cape to warmer waters in the east. The spectacle draws divers and an array of predators: birds, larger fish, and a variety of sharks, including great whites, dolphins, and seals.
www.sardinerun.com

**9 YONAGUNI MONUMENT**
Yonaguni Island, Japan

Less than a half mile (0.8 km) off the island and 80 feet (24 m) deep lies a mysterious landscape filled with impressive staircase-like formations guarded in winter by schools of hammerhead sharks. While most scientists agree that the monument is just a remarkable natural structure, some believe that the precision-cut "stairs" are the ruins of mythical Atlantis.
www.morien-institute.org/yonaguni.html

**10 MAROVO LAGOON**
New Georgia Islands, Solomon Islands

A double barrier reef encloses the calm waters of one of the world's largest lagoon systems and creates a variety of habitats for pelagics (jacks, tuna, sharks) as well as tropical reef fish. Divers can also explore caverns and World War II shipwrecks.
www.visitsolomons.com.sb

The underwater statue in Cancún is far more than a curiosity. Soon enough, she'll be a foundation for coral growth.

# THE OUTBACK

*My affection for the outback is, frankly, a mystery to me. Nearly every-thing about it is alien or alarming to my nature. It exceeds by a consider-able margin my personal requirements for warmth . . . Uluru apart, most of the interior is just unremittingly unremitting. And yet I love it all.*
—BILL BRYSON, AUTHOR OF *IN A SUNBURNED COUNTRY* & OTHER BOOKS

A three-hour drive from Perth, the Pinnacles rock formations—some poking up more than 11 feet (3.5 m) high—at Nambung National Park are millions of years old.

The aboriginal rock art at Ubirr in Arnhem Land's Kakadu National Park is anywhere up to 1,500 years old.

AUSTRALIA

# ARNHEM LAND

Take a starlit boat tour through a pristine wetland teeming with life.

The vast, remote, and primeval wilderness of Arnhem Land, located in the eastern half of the Northern Territory's northern peninsula, was named after the boat of Willem van Colster, the region's first Dutch visitor. Visitors today are relatively scarce; however, those who make the journey will find fair recompense. The area's biggest draw is Kakadu National Park, Australia's largest national park.

About three hours southeast of Darwin, Kakadu awaits a pristine, tropical, 7,825-square-mile (20,266 sq km) expanse of eucalyptus woodlands, floodplains, coastal mangroves, and billabongs filled with waterfowl and blanketed in lilies. The park's defining landmark is the dramatic Arnhem Land escarpment, a 400-mile (640 km) line of massive sandstone cliffs, over which spills the South Alligator River. Visit from December to March, when runoff from the monsoon rains pours over the cliffs in a series of spectacular waterfalls.

Indigenous-owned Gagudju Dreaming leads cruises through Kakadu's most famous wetland, the Yellow Water Billabong. Guides point out wetland inhabitants along the way: whistling-ducks, magpie geese, kingfisher, crocodiles, and buffalo grazing in the floodplains. On the starlit tour, sounds and scents are the main attractions. Close your eyes and listen to the calls of nocturnal birds. Breathe in the earthy plantation smells. Scan the night sky as local storytellers share aboriginal night mythology.

■ **PLANNING** Arnhem Land www.discoveraustralia.com.au. You can visit Arnhem Land on your own, but an organized tour is recommended. **Kakadu National Park** www.kakadu.com.au. **Gagudju Dreaming** www.gagudju-dreaming.com.

## ∽ IN THE KNOW ∽
### ABORIGINAL ART IN KAKADU NATIONAL PARK

Thousands of rock-art murals, which decorate Kakadu's hidden gorges, rock shelters, cliffs, and caves, tell us that Aborigines have inhabited this terrain for 40,000 years. Their art illustrates a world of ancestral beings—giant kangaroos, lizards, snakes, sea creatures, and grubs—during the Dreamtime of creation and reveals a deep spiritual connection with the land. Every Aborigine is responsible for "holding" fragments of a mythological mosaic known as the Dreaming—creation stories of how their land was formed and how people, plants, and animals came to be as they are today.

# MILFORD SOUND

Take flight over a lush New World paradise that is by turns pure and grandiose.

Few places offer the kind of idyllic beauty found in Milford Sound. Carved into the southwestern corner of New Zealand's South Island, this 14-mile (22 km) fjord boasts an almost ridiculous panoply of rainbows, sun-kissed waterfalls, mossy rain forests, whales, penguins, dolphins, and wispy, cloud-crowned peaks.

The Maori call it Piopiotahi, meaning "single thrush." Polynesian legend says that the deity Tu Te Raki Whanoa carved the fjord with his magic adze. The result, a sort of subtropical Maori Matterhorn, was considered his finest work and remains one of New Zealand's greatest wilderness destinations. Overseeing the whole affair, the rocky, angular 5,551-foot-high (1,692 m) Mitre Peak. The protected area is just one of ten that make up the 10,039-square-mile (26,000 sq km) rain forest and marine reserve called Te Wahipounamu.

It takes a bird's-eye view to grasp the majesty of the Milford Sound fjord. Queenstown flightseeing outfitters take visitors on aerial tours over the Fiordland's highest peaks and their glaciers. On the flight from Queenstown to Milford, view the entire sound all the way to the Tasman Sea, including Mitre Peak and the Bowen and Stirling Falls. The return trip soars over Sutherland Falls and the crystal clear lakes of Fiordland National Park.

■ **PLANNING** **Milford Sound** www.milford-sound.co.nz. There are no roads or cell phone service in the reserve. **Milford Sound Scenic Flights** www.milfordflights.co.nz. Aerial tours offered.

## ∿ IN THE KNOW ∿
### MOA OR LESS

Although the beloved, endemic kiwi is New Zealand's undisputed national symbol, it is the large, flightless moa that garners the most headlines. The moa is believed to have gone extinct in the 13th century, but rumors about the bird's survival have persisted since the late 19th century, particularly in the southwest and Fiordland near Milford Sound. As recently as 1993 and 2008, locals, scientists, and cryptozoologists have made credible claims asserting that the densely wooded habitat plays host to colonies of this ancient species. No evidence, however, has led to an official investigation of the bird's existence.

The waters of Milford Sound teem with whales and dolphins.

# URBAN SPACES

## *Cities for the Ages*

The great cities of the world stimulate and enrich us. They offer an energizing blend of style, creativity, tradition, art, and opportunity found nowhere else. Even as they embrace their past, they foster a spirit of renewal and invention that continually re-imagines the urban landscape. Their contributions to global culture are essential to our collective consciousness.

The skyscraper at 555 California Street offers the ideal vantage point for taking in San Francisco's distinctive landmarks and the bay beyond.

Vanier Park provides the perfect perspective on Vancouver's place in the natural world—between bay and mountains.

## BRITISH COLUMBIA, CANADA

# VANCOUVER

Commune with nature in one of North America's most beautiful cities.

The great outdoors is not so much on Vancouver's doorstep as in its front room. It's no wonder that Greenpeace was founded here in 1969, or that innumerable surveys report Vancouver as the city with the world's highest quality of life. Add a multiethnic population, a booming port, and the inrush of global money attracted by a prime Pacific Rim position, and you have a very dynamic city indeed.

Long-term resident Douglas Coupland, author of *Generation X,* says Vancouver is North America's most "atypical city," dishing up a wide range of cultural and other attractions: nude beaches, powder skiing, whale-watching, dim sum feasts. "In one day here you can climb cliffs, deep-sea dive, shop for Indian saris, and pick cranberries," says Coupland. Put it all together, and you have a "funky, glitzy, outdoorsy, high-tech, prim, hippie, glass-covered sort of place."

Come to grips with the city's natural beauty during a walk through Stanley Park, a 988-acre (400 ha) oasis of forest, beaches, and untamed landscapes. Its fringes may be domesticated—the 7-mile (10.5 km) perimeter seawall is popular with walkers, joggers, and cyclists—but elsewhere lonely trails meander past lakes and through vast stands of fir, cedar, and Western hemlock. Wildlife abounds, and birdsong fills the air. You'll feel the truth of actress Isabella Rossellini's observation that "in New York you get pigeons, in Vancouver . . . eagles."

■ **PLANNING Vancouver** www.tourismvancouver.com. **Stanley Park** www.vancouver.ca/parks. Note that the seawall has designated lanes. Cycling and in-line skating lanes are closest to the water and one way (counterclockwise) only.

## ～ IN THE KNOW ～
### MUSEUM OF ANTHROPOLOGY

For thousands of years before the arrival of outsiders, the coast around present-day Vancouver was the preserve of the Tsawwassen, the Squamish, and other indigenous peoples. Memorials to their sophisticated cultures can be found in the world-class Museum of Anthropology (*www.moa.ubc.ca*), designed by the eminent Vancouver-born architect Arthur Erickson (1924–2009). Pride of place goes to the totems and other monumental carvings in the Great Hall, but don't miss Vancouver's most celebrated work of art, "The Raven and the First Men," an immense sculpture by First Nations artist Bill Reid (1920–1998).

# MONTREAL

Find culinary pleasure in the city that seems to have invented the idea.

A bout Montreal's allure, local author Adam Gollner observed, "It's the only place in the Western world where you can still be a bohemian." A midsize metropolis, Montreal has the leisurely pace of a patchwork of inter-connected villages, ideal stomping grounds for the latter-day boulevardier. No other place has mastered the notion of joie de vivre quite like Montreal, and the best way to partake in its characteristic whim and indulgence is to play flaneur—and eat with abandon.

Like the city itself, Montreal's restaurants are lively, friendly, hedonistic. Kick off your caution-to-the-wind gastronomic tour at Schwartz's deli, the venerable charcuterie Hébraïque on Boulevard St. Laurent. (Here, meats come in three degrees of fattiness, and a frankfurter is considered a side dish.) Head also to Au Pied de Cochon, one of the city's most iconic restaurants, known for such rich dishes as foie gras poutine, stuffed pig's feet, and tripe pizza—all of which should come with their own medical-alert bracelets. (If the dishes inspire, the restaurant also offer cooking lessons.) And don't leave without a trip to Fairmount Bagel in the city's Mile End neighborhood. This establishment is beloved for its petite, sesame-covered bagels.

■ **PLANNING** **Montreal** www.tourisme-montreal.org. **Schwartz's** www.schwartzsdeli.com. **Au Pied de Cochon** www.restaurant aupieddecochon.ca. **Fairmount Bagel** www.fairmountbagel.com. Open 24 hours a day.

---

## ⚜ BEST OF THE BEST ⚜
### Old Montreal's Most Stylish Hotels

Montreal's innate sense of Gallic style means that the city has never wanted for elegant hotels. Today, the most fashionable place to check your suitcase is in the cobbled neighborhood of Old Montreal (sprawling along the St. Lawrence River, southeast of downtown), where heritage buildings have been converted into fashionable boutique hotels. Housed in a for-mer fur warehouse dating from 1723, **Les Passants du Sans Soucy** (*www.lesanssoucy.com*) flaunts its original stone walls and beamed ceilings. **Hotel Nelligan** (*www.hotelnelligan.com*), named after Victorian Quebecois poet Émile Nelligan, is made up of three 19th-century heritage buildings, while the grand, neoclassical **Le Place d'Armes** (*www.hotelplacedarmes.com*) overlooks the square.

For a quiet escape from the city below, lovers and others head for Mount Royal Park.

# SAN FRANCISCO

Hike along the Northwest coast into the city's wilds.

A fantasy of elegance, opulence, and eccentricity, San Francisco overflows with treasures, both urban and natural. In this city of hills (anywhere from 42 to 53 of them, depending on who's counting), the best way to take in the sights is as the locals do—on foot. Among the most precipitous—and hikeworthy—of the city's peaks is Telegraph Hill, dominated by 210-foot-tall (64 m) Coit Tower. At the top of the tower, soak in views of Fisherman's Wharf, the Golden Gate Bridge, and Alcatraz, and then descend 800 steps down the hill to the sound of wild parrots calling to each other.

To really experience San Francisco's history and natural setting at their best, however, head out to the spectacular Land's End Trail, which begins near the ruins of Sutro Baths, a late 19th-century bathing complex on the city's wild and rocky northwestern tip. The trail hugs the cypress-shaded cliffs north and east along the Golden Gate Channel for 3.5 miles (5.6 km), offering million-dollar views of the Marin headland and promising surprises at every turn, from secluded beaches and pretty gardens to historic shipwrecks and gun batteries.

Spy cormorants and other shorebirds roosting on the rocks, or seals and dolphins playing in the surf.

■ **PLANNING San Francisco** www.sanfrancisco.travel. **Coit Tower** www.sfrecpark.org. Parking is extremely limited; there is a fee to ride the elevator to the top of the tower. **Land's End Trail** www.parksconservancy.org/visit. Most of the trail is unpaved, and there are a couple of steep stairways.

## ❦ BEST OF THE BEST ❦
### Views of the Golden Gate Bridge

One of the world's most beautiful bridges, the Golden Gate Bridge spans the mouth of San Francisco Bay, linking the San Francisco peninsula with Marin County to the north. For fabulous views on the San Francisco side, try **South Vista Point** (off Lincoln Blvd. or U.S. 101) or **Fort Point** (off Lincoln Blvd.), which looks from below along the seawall. On the Marin side, head for the cove at **East Fort Baker** (U.S. 101 north to Alexander Ave. exit; at Bunker Rd. follow signs to Bay Area Discovery Museum), or try **Conzelman Road** (U.S. 101 north to Alexander Ave. exit; left at Bunker Rd., left on McCullough Rd., left on Conzelman Rd.) for a great prospect from the Marin Headlands.

The view from Alamo Square, atop one of San Francisco's many hills, is best at sunset, when the city's lights come on.

The Mile-High City blends equal parts cow town and ultramodern metropolis.

# COLORADO
# DENVER

Go beyond the city's cowboy past to find the avant-garde.

Located 1 mile (1.6 km) above sea level on the open plains at the base of the Rocky Mountains, Denver is, and long has been, the hub of the Rockies. Denverites, fiercely proud of their Old West heritage, don their well-worn cowboy hats for the annual longhorn cattle drive through downtown. As

Tom Noel, a history professor at the University of Colorado Denver, says, "We're still a cow town."

However, there's more to this thriving metropolis than sentimental cowboys—who, by the way, you'll find chowing down on buffalo prime rib at Denver's oldest restaurant, the Buckhorn Exchange, and replacing their plaid shirts at the 110-year-old Rockmount Ranch Wear shop. Denver is also home to cutting-edge architecture, Broadway-caliber theater productions, and an impressive arts scene.

"Between New York and Los Angeles, there are few places where you can get a cosmopolitan art experience, and one is Denver." Local artist Clark Richert's bold claim certainly rings true when admiring pioneering installations and photography in the Museum of Contemporary Art Denver. The Denver Art Museum houses an equally rich collection of world art, housed in Daniel Libeskind's spiky, titanium-covered building, which evokes the craggy Rockies.

■ **PLANNING** Denver www.denver.org. **Buckhorn Exchange** www.buckhorn.com. **Rockmount Ranch Wear** www.rockmount.com. **Museum of Contemporary Art Denver** www.mcadenver.org. **Denver Art Museum** www.denverartmuseum.org.

## ❧ BEST OF THE BEST ❧
### Denver's Microbreweries

Colorado leads the United States in beer production, with behemoths like Coors calling Denver home since the 1870s, but aficionados should focus on the city's microbreweries. The **Wynkoop Brewing Company** (www.wynkoop.com) is Denver's original brewpub and now one of the world's largest. **Falling Rock Taphouse** (www.fallingrocktaphouse.com) has Colorado's most extensive selection of state-brewed beer. **Cheeky Monk** (www.thecheekymonk.com) pays homage to Belgian beers, while **Vine Street Pub** (www.mountainsunpub.com) is the city's grooviest newcomer, serving veggie burgers with its award-winning brews. Ask what's on the revolving "nitro" tap—filtered but unpasteurized beer pressurized with nitrogen, making for a smoother drink.

Once home to steel mills, the Monongahela now hosts daytime kayakers and nighttime lights.

# PITTSBURGH

Witness an extreme metropolitan makeover.

Pittsburgh's 21st-century face is as fresh as the rivers that course through its heart. While the Allegheny, Monongahela, and Ohio remain hardworking rivers, they're cleaner and greener now. With steel mills banished, the legacy of robber barons like Andrew Carnegie now lies in the city's handsome architecture and museums—including the one devoted to pop artist Andy Warhol, a native son. Don't miss downtown landmarks by American architects Henry Hobson Richardson and Philip Johnson, the energetic theater district, or the spectacular Phipps Conservatory, a Victorian greenhouse with an indoor cliffside forest.

European-style neighborhoods spiked with onion-domed churches and cobbled streets crown Pittsburgh's rugged hills. "It must have been laid out by a mountain goat," complained newspaper columnist Ernie Pyle, who visited in 1937. Pittsburgh's streetscapes still bear witness to the ethnic roots of 19th-century immigrants who settled by its rivers, close to its steel mills. Today, its riverfront has been converted for recreation—downtown offers 30 miles (48 km) of level waterside trails. Pedal a bike or paddle a kayak for an up-close look at Pittsburgh's surprising reinvention. Or join commuters on the Duquesne Incline, a cable car ride to the top of Mount Washington, 36 feet (100 m) above the city, for a nighttime view.

## ～ IN THE KNOW ～
### VANKA MURALS

Immigrant history is enshrined in the striking murals of St. Nicholas Croatian Catholic Church. Bold modernist murals by painter Maxo Vanka tell the story of the Croatian peasants who journeyed to the United States and mourned the factionalism that destroyed their homeland. Now in the process of being restored, the murals are interpreted every Saturday in docent-led tours of the church, which is located on Maryland Avenue, 5 miles (8 km) from downtown. Tours last about one hour. Visit the mural website, www.vankamurals.org, for more details about the effort to restore the murals.

■ **PLANNING** Pittsburgh www.visitpittsburgh.com. **Andy Warhol Museum** www.warhol.org. **Phipps Conservatory** www.phipps.conservatory.org. **Duquesne Incline** www.duquesneincline.org. Opened in 1877, the Duquesne Incline still features the original wooden cable cars.

# WASHINGTON, D.C.

Venture beyond monumental sights to discover the District's true nature.

Washington, D.C.'s, namesake, the first President of the United States, envisioned a great urban area rising on a providential river. Once viewed as a dozing, one-dimensional city of policy wonks and lawyers, the nation's capital now claims its place among the world's great cities—defiantly transcending its role as a bland backdrop to the grandeur of the monuments and museums.

The city's core remains the federal area that George Washington commissioned. Around it cluster leafy parks lined with gorgeous Victorian row houses. Spacious boulevards, low buildings, and sight lines anchored by Pierre-Charles L'Enfant's ceremonial circles give the remarkably bright and airy city an unusually European skyline and an approachable human scale.

The District was designed with walkers in mind, so stroll the interconnected neighborhoods beyond the National Mall—Adams Morgan, Dupont Circle, the U Street Corridor, Cleveland Park, Penn Quarter, Chinatown, H Street, Georgetown, and beyond—to bring Washington clearly into perspective. East of the Capitol, find a perch on the Brookland heights occupied by the Basilica of the National Shrine of the Immaculate Conception. The bitten-off diamond city spreads before you, the white dome still grand at this distance, but not so dominating as it remains part of a larger picture.

■ PLANNING Washington, D.C. www.washington.org. Metro, the District's efficient rapid transit system (www.wmata.com), offers daily or weekly passes. Basilica of the National Shrine of the Immaculate Conception www.nationalshrine.com.

## BEST OF THE BEST
### Green Spaces

The surprisingly green District boasts some of the nation's finest leafy delights. The **United States Botanic Garden** (www.usbg.gov) is a soothing oasis in the shadow of the Capitol; 4,000-plus plants are displayed in the glass-paneled conservatory. **Rock Creek Park** (www.nps.gov/rocr), running in a long strand of hilly woods and meadows from the National Zoo to the Maryland border, is more than twice the size of New York's Central Park. The **Chesapeake and Ohio Canal towpath** (www.nps.gov/choh), a 184.5-mile (297 km) path that follows the canal on the north bank of the Potomac River, is a favorite of singer-songwriter Mary Chapin Carpenter, a D.C. native: "It's perfect for a quiet walk with the dogs, a bike ride, a morning run, or an evening stroll with the lights of Washington in the distance."

Rent a pedal boat for views of the Jefferson Memorial and the cherry trees from the Tidal Basin.

# NEW YORK CITY

Play with modern locals in Central Park or delve into the lives of New Yorkers past at one of the city's museums.

New York City is on 24 hours a day. Life here means high speed, big nights, quiet mornings, Broadway glitz, buttoned-down Wall Street, five boroughs, rush, rush, rush, stop! In other words, New York is a million worlds in one, a city that refuses to be pigeonholed. And, perhaps more than any other destination in the world, it's very love it or leave it.

Condemn New York City as a place detached from nature, and a local will point you toward the prehistoric caves of Inwood Hill Park or the 160-square-mile (414 sq km) New York City Water Trail, where you can pilot a kayak. Complain that the city is crowded, without a moment's peace, and some guy at the local diner will suggest you spend a few minutes

More than a million walkers, bikers, and runners borough-hop across the Brooklyn Bridge every year.

walking the miles of pathways that wend through Brooklyn's historic Green-Wood Cemetery.

So, do as New Yorkers do: Get to know the city's neighborhoods. In town for a week? Choose three neighborhoods. Maybe four. Spend a day or two in each. Walk up the avenues. Wander the side streets. Select a random pizza place, food cart, or coffeehouse and pronounce it the best in the city. (But say it out of earshot of any locals. They're nicer than you've heard but three times as opinionated.)

By day two or three you'll see that each neighborhood is its own New York. The city is no perfect jigsaw puzzle. Smash some pieces together and create your own map. As the

The Tenement Museum on the Lower East Side leads tours of the neighborhood's immigrant history.

## MELTING POT

Room by room, layer of wallpaper by layer of wallpaper, the stories have been unearthed. The place that now houses the Tenement Museum has been changed both completely and not at all since founders Ruth Abram and Anita Jacobson walked inside the shuttered building in 1988. On their first visit, they found evidence of the city's rich immigrant history, of the immigrant families that moved into the building from Germany and Ireland, from Greece, from Italy, and beyond.

Now docents—lively storytellers all—lead visitors on themed tours of the building's apartments. This is New York City's history. This is American history.

## PERFECT PROMENADE

The elevated park known as the High Line earned rave reviews from the day it opened in June 2009. Stretching from the Meatpacking District to West 34th Street, this erstwhile elevated cargo railway was saved from demolition by neighborhood activists. Join locals for one of the city's most pleasant strolls, with gardens, benches, artwork, and views of the Hudson River. You'll feel like you belong.

■ **PLANNING** **New York City** www.nycgo.com. **New York City Water Trail** www.nycgovparks.org/facilities/kayak. **Inwood Hill Park** www.nycgovparks.org/parks/inwoodhillpark. **Central Park** www.centralparknyc.org. The Central Park Conservancy app details the park's many secrets and places to explore. **Tenement Museum** www.tenement.org. Guided tour only. Reserve tour tickets in advance; they sell out quickly. **The High Line** www .thehighline.org. The High Line is wheelchair accessible. Elevator access is available at the 14th, 16th, 23rd, and 30th Street entrances. Other entrances—Gansevoort, 18th, 20th, 26th, and 28th Streets—are by staircase only.

Broadway tune from the 1940s musical *On the Town* says, "It's a helluva town."

## BACKYARD WONDER

A true backyard to those who live uptown, Central Park is part playground, part thoroughfare (by foot, car, or even horse), part massive art piece, and always changing. The park—which stretches from 59th Street to 110th Street and from Fifth Avenue to Central Park West—is 6 miles (9.7 km) around. Within its confines exist seven bodies of water, 250 acres (101 ha) of lawns, and 136 acres (55 ha) of woodlands.

Though at its busiest on spring and summer days, the 843-acre (341 ha) park is never without company. About 38 million people visit the park each year. There's no better place in New York to grab some space of your own without feeling lonely.

"I'm a fanatic of Central Park," says Eric Ripert, chef-owner of Michelin-starred Le Bernardin (and resident of the Upper East Side). "I know the saxophone player and the Rollerbladers. I know everyone over there."

## PLACES THAT CHANGED ME

*Nora Ephron, novelist & film director*

I suppose I could live somewhere else, but I never feel at home anywhere but New York City. Those of us who didn't grow up in New York have such a deep sense of this: Of growing up somewhere else and then coming here and just absolutely knowing that this is where we belong and where we belonged all along. It's the way you feel when you fall in love with the love of your life. You're just so sure . . . The truth is that if you unpack your bags in New York, you live here.

New York City's biggest backyard, Central Park, is part playground and part thruway for residents and visitors alike.

# AMAZING CITY VIEWS

Find postcard-perfect views from urban parks, hotel lounges, and even a chair carved from sandstone.

## 1 KERRY PARK
### Seattle, Washington

It's almost as if one of Seattle's artists designed the view from this hillside park: the Space Needle–dominated downtown, ferries chugging across Elliott Bay, and on a clear day, Mount Rainier looming in the distance.
www.wwww.seattle.gov/parks

## 2 ADLER PLANETARIUM
### Chicago, Illinois

Adler Planetarium may specialize in galaxy gazing, but its location on a finger of land that juts into Lake Michigan makes it perfect for taking in Chicago's architectural stars, from the Willis Tower (formerly called the Sears Tower) to the John Hancock Center and the solid red CNA Center.
www.adlerplanetarium.org

## 3 CORCOVADO MOUNTAIN
### Rio de Janeiro, Brazil

At 125 feet (38 m) tall, Rio's Christ the Redeemer statue opens his arms to the city from the rocky peak of Corcovado. Take the Corcovado Rack Railway up to the viewing platform and look down to see homes and high-rises curve around the forests, seas, and mountains of this tropical city.
www.corcovado.com.br

## 4 HAMPSTEAD HEATH
### London, England

Rustic Hampstead Heath, a nearly 800-acre (320 ha) swath of rolling hills and woodlands in north London, is renowned for its panoramic vista over the capital. Seek out Parliament Hill, where kite fliers grapple with steady breezes, and the sweeping views south include St. Paul's Cathedral, the Docklands skyscrapers . . . and everything else to distant Surrey.
www.visitlondon.com

## 5 ARC DE TRIOMPHE
### Paris, France

In 1806, Napoleon commissioned this 164-foot-high (50 m) arch to honor a military victory; today, visitors can march to the top. Look southeast to see the grand Champs-Élysées make its way toward the Tuileries Garden. The Eiffel Tower rises to the south, and skyscrapers of la Défense cluster to the west.
http://arc-de-triomphe.monuments-nationaux.fr

## 6 FISHERMAN'S BASTION
### Budapest, Hungary

Named for the fishermen who defended this street in the Middle Ages, this terrace twists up Buda's Castle Hill in a graceful cluster of turrets and winding stairs fit for a fairy-tale princess. The arched windows beautifully frame the city below: Just across the Danube River, the country's parliament building stands at attention.
www.budapestinfo.hu

## 7 INTERCONTINENTAL HONG KONG
### Hong Kong, China

This hotel, which juts into Victoria Harbor, has unparalleled views of one of the world's great trade centers. Visit the three-story windows of the InterContinental's Lobby Lounge at sunset, when the glazed skyscrapers light up like slender gemstones. The water beneath them mirrors the urban glow.
www.hongkong-ic.intercontinental.com

## 8 THE BUND
### Shanghai, China

With the orb-festooned spire of the Oriental Pearl Tower and the swooping sharp lines of its neighboring skyscrapers, the Pudong district looks as if it were plucked from a science fiction novel. Head across the river to the waterfront area for out-of-this-world views of some of the country's tallest structures.
www.cnto.org/shanghai.asp

## 9 MORI TOWER
### Tokyo, Japan

Part of a megacomplex that includes residences, an art museum, and an arena, Mori Tower's Sky Deck is an open-air perch in this city of about nine million. Just to the east, the Tokyo Tower—Japan's slightly taller answer to Paris's Eiffel Tower—glows red at night, while the skyscrapers around it line up in bright geometric patterns.
www.roppongihills.com

## 10 MRS. MACQUARIES POINT
### Sydney, Australia

From the harborside path leading to Mrs. Macquarie's Chair—a sandstone bench carved about 200 years ago—you can see across the city's harbor to the blossoming opera house, the steel arch bridge, and Australia's most prominent skyline.
www.rbgsyd.nsw.gov.au

Hungary's Parliament Building is among the sites on view from Budapest's Fisherman's Bastion.

One of the highlights at the Palacio de Bellas Artes, off Alameda Park, is a Tiffany stained-glass curtain depicting a panorama of the valley of Mexico.

MEXICO

# MEXICO CITY

Embrace the city's contradictions in one of its most stylish neighborhoods.

Mexico City, often disparaged as dirty and chaotic, is a complex, vibrant, and fascinating megalopolis made up of dozens of villages merged together over the past hundred years. Today, it encompasses more than 350 neighborhoods, each a beguiling convergence of historic (the Zócalo, site of the Aztec capital of Tenochtitlan, settled 678 years ago; Alameda Park, the city's oldest green space, created in the 16th century on the site of an Aztec market) and modern (high-design boutique hotels, vintage furniture emporia). Here sheer urban energy (driving here feels like an adrenaline-charged extreme sport) thrives alongside languor (lunches are a sacred, tequila-doused ritual of relaxation and conversation).

To take in the contradictions at their most seductive, head to Condesa, among the city's most fashionable neighborhoods. At its heart is the oval-shaped Parque México, where locals and visitors take yo-yo lessons and flamenco classes, and take their dachshunds for promenades under the shade of flowering jacarandas. Wend your way through side streets lined with pastel-painted Spanish colonial apartment buildings and 1920s neoclassical mansions to discover art galleries, cevicherías (seafood restaurants), mezcalerías (places for drinking mescal), and stylish dining rooms where celebrity chefs specialize in new-wave Mexican food.

## ❧ BEST OF THE BEST ❧
### Top Female Chefs

Mexico City is glutted with fine restaurants, many of which are helmed by female chefs. In Polanco are chef Carmen "Titita" Ramírez Degollado's **El Bajío** (www.carnitaselbajio.com.mx), where you'll find lusty-flavored regional fare (try the mole de Xico), and chef Martha Ortiz's **Dulce Patria** (www.dulcepatria mexico.com), where diners can tuck into avant-garde takes on Mexican classics like Oaxacan cheese-and-epazote empanadas. For lunch in Condesa, don't miss chef Gabriela Cámara's seafood shack, **Contramar** (www.contramar.com.mx), which has the casual, salt-air vibe of a beachside palapa (thatched-roof shelter).

■ **PLANNING Mexico City** www.mexicocity.gob.mx. **Parque México** The park is located about 1,640 feet (500 m) north of the Chilpancingo metro station or 0.6 mile (1 km) south of the Sevilla metro station. Free tango classes are offered Sun. at 5 p.m.

# SANTIAGO

Escape bustling downtown with a climb back in time.

Nearly a third of Chile's population lives in the capital city, Santiago, where nightlife thrives and museums include La Chascona, the home of poet Pablo Neruda. Avenida O'Higgins, the city's main thoroughfare, parallels the Mapocho River and connects the major neighborhoods: newly hip Barrio Brasil; neoclassical París-Londres; historic downtown; bohemian Bellavista; and modern Las Condes. "Santiago is a modern, easygoing, and relaxed city with low crime," says travel writer and Chilean resident Kristina Schrek, "and the summer is especially delightful with near-perfect temperatures and lots of people outdoors enjoying themselves."

Conquistador Pedro de Valdivia founded Santiago in 1541, when he viewed the area from the top of what is now known as Cerro Santa Lucía. Today this historic hill at the center of the city offers a panoramic vista that encompasses the urban skyline, with the Andes Mountains forming a dramatic backdrop. Begin the climb at the Terraza Neptuno, where twin staircases wrap around an ornate fountain featuring the Roman sea god. Follow meandering cobblestone walkways and steep, sometimes uneven stairways past lushly landscaped gardens and pretty plazas, historic buildings, and monuments to the summit of this once barren outcrop.

■ **PLANNING** Santiago www.chile.travel. **La Chascona** www.fundacionneruda.cl. **Centro Cultural Palacio la Moneda** www.ccplm.cl. **Cerro Santa Lucía** The climb to the top takes about 20 minutes and is sometimes slippery; wear sturdy shoes. An elevator also runs up the east side of the hill.

## ∽ IN THE KNOW ∽
### VILLA GRIMALDI

To get a better idea of the lengths a government will go to in order to suppress its people, spend a day at the sobering Villa Grimaldi *(www.villagrimaldi.cl),* located in the suburbs of Santiago. Now known as the Park for Peace, the main house and its surroundings were used as a torture center for dissidents under the dictatorial regime of Augusto Pinochet in the 1970s. Today, survivors like Pedro Matta give the tours here. They point out where they were held captive and lead visitors around the villa's grounds, which are now filled with art memorializing friends long gone.

A fountain of Neptune stands at the start of the ascent up Santiago's Cerro Santa Lucía.

# RIO DE JANEIRO

Dance in the sun and in the streets to the sounds of a city in love.

When in Rio, don't forget to look down: The city's beaches are lined with gorgeous black-and-white Portuguese pavement.

Sensuality appears to be the lifeblood of Rio. Here, people seem to hurry in slow motion—a movement attainable only in the more exotic parts of the world. And baring nearly all is a national pastime. No trip to the Cidade Maravilhosa (Marvelous City) is complete without a visit to the iconic Pão de Açúcar (Sugar Loaf). Take the two-stage tram ride to the summit. Or skip the ride and hike up with a guide. To really savor Rio's voluptuousness, however, head to the city's curving beaches and pulsing nightclubs.

## LIFE ON THE BEACH

On Ipanema Beach, like its even more famous sister,

Copacabana, dark-eyed men sporting perfect tans and sparkling teeth flaunt chiseled physiques, and your nostrils burn with the tang of sea salt, bus fumes, and roasting *churrasco,* the local version of barbecue. "Aaaahh, the beach, the beach. You must go to the beach. Life here is lived on the beach," says one retired resident. Stroll the trademark black-and-white paved beach promenade, check out the adrenaline-pumped volleyball teams and fearless surfers, and feast on a cornucopia of street food. The beach is informally divided into *postos,* or lifeguard stations. Posto 9 draws the arty, intellectual crowd, while posto 10 is great for families with children.

## BOSSA NOVA NIGHTS

When it comes to being sexy, Rio just can't help itself. The city's hip-swiveling jubilance and seductive languor find perfect expression in its music. Check out Palpite Feliz, a "real" samba club in the Vila Isabel neighborhood. Here, you can enjoy bands like Tio Samba, a throwback to the early days of Brazilian dance music. Eleven members perform on trombone, tuba, guitar, *cavaquinho* (similar to a ukulele), saxophone, clarinet, vocals, percussion, and tambourine. Farther south toward the beach the infectious

## PLACES THAT CHANGED ME

*Heloisa Pinheiro, inspiration for the international hit song
"The Girl From Ipanema"*

Rio is a beautiful postcard. God graced us with her never-ending natural beauty, from the mountains to the sea. The excitement begins at the beaches—frescobol, volleyball, soccer, peteca, surfing. At New Year's the beach becomes a stage of fire—with fireworks and bonfires—of religious Umbanda circles, and of invocations with flower offerings in the seas to the saint Yemanj. I love the beaches, especially Ipanema—the one that launched me to the world . . . This place is happy-go-lucky. Rio welcomes everyone with love, and my love for it has no limit. I love Rio passionately in life and, as it says in the song, it is the most beautiful and cute little thing.

bossa nova anthem "The Girl From Ipanema" is best celebrated with an icy *chopp* (draft beer) at Garota de Ipanema, the restaurant where Tom Jobim and Vinicius de Moraes penned the song for local beauty Heloisa Pinheiro in 1962. Its stanzas grace the wall. Across the street you'll find Vinicius, a piano bar, and, nearby, Toca do Vinicius, with

impromptu (and free) evening performances by such beloved singers as Claudia Telles.

■ **PLANNING** Rio de Janeiro www.rioguiaoficial.com.br. Cable cars leave for Pão de Açúcar from the Praça General Tibúrico. To enlist a guide, consult www.riohiking.com.br. **Ipanema** www .ipanema.com. **Vinicius** www.viniciusbar.com.br. **Toca do Vinicius** www.tocadovinicius.com.br.

Travel by taxi or cog railway to the top of Corcovado Mountain for unparalleled views of Rio de Janeiro and Guanabara Bay beyond.

# BUENOS AIRES

Watch the locals from the Obelisco, and then dine like them, too.

Called by many the Paris of South America, Buenos Aires was founded twice by the Spanish on the Río de la Plata—unsuccessfully in 1536 and again in 1580. The soaring Obelisco at the intersection of Avenida 9 de Julio, the world's widest boulevard, and Avenida Corrientes, lined with neon-lit art deco theaters, commemorates the 400th anniversary of the city's first founding. At the monument's base, you'll find everything from holiday concerts to cheering soccer fans.

Few things define *porteños,* as locals call themselves, like a great steak dinner. Locals crowd into *parríllas,* or steakhouses, in search of Argentina's famous grass-fed beef. One of the best is at El Obrero, founded by two Spanish brothers in La Boca, the city's colorful Little Italy. The brothers' descendants continue the tradition. The smell of charcoal and meat permeates the restaurant, which boasts reasonable prices and great local ambience. Its walls are lined with pennants and other memorabilia from the Boca Juniors soccer team, whose nearby stadium is where Diego Maradona rose to international fame. Mixing casual with formal, Cabaña Las Lilas overlooks the Puerto Madero renovated waterfront. At La Cabrera, in fashionable Palermo Viejo, choose to dine outside and watch the sidewalk life in action. You can't go wrong at any of these places.

■ **PLANNING** Buenos Aires www.argentina.travel. **Obelisco** Lines B, C, and D of the metro have stops near the monument. **El Obrero** www.bodegonelobrero.com.ar. **Cabaña Las Lilas** www.laslilas.com. **La Cabrera** www.parrillalacabrera.com.ar.

## ⚘ BEST OF THE BEST ⚘
### Beaux Arts Architecture

Buenos Aires dazzles with beaux arts buildings, remnants of the city's golden age at the beginning of the 20th century. The best examples line Avenida de Mayo, the city's ceremonial route connecting the **Casa Rosada** and **Presidential Museum** (*www.presidencia.gov.ar*), where Evita Perón made her famous speeches, to the massive granite **Congreso** (*www.congreso.gov.ar*), its interior adorned with imported marble, bronze, and stained glass. Don't miss **Palacio Barolo** (*1370 Av. de Mayo, www.pbarolo.com.ar*), whose dome glistens at night with 300,000 little lights. The Casa Rosada overlooks the Plaza de Mayo on Calle Balcarce.

Puerto Madero, the newly revitalized waterfront district in Buenos Aires, offers lively bars and restaurants—and gorgeous skyline views.

Built in 1906, Belfast City Hall reopened in 2009 after a two-year renovation.

## NORTHERN IRELAND
# BELFAST

Find hope and renewal where the Lagan meets the Irish Sea.

Northern Ireland's capital retains the grand image of its Victorian-age dominance in the copper-domed Belfast City Hall and the proper promenades of the Botanic Gardens. The Grand Opera House, built in 1894, was bombed repeatedly in the 1990s, at the height of what locals call the Troubles. The Good Friday Agreement of 1998 quelled centuries of Protestant-Catholic strife, and the theater now stands, restored to its former glory. Eschewing violence and emphasizing its seafaring tradition, Belfast's new spirit is tranquil and hopeful.

Mention the *Titanic* in Belfast, where the mighty vessel was built, and you'll get a typically deadpan response. "She was all right when she left here," locals will joke. Yet with the Titanic Quarter, a $152 million attraction celebrating the ship, even the city's waterfront has been reborn. The monuments that now rise in the former shipbuilding district on this misty waterfront are glassy new theaters and hotels, and the River Lagan, a fetid sewer in decades past, now jumps with fish—and visitors. Take a cruise upriver, beneath Andy Scott's 2007 angelic 50-foot (15 m) wire sculpture titled "Beacon of Hope" at the end of the Queen's Bridge to appreciate a city rebuilding itself with spirit and wit.

■ **PLANNING** Belfast www.gotobelfast.com. **Botanic Gardens** www.belfastcity.gov.uk. **Grand Opera House** www.goh.co.uk. **River Lagan Cruises** www.laganboatcompany.com. **Titanic Quarter** www.titanic-quarter.com.

---

### ✵ BEST OF THE BEST ✵
#### Crown Liquor Saloon

The Crown Liquor Saloon, a gaslit gin palace with "snugs," or small private rooms, for a cozy pint, has been a local tradition since sailors caroused in the red light district along Great Victoria Street. Settle into one of the saloon's private compartments, amid mosaics and mirrors, and ring the antique bell to place your order. Make sure to order a plate of icy fresh oysters and the house specialty of champ—potatoes mashed with green onions—to accompany your draft. The saloon is located at 46 Great Victoria Street. Visit www.crownbar.com for a menu.

IRELAND

# DUBLIN

*In my Dublin, swallows call as they swoop from tree to tree in Dartmouth Square. And in my Dublin, a late-night stroll to the store for a quart of milk takes me past Georgian row houses veiled in a light mist, reminding me just how far I've traveled from my New Jersey roots to find home.*

—ANDREW McCARTHY, *NATIONAL GEOGRAPHIC TRAVELER* MAGAZINE EDITOR AT LARGE

Until 2000, the cast iron Ha'penny Bridge, restored between 2001 and 2003, was the only pedestrian bridge across the River Liffey.

# LONDON

Share in the colorful royal pageantry, explore an age-old market, and float through the heart of the city.

"B y seeing London I have seen as much of life as the world can show," Samuel Johnson wrote in the 18th century. Though Dr. Johnson would be hard-pressed to recognize the modern city, his words transcend the centuries. Like any great city, London must juggle the demands of past and present by clinging to the things that help make it great, while embracing the changes that will ensure future greatness.

## CHANGING THE GUARD

Heads in the crowd turn toward the crisp sound of soldiers marching in step. Punctual to the minute, a detachment of guards, resplendent in scarlet uniforms and distinctive busbies, or bearskin hats, approaches Buckingham Palace. In front of the palace a separate detachment awaits. Officers approach and touch gloves, symbolically

An impressive engineering marvel, Tower Bridge also plays the role of recreational activity hub.

transferring the keys to the palace and the responsibility for protecting the monarch.

The Changing the Guard has taken place since 1837, when Queen Victoria moved into what was then known as Buckingham House. Five regiments have the honor of protecting Buckingham and nearby St. James's Palace, the official center of the royal court. Soldiers in the Guards are drawn from working regiments, and many of today's Guards have seen active duty in Iraq or Afghanistan. A detachment remains in place for 24 hours, and individual soldiers are on duty for two hours at a time. When the 24 hours are up, a detachment of the New Guard departs on foot from Wellington Barracks to relieve the Old Guard—and the Queen and her palaces are protected for another day.

The Queen's Life Guard, mounted cavalry troops, watch over the official entrance to St. James's Palace and Buckingham Palace.

## NOTTING HILL & PORTOBELLO ROAD

Time was when Notting Hill was one of the poorest areas in London. Not anymore. Its earthy, bohemian atmosphere and cheap rents attracted artists, writers, and then more affluent residents. Today its streets contain some of the most expensive real estate in the capital. But much of its original charm remains, thanks in large part to Portobello Road, which runs through the neighborhood's heart. The street's fruit and vegetable stalls, along with its Saturday antiques market, provide a gritty, blue-collar edge that cuts through the area's pretensions. Excellent small boutiques have opened here and on nearby Westbourne Grove, one of the city's finest emerging shopping destinations, but most visitors are still more likely to enjoy swapping banter with the market traders or searching for a dusty bargain in the labyrinth of antique stalls. Farther up the street, toward Golborne Road, the spirit of "old" Notting Hill is alive and well. Among the vintage clothing stalls and piles of junk laid out for sale, you really might find a treasure.

## A BOAT ON THE RIVER

The Thames is one of the reasons London is where it is—the

Romans built a bridge near present-day St. Paul's Cathedral—and one of the reasons for its prosperity. A million people worked on the river in 1900 in what was then the world's busiest port, bolstered by trade with the British Empire. By the 1980s, though, the docks were all but derelict, their surroundings desolate, and the river itself horribly polluted. But today, after far-reaching changes, a hundred species of fish live in the river; bridges have been overhauled (and new ones built); the Docklands area in the east, especially around Canary Wharf, has been regenerated; and old landmarks, notably the Bankside Power Station—now the Tate Modern art gallery—have been transformed.

Several boating options are available. Take a short, urban journey downstream past the City of Westminster and the City of London, or venture farther to the maritime attractions at Greenwich; or make a longer rural journey upstream, gliding past Somerset House and Battersea Power Station though increasingly green areas of outer London to Kew Gardens and Richmond Park. You could even take a speedboat far downstream, through Docklands and on to the futuristic flood defenses of the Thames Barrier.

■ **PLANNING London** www.visitlondon.com **Changing the Guard** www.royal.gov.uk. Takes place on alternate days in winter, daily in summer; may be canceled in bad weather. **Notting Hill & Portobello Road** www.portobellomarket.org, www.rbkc.gov.uk/street markets. **Food Market** Section from Elgin Crescent to Talbot Road; daily except Thurs. & Sun. **Antiques Market** Chepstow Villas to Elgin Crescent; Sat. 6 a.m.–3 p.m. **London Eye River Cruise** www.londoneye.com. **Westminster Passenger Service Association** www.wpsa.co.uk; trips to Kew and Hampton Court. **Crown River Cruises** www.crownriver.com. **Thames River Services** www.thamesriverservices.co.uk. **London RIB Voyages** www.londonribvoyages.com; speedboat trips.

## PLACES THAT CHANGED ME
### *Anna Quindlen, Pulitzer Prize-winning columnist & author*

I have . . . been to London too many times to count in the pages of books, to Dickensian London rich with narrow alleyways and jocular street scoundrels, to the London of Conan Doyle and Margery Allingham with its salt-of-the-earth police officers, troubled aristocrats, and crowded train stations. Hyde Park, Green Park, Soho, and Kensington: I had been to them all in my imagination before I ever set foot in England. So that by the time I actually visited London in 1995 for the first time, it felt less like an introduction and more like a homecoming.

The London Eye has been spinning across the Thames from Big Ben since March 2000.

# POMP & CEREMONY

Witness history, tradition, and pride coalesce.

## 1 TOMB OF THE UNKNOWNS
Arlington, Virginia

To stand guard at the Tomb of the Unknowns at Arlington National Cemetery is considered a great honor. Echoing the solemn 21-gun salute, a sentinel paces as many steps past the marble sarcophagus, stops, and faces it for 21 seconds. This routine is repeated between the changing of the guard every 30 to 60 minutes.
www.arlingtoncemetery.mil

## 2 DAY OF THE DEAD
Mexico

Laugh death in the face on Día de Los Muertos, an upbeat festival rooted in the ancient traditions of Mexico's indigenous Maya, Aztec, and Nahuatl people. Families carry brooms, flowers, and food to local cemeteries to freshen up the graves of departed loved ones, while shops fill with ghoulish treats to be gobbled up during all-night fiestas.
www.dayofthedead.com

## 3 BELTANE FIRE FESTIVAL
Edinburgh, Scotland

The spirit of the ancient Celts burns bright at Edinburgh's Beltane Fire Festival, heralding the start of summer in the Celtic year. Revived in modern times, Beltane means different things to different people: It's a celebration of the seasons, a religious observance of pagan origin, or simply an opportunity to join in a popular and powerful event. Catch the festival's bonfires and processions atop central Edinburgh's Calton Hall every April 30.
www.beltane.org

## 4 BASTILLE DAY MILITARY PARADE
Paris, France

Gallic hearts swell with pride on La Fête Nationale, July 14, when Parisians rose up and stormed the Bastille prison, thus starting the French Revolution. The highlight is Europe's oldest and largest military parade, when France's entire armed forces seem to cruise down the Champs-Élysées.
http://en.parisinfo.com

## 5 ROYAL AKWASIDAE FESTIVAL
Ghana

Held every six weeks at the royal palace in Kumasi, this celebration features a long line of dignitaries—sword bearers, musket bearers, men with ostrich-feather fans—who pay homage to the king, who may ride out in a palanquin to greet his admirers.
www.touringghana.com

## 6 SETO MACCHENDRANATH BATHING CEREMONY
Kathmandu, Tibet

During the annual bathing ritual at Seto Macchendranath, an ancient temple for both Buddhists and Hindus, Nepalese priests cleanse an idol of the deity with holy water and a mixture of butter, honey, milk, curd, and sugar. The bathwater is then sprinkled over the devoted as blessings.
www.welcomenepal.com

## 7 WATER SPLASHING FESTIVAL
Xishuangbanna, China

Observed with gusto by the Dai ethnic minority, the Water Splashing Festival involves three days of lighthearted celebration of purification for the new year. Dragon-boat races are held on the Lancang River, and at night, illuminated lanterns float on the water. The symbolic dousing begins—first a ceremonial pour on a Buddha statue, then a free-for-all among giggling crowds in the streets.
www.china.org.cn

## 8 LUNAR NEW YEAR
South Korea

The hottest festivity on the South Korean calendar is the three-day Lunar New Year, when families cast off their house demons, dress up in colorful *hanbok* (traditional clothes), eat traditional *ttokkuk* (rice cakes), and make pilgrimages to their hometowns.
http://english.visitkorea.or.kr

## 9 TEA CEREMONIES
Japan

Choreographed rituals, Japanese tea ceremonies go back to at least the ninth century, when a Buddhist monk brought the fragrant leaf from China. Still performed in magnificent pagodas such as Shokin-tei near Kyoto, the custom is more about artful gesture and hospitality than about drinking tea.
www.japanese-tea-ceremony.net

## 10 OPENING CEREMONIES
Olympic Games

First held in 1908, the opening ceremony of the Olympic Games has evolved into a spectacular, performance-based event. Traditionally, runners carry the torch from the ancient site of Olympia; Greek athletes always lead the Parade of Nations into the stadium.
www.olympic.org

The Dai people of Xishuangbanna, in China's Yunnan Province, wish good luck in the coming year by throwing water at each other.

# FRANCE
# PARIS

Stroll through flea markets and patisseries, or hop on the Métro for some unique art.

Home to haute couture, masterpieces of art and architecture, temples of fine dining, and bohemian cafés, the City of Light is considered by many to be the world's most beautiful city. Among its most illustrious sights are the imposing Arc de Triomphe, marking the crossroads of 12 streets and memorializing military victory; one of the

world's greatest art collections at the Louvre; and the Notre-Dame's splendid Gothic architecture. To get to know a different side of France's capital, hit the neighborhoods—"I . . . [love] stumbling into neighborhoods and watching the special quality of the light as it hits familiar places at different times of the day," Pulitzer Prize–winning author David Halberstam

In Paris, many of the Métro stations provide some serious eye candy.

wrote. Patisseries, flea markets, and the Métro are great places to start.

## PATISSERIES

The perfect Parisian patisserie: Is it a grand establishment with centuries-old baking traditions? A nouveau spot that blends daring flavors and artistry? Or the neighborhood gem that locals hope will remain their secret? With such a delectable question, the answer is simple: all of the above. Among the most celebrated is Ladurée in the 8th arrondissement. When it opened in 1862, Ladurée was one of the city's only tea salons. Today, it's the most popular. With magnificent belle epoque styling, the salon de

If you're after something special, head to Paris's flea markets early in the day, before the crowds.

thé owes a great deal of its following to the *macaron,* the pretty meringue cookie that is as iconic to the French as the cupcake is to Americans. There's also Philippe Conticini's Pâtisserie des Rêves on tony rue du Bac in the 7th arrondissement. Against a candy-colored backdrop of pink, green, and tangerine, glass domes descend from the ceiling to protect individual cakes that are displayed on a central table like fine art. And then there's Stohrer on rue Montorgueil in the 2nd arrondissement, founded in 1730 by Nicholas Stohrer, King Louis XV's pastry chef. He also created the baba au rhum dessert when he splashed a dry Polish brioche with sweet Malaga wine. Don't care for rum-soaked cake? You can leave the historic patisserie with almost any French classic, from raspberry tarts with perfectly aligned berries dusted with sugar to Puit d'Amour cake filled with vanilla custard. It's no wonder chef and author Julia Child remarked of Paris, "And the food—there's nothing quite like it anywhere else."

## BROWSING FLEA MARKETS

The *puces,* or flea markets, located at the *portes* (gates) of Paris, are a treasure trove for anyone who enjoys the thrill of hunting for that perfect find. Most famous is the Saint-Ouen, where you can pick through the antiques, clothing, and objets d'art of more than 2,000 exhibitors. Avoid the main drag, which tends to be full of tourists and T-shirts, and beeline instead for the warren of narrow passages surrounding the market, which remain as intriguing as a Moroccan suq. Montreuil is the place for knickknacks, secondhand bikes, furniture, and clothes. Vanves is essentially a secondhand market overflowing with everything from old toys to paintings.

## PARIS BY MÉTRO

Explore Paris's artistic flamboyance at some of the city's most interesting Métro stops. Not all are alike. Some have been decorated in accordance with their location: Louvre-Rivoli is a tasteful mini-museum furnished with reproductions of works from the Louvre, while Varenne has statues by Rodin. Gare de Lyon, on the newest line, 14, has a tropical garden; the Arts et Métiers stop looks like the inside of a submarine; and the Concorde station has the Declaration of the Rights of Man written out on its tiled walls. Perhaps the coolest of all are the ghost stations. Keep your eyes peeled as the trains on Line 8 or 9 pass between Strasbourg–St.-Denis and République to see the long-closed Saint-Martin station, its tiles now covered in graffiti.

■ **PLANNING** **Paris** www.parisinfo.com. **Ladurée** www.laduree.fr. **Pâtisserie des Rêves** www.lapatisseriedesreves.com. **Stohrer** www.stohrer.fr. **Saint-Ouen** Métro: Porte de Clignancourt. **Montreuil** Métro: Porte de Montreuil. **Vanves** Métro: Porte de Vanves. For more flea market options, go to www.parispuces.com. You can also visit the city's vintage boutiques with the help of Ooh La La Vintage (www.oohlalavintage.com). **Ademas** ademas.assoc.free.fr. Tours of the Métro, including a ghost station.

## ⚜ BEST OF THE BEST ⚜
### Art in the City

Few cities can compete with Paris's allure to artists through the ages, so it's no wonder that you'll find some of the world's best artwork here. Above all, seek out da Vinci's famous "Mona Lisa" (Louvre) and Monet's "Water Lilies" (Musée de l'Orangerie) and "Impression, Soleil Levant" (Musée Marmottan Monet), which gave its name to an entire art movement. David's "The Coronation of Napoleon" (Louvre), van Gogh's "Bedroom in Arles" (Musée d'Orsay), and Manet's "Luncheon on the Grass" (Musée d'Orsay) complete a very short list of masterpieces.

Find many of the city's quaintest restaurants and cafés along rue Montorgueil.

# GERMANY
# BERLIN

Try to keep up in a city changing by the minute.

Two decades ago Potsdamer Platz was a windswept field where flea-market vendors stood in the mud selling rubber boots, old uniforms, and, if you winked, Polish vodka. That, of course, was then. The market has given way to a showstopper of glass and steel created by the world's top architects.

The maestro of reinvention, Berlin is bent on memorializing its past while limning a fresh silhouette of the future. "Paris is always Paris, but Berlin is never Berlin," quipped former French culture minister Jack Lang.

A burned-out hulk during the Cold War, the historic Reichstag now sports a snazzy glass dome designed by Norman Foster. Where the GDR-era Palast der Republik once stood, a replica of the Hohenzollerns' city palace will soon rise again, like a Prussian phoenix. Farther south in the Kreuzberg district, an Old World baroque facade obscures the jagged, zinc-paneled core of the Jewish Museum Berlin.

In a city that morphs this fast, keeping up with the nightlife is a 24-hour job. "The professionally trendy wait for the word on the street," says writer Frank Heibert, "and head for underground clubs that pick up and move every week."

Among more stable venues is Berghain, a techno temple lodged in a decommissioned power station. For something more redolent of Berlin's gentler, soft-core past, head to Bar Jeder Vernunft for saucy stagings of cabaret.

■ **PLANNING Berlin** www.berlin.de. **Reichstag** www.bundestag. de. **Jewish Museum Berlin** http://jmberlin.de. **Berghain** http://berghain.de. **Bar Jeder Vernunft** www.bar-jeder-vernunft.de.

## PLACES THAT CHANGED ME

*Jeremy Gray, National Geographic writer*

In 1985, the capital of the German Democratic Republic was a place charged with intrigue. Hairs on the back of my neck screamed and I felt like a Western spy as I passed the border guards at Friedrichstrasse. On Unter den Linden I watched goose-stepping soldiers at the Neue Wache. I remember how the locals, aware of the Stasi's roving cameras, avoided me like the plague. Finding little worth buying, and wondering if I'd really just seen a model city of socialism, I stuck my leftover Ostmarks in a charity box.

# BARCELONA

Embark on a flight of architectural fancy.

Cradled between the Mediterranean and the Serra de Collserola hills, Barcelona stands apart from Spain. The free-spirited capital of the self-governing and fiercely independent northeastern Catalonian region traces its history back two millennia. It began as a Roman outpost and emerged as one of Europe's most dynamic cities.

Eccentric Catalonian-born architect Antoni Gaudí and fellow artists Pablo Picasso, Salvador Dalí, Joan Miró, and Antoni Tàpies called Barcelona home, their masterpieces fueled by the city's innate creative energy. The result is a fanciful cityscape steeped in design—from playful sculptures and fantastical architectural swirls to palm-shaded squares with neoclassical facades and acres of parks and gardens on Montjuïc, the hill overlooking Barcelona from the southeast.

The best way to get to know Barcelona is to dance with her, slowly, passionately. Walk from the original Roman settlement, much of it still intact under the narrow streets of Barri Gòtic, the old city's Gothic Quarter, to the palaces and churches of Barcelona's 12th- and 13th-century golden age and on to the 19th-century L'Eixample neighborhood, where every avenue seems to be lined with flights of architectural fancy.

■ **PLANNING Barcelona** www.barcelonaturisme.com. Barcelona Turisme's themed trails, along with an extensive metro and bus system, make it easier to navigate this somewhat indecipherable city at your own pace.

## PLACES THAT CHANGED ME

*Paul Goldberger, Pulitzer Prize-winning architecture critic*

Several years ago I spent one of the happiest days of my life in Barcelona, and nothing happened . . . I went nowhere farther than my feet could take me, and I felt more intensely connected to urban life than I have anywhere else in the world. I spent the day as I did as an undergraduate touring Europe for the first time—I walked the streets from early morning until late at night, stopping only to eat or enter whatever buildings I could. I had more energy at midnight than in the morning, because in Barcelona energy builds, in lilting stages, throughout the day, as the city becomes more a part of one's inner being.

Opened in 1922, Antoni Gaudí's Parc Güell is a land of enchantment in a city already teeming with magic.

# SANTIAGO DE COMPOSTELA

*The old city is graceful and lovely, its streets narrow and twisting and cobbled, with bright shop windows revealing all sorts of temptations: chocolates, toys, wine, necklaces, books. Eager as I am to reach the cathedral, I linger at every corner; I see few things that I don't image myself buying.*

KATHRYN HARRISON, AUTHOR OF *THE ROAD TO SANTIAGO* & OTHER BOOKS

The sacred way of St. James ends at Santiago de Compostela, where winding, medieval streets lead to the city's famed cathedral.

# PLACES TO LISTEN TO MUSIC

Embrace the rhythm and join the dance.

## 1 JAZZ CLUBS
### Chicago

Jazz is the lifeblood of the Windy City and the first thing you'll hear at O'Hare Airport when you arrive. Blue Chicago on Clark showcases female vocalists, Von Freeman blows his celebrated tenor at New Apartment Lounge, and Meyers Ace Hardware is where Louis "Satchmo" Armstrong soloed among the fork hammers.
www.jazzinchicago.org

## 2 GRAND OLE OPRY
### Nashville, Tennessee

Since 1925, this cultural icon has rolled out the biggest stars in country, bluegrass, folk, gospel, and comedy at the Grand Ole Opry House, including country music legends Johnny Cash, Dolly Parton, and Hank Williams.
www.opry.com

## 3 REGGAE SUMFEST
### Montego Bay, Jamaica

Joined at the hip, Jamaica and reggae scale an emotional peak at the four-day Reggae Sumfest, luring thousands of fans to the Bob Marley Entertainment Center. Either side of the festival, Caribbean vibes continue to emanate from laid-back harbor bars like Mobay Proper.
www.reggaesumfest.com

## 4 CARNAVAL
### Salvador, Brazil

This ecstatic goodbye to seasonal abstinence may reverberate deepest in Salvador, on the stunning Bahia Bay. Typical music is *axé*, stirring an earthy pot of Caribbean calypso, samba, and reggae, and blared out to massive crowds trailing behind the *blocos* (trucks). *Tríos elétricos*—amp-stacked floats with musicians playing up top—originated here.
www.bahia-online.net

## 5 CAFÉ TORTONI
### Buenos Aires, Argentina

Founded in 1858, the city's oldest coffeehouse exudes a timeless elegance and lays a somewhat contentious claim to being its most famous tango venue. Performances on the basement stage, La Bodega, are unexpectedly affordable.
www.cafetortoni.com.ar

## 6 ALFAMA DISTRICT
### Lisbon, Portugal

While Portugal's haunting national song, fado, can be heard all over this lovely city, the eastern quarter of Alfama hits the highest notes. In a laundry-festooned street where fishermen sell their catch from doorways, Baixa is a tiny, earthy bar where the cook and local taxi drivers croon their hearts out.
www.visitlisboa.com

## 7 WIENER KONZERTHAUS
### Vienna, Austria

Inaugurated by Kaiser Franz Joseph in 1913, this renowned four-hall venue with velvet acoustics is the stomping grounds of the Wiener Symphoniker. Reserve weeks in advance to see Vienna Mozart Orchestra, whose musicians perform in 18th-century wigs and costumes in the atmospheric Mozartsaal.
http://konzerthaus.at

## 8 DAKAR
### Senegal

This vibrant port city (and the west African nation's capital) has long been famous for a rich mélange called *mbalax,* a seamless fusion of Afro-Cuban music, jazz, funk, rock, and French pop with African drumming and hurricane-throated song. Choice places to hear mbalax's unique and infectious sound are Club Thiossane, owned by music legend (and, as of 2012, government cabinet member) Youssou N'Dour, and the Alizé Club.
www.au-senegal.com

## 9 HO CHI MINH CITY
### Vietnam

If you haven't tuned in since Uncle Ho's day, the music scene in the former city of Saigon absolutely kicks it. There's something here for every ear, from vintage Hendrix to Latin, classical to Vietnamese folk, flamenco to country and western. Put the Acoustic Bar, Carmen, and Yoko on your boogie list.
www.vietnamtourism.gov.vn

## 10 TE MATATINI NATIONAL FESTIVAL
### New Zealand

Every two years, more than 50,000 fans make a pilgrimage to Te Matatini, the world's biggest festival of Maori performing arts. Led by tribal experts of *haka*—an awe-inspiring, multipurpose dance for war, honor, and welcoming—the event revolves around competitions of New Zealand's top talent. The location changes each time.
www.tematatini.co.nz

One of Chicago's oldest jazz clubs, Jazz Showcase, in historic Dearborn Station, features legendary performers and the hottest up-and-comers.

# ROME

Enjoy a Roman holiday, mixing the secular with the spiritual.

Piazza Navona is the place to sample *tartufo,* a delectable chocolate ice-cream treat.

today, attesting to the glory that was Rome and lending to its everlasting allure.

## LA DOLCE VITA

Few cities make it easier to wallow in la dolce vita than Rome. Audrey Hepburn and Gregory Peck did it in the 1953 movie *Roman Holiday;* thousands do it every day. The place to start is the mostly pedestrian Centro Storico, where streets spill onto sun-filled plazas. Cafés and trattoria tables beckon beside the 2,000-year-old Pantheon, just a short trek over from the Roman Forum and Colosseum. Located near the Spanish Steps, the historic Antico Caffe Greco—the former stomping grounds of writers like Stendhal, Goethe, and Byron—still captivates with its romantic charm. Up the way, at the end of luxury boutique–flanked Via Condotti, it's time for another gelato before climbing the palm-fringed Spanish Steps to graceful Trinità dei Monti, the iconic, twin-towered church built in 1502. Sneak over to the 18th-century Trevi Fountain at night, after the crowds have thinned, and watch how the monumental fountain morphs into a sensuous backdrop of shared community celebrating Roman life.

Another dolce vita hot spot, Piazza Navona—with its three graceful fountains, including Bernini's exuberant baroque Fountain of Four Rivers—sits atop an ancient Roman

Lucian, the second-century Greek rhetorician, described Rome as "a bit of Paradise." Fifteenth-century Tuscan scholar Gian Francesco Poggio Bracciolini praised the city as the "most beautiful and magnificent of all those that either have been or shall be." These opinions about the Eternal City survive, and why not? Almost 3,000 years of history, layer upon layer of it, testify not only to the genius, perseverance, and adaptability of the peoples who founded Rome and developed it through the ages, but also to that of those who followed. The city's vast number of archaeological sites, ancient monuments, and early structures still exists

## PLACES THAT CHANGED ME

*Johann Wolfgang von Goethe, excerpt from* Italian Journey

My desire to reach Rome quickly was growing stronger every minute until nothing could have induced me to make more stops . . . Now I have arrived, I have calmed down and feel as if I had found a peace that will last for my whole life. . . . The sky is now wonderfully serene. Rome is slightly foggy in the morning and the evening, but on the hills of Albano, Castello and Frascati, where I spent three days last week, the air is always limpid and pure. *There* is a nature for you which is worth studying!

racetrack built in A.D. 86. Musicians, artists, and lots of cafés make this pedestrian outdoor living room an excellent spot for people-watching.

## RELIGIOUS ROME

No visit to Rome would be complete without visiting a few of its many churches and basilicas: the Basilica of St. John Lateran, the medieval Basilica of San Clemente, vast Santa Maria Maggiore, and, of course, St. Peter's Basilica and the Vatican—all repositories of relics and magnificent art. "In one unique location of only 108 acres [43 ha]," says Edmund Cardinal Szoka, President Emeritus, Pontifical Commission, Vatican City State, "2,000 years of religious, cultural, and artistic history come together to reveal the splendor of God." For a touch of mystery, explore the ancient Christian burial sites tunneled under the Old Appian Way. The murky catacombs of St. Callistus hold some 170,000 graves, the crypt of St. Cecilia, and paintings from the second and third centuries A.D.

■ **PLANNING Rome** www.turismoroma.it. **Antico Caffè Greco** www.anticocaffegreco.eu. **Basilica of San Clemente** www.basilica sanclemente.com. **St. Peter's Basilica and the Vatican** www .vatican.va. **Catacombs of St. Callistus** Closed noon–2:30 p.m. daily. Closed Wed. and during Feb. Admission fee.

Roman ruins sit close to the city's cafés and more modern attractions.

# VENICE

*When I visit Venice nothing makes me happier than a walk into Piazza San Marco, where for centuries artists, lovers, and such writers as Byron and Dickens have met at outdoor tables to sip caffè. Especially in winter, when mornings are steeped in fog and the city assumes a dreamlike quality.*

—DALE CHIHULY, GLASS SCULPTOR & U.S. "NATIONAL LIVING TREASURE"

Settle in for a coffee in Piazza San Marco, where café orchestras compete for your attention.

# SOFIA

Drink to the past.

Sofia is as young as European capitals get. The city really arrived on the world stage only in the 19th century, when it was chosen as the capital of newly independent Bulgaria. At its heart stands the gleaming gold dome of the St. Alexander Nevsky Cathedral, built a century ago to commemorate the Russian soldiers who fell in the battle to liberate Bulgaria from the Ottoman yolk in the 19th century.

Few visitors, however, realize that a permanent settlement has thrived here for several thousand years. The highly evolved Thracian civilization resided in the territory of modern-day Bulgaria between the seventh and second centuries B.C., settling the site of present-day Sofia. Why were they drawn here? Hot springs—an attraction that continues to appeal. To summon your inner Thracian, join the locals as they congregate at the Sofia Public Mineral Springs in the center of town to fill up their drinking bottles with free mineral-rich water. Or, check out the National Archaeological Museum, which occupies the former Grand Mosque and houses an astounding assortment of Thracian weaponry, gold and silver jewelry, and bronze masks unearthed in recent archaeological digs.

■ **PLANNING** **Sofia** www.sofia.bg. Sofia's crowded center is best enjoyed on foot, so wear comfortable walking shoes. Vitosha, a 7,500-foot (2,290 m) mountain peak, rises south of the city and is visible from nearly anywhere, providing a quick and easy way to get your bearings. **National Archaeological Museum** www.naim.bg.

## IN THE KNOW
### BULGARIAN CUISINE

Despite its youth, Sofia is the perfect setting to enjoy centuries of Bulgarian culinary traditions. Like the cuisines of its Turkish and Serbian neighbors, Bulgarian cooking involves a lot of sumptuously grilled meats, mostly pork and lamb. The country's signature dish is *shopska* salad, an addictive concoction of garden-fresh tomatoes, cucumbers, onions, and chopped red peppers, topped with a pleasantly salty, grated sheep's cheese called *sirene*. Salads usually start a meal and are almost always accompanied by a shot of *rakia*, or fruit brandy, usually made from fermented plums or grapes. For dessert, there's baklava, or try *mekitsi*—lightly fried dough dusted with powdered sugar.

Built atop ancient Roman thermal baths, the elegant Sofia Public Mineral Baths served as the city's public baths from 1913 to 1986.

Only a few columns remain of the colossal Temple of Olympian Zeus, which was larger than the Parthenon.

GREECE
# ATHENS

Peel back the layers of history upon which the city stands.

Thinking of bypassing Athens and heading straight for the islands? Think again. The Big Olive is more than a collection of old stones. Here past and present coexist so harmoniously that it's hard to tell where one ends and the other begins. The city's great museums—the National Archaeological Museum, the Byzantine & Christian Museum, the Museum of Cycladic Art, and the Benaki Museum—tell the story of Athens, but the best way to capture the city's complex melding of cultures and eras is to head out onto the streets, or under them.

Start with a visit to the bright and modern Syntagma metro station, where commuters rush past displays of artifacts discovered during the station's construction in the early 1990s. Ride the metro to the Acropolis station and walk the sacred rocky outcrop. Then stroll over to nearby Plaka, where ancient monuments, Byzantine churches, Turkish mosques, and even an island village (Anafiotika) rub shoulders with art galleries, designer graffiti, posh antique shops, kitsch souvenir emporiums, old-fashioned tavernas, and loud cafés. From here the bustling Monastiraki flea market, a bazaar since Socrates' day, is just a short amble away.

■ **PLANNING** Athens www.breathtakingathens.com. **National Archaeological Museum** www.namuseum.gr. **Byzantine & Christian Museum** www.byzantinemuseum.gr. **Museum of Cycladic** Art www.cycladic.gr. **Benaki Museum** www.benaki.gr. **Athens Metro** www.ametro.gr.

## ❧ BEST OF THE BEST ❧
### Hilltop View of Athens

For a truly memorable experience, pack a picnic and head to the top of **Lycabettus Hill.** This limestone outcrop reaches nearly 1,000 feet (305 m) above the city and promises a superb view. You can climb the hill, but most visitors prefer the two-minute funicular ride to the summit. At the top you'll find Agios Georgios (a blazing white church), a café, and a stunning panorama that encompasses the Acropolis and the Port of Piraeus and reveals the extent of this city of four million souls. The Athenian connection to the sea and the mountains that surround it, the famous Attic light that has inspired so many artists and poets, and the beauty of the city's ancient and modern monuments, spotlighted and tranquil at night, all reveal themselves.

With the Atlas Mountains as a backdrop, the peaceful Menara imperial garden in Marrakech rustles with the sound of olive and fruit trees.

# MARRAKECH

*Morocco is a garden, and before us, as we go toward Marrakech, we see the garden wall. It is some 12,000 feet high. The Atlas Mountains shoot up abruptly from the plain to snowy heights. Behind it is the Sahara. Before it, like a small stage against a stupendous backdrop, is the city of Marrakech.*

—WILLARD PRICE, *NATIONAL GEOGRAPHIC* MAGAZINE, JULY 1943

# TURKEY
# ISTANBUL

Let centuries of history (and *hammams*) work their magic.

The site of grand dreams ever since Christian emperors sought to establish a new Rome here in the fourth century A.D., Istanbul is often considered the bridge—both literal and metaphorical—between Europe and Asia. It's certainly one of the world's most complex cities, the magnetic center of a country that is 98 percent Islamic yet increasingly famous for its watermelon martinis and as a showplace of fashion. As Turkish university director Metin Heper puts is, "The cultural features of East and West combine in such a picturesque and harmonious manner that the so-called clash of civilizations is so unreal and multiculturalism so possible."

Despite the city's increasing modernization, its compact historic core—the Sultanahmet district—continues to mesmerize. The stunning Blue Mosque, Hagia Sophia, and sprawling grounds of Topkapi Palace are must-sees on any visitor's itinerary. After a long day of sightseeing, treat yourself to a traditional Turkish bath, or hammam. In Sultanahmet, steam and scrub your way to health and happiness at either of two historic hammams: Try Cemberlitas Hamami, designed by royal architect Sinan in 1584; or Cagaloglu Hamami, built in 1741.

■ PLANNING Istanbul english.istanbul.com, www.kultur.gov.tr. Cemberlitas Hamami www.cemberlitashamami.com.tr. Cagaloglu Hamami www.cagalogluhamami.com.tr.

## ~ IN THE KNOW ~
### CRUISING ISTANBUL BY FERRY

Istanbul's sense of ceaseless movement doesn't stop at the water's edge. Eminonu, on the Europe side, and Karakoy, on the Asian shore, serve as the main ferry hubs, although a more intimate point of departure is the smaller station Halic (Golden Horn), a little west of Eminonu. Buy a dollar token and pass the turnstile to enter a sort of floating social club. Commuters, fresh-faced naval cadets, pilgrims going to the scenic mosque at Eyup, courting lovers, and stocky men in flat caps all rub shoulders on the hard white wooden benches, as waiters bearing glasses of orange juice and apple tea jounce past. Visit www.ido.com.tr for a ferry schedule.

From the glorious perch of Istanbul's Suleymaniye Mosque, head downhill for a fish sandwich from one of the boats jostling in the Bosporus.

## ISRAEL
# JERUSALEM

From ramparts above, observe the day-to-day life of three different religions at the crux of Middle East strife.

Within the ancient walls of Jerusalem's Old City, monuments celebrating three of the world's most significant religions coexist, including the gilt Dome of the Rock, sacred to both Muslims and Jews, the Western (or Wailing) Wall, the most holy place for prayer in Judaism, and the Church of the Holy Sepulchre, the death and burial site of Jesus Christ. "By far the most interesting half-acre on the face of the earth" is how 19th-century missionary W. M. Thomson summed it up.

To truly get at its soul, climb upon the ancient stone ramparts that surround the Old City and take a stroll, peering down at the goings-on through loopholes meant for Crusades-era archers to aim their arrows. You'll see in the twisting labyrinth of lanes how the markets, homes, schools, and sites central to the beliefs of Christianity, Islam, and Judaism don't mix together. Instead, each group tightly clings to its own crisply designated, tightly packed quarter—a microcosm of conflicted religious life in the heart of the Holy Land. But you'll also spy tidbits of everyday life—women in head scarves hanging laundry, kids in yarmulkes or uniforms tossing soccer balls, men in tunics or collars headed toward their place of worship—and other reminders that life goes on.

■ **PLANNING** Jerusalem www.goisrael.com. **Jerusalem Walls** Access the walls at Jaffa Gate. Call 02/625-4403 for more information.

## ∽ IN THE KNOW ∽
### SATAF NATURE TRAIL

Blessed with clear mountain air and fig trees fed by a natural spring, the restored village of Sataf, a ten-minute drive west of Jerusalem, is an ancient farming site with caves and archaeological digs that provides a glimpse of days gone by. Thousands of years ago, hilltop farmers took rocks from the slopes, some as big as Western Wall boulders, to sculpt terraces where they raised grapes, olives, and spices. One trail leads from the mountaintop through the terraces to the spring, where Jerusalemites still till the soil. On two- to four-hour hikes you'll likely catch sight of local chukars (small pheasant) and enjoy sweeping views of the Valley of Rephaim, where David fought the Philistines. Check locally for bus schedules to Sataf and the nature trail.

Traditional sailboats called feluccas reveal the calm thread at the heart of this otherwise hectic city.

# EGYPT
# CAIRO

See how the frenetic city reveals itself slowly and on its own terms.

Cairo has been a city of pharaohs and caliphs, of pashas and emperors and presidents, of Christians and Muslims. Today, of course, Cairenes are focused on the future, not the past, and traces of the city's recent turbulence can be seen in Tahrir Square. Truly understanding this fast and furious, filthy and fascinating city takes time and patience.

Start at the legendary Egyptian Museum in Tahrir Square.

Here you'll meet the mummies of ancient Egypt (including King Tut, of course) as well as more than 120,000 other relics—the mother of all Victorian curio cabinets. Then venture out to tranquil Roda Island for atmospheric views of the Nile and a look at the ancient Nilometer, used to measure floods. Coptic Cairo, a walled village with Roman vestiges and early churches, is just across the way via a wooden footbridge. You'll find the Cairo of Ali Baba and Aladdin in Khan al-Khalili, one of the world's largest suqs (markets), where you'll need to bargain for anything you wish to buy. If you think the price is too high, do like an Egyptian and walk away or at least make a pretense of doing so—you may be surprised by how quickly the price comes down! To find peace amid the bustle, head for Al-Azhar Mosque, which has been the spiritual heart of Egypt for more than a thousand years.

■ **PLANNING Cairo** www.egypt.travel. **Coptic Cairo** www .coptic-cairo.com. **Khan al-Khalili** Although some vendors take credit cards, most do not, so bring cash. The bazaar is closed on Sun. **Al-Azhar Mosque** This is an active place of worship; dress modestly.

## ∾ IN THE KNOW ∾
### EGYPTIAN FAST FOOD

Guidebooks wax poetic about the pleasures of Cairo's legendary coffeehouses, like El Fishawy. But for a real local hangout, head to Gad, Cairo's own Egyptian fast-food chain. Found at busy intersections and boulevards throughout town, these outlets sport big red signs announcing cheap, simple fare and an easygoing, friendly vibe. The staff will help you sort through the options: shawarma meat sandwiches, *fuul* (Egypt's traditional fava bean dish), *tamaya* (a kind of falafel), and even the pizzalike flat bread called *fetir*, along with many other popular favorites. Some locations even offer sit-down dining upstairs (the ground floor is just for takeout).

# DUBAI

Immerse yourself in the Old World traditions of this epicenter of ultramodern culture.

A desert mirage come to life, the miracle city of Dubai combines Las Vegas glitz with warm Arab hospitality. Home to the world's tallest building, the Burj Khalifa, this city offers a life of luxury about which "over the top" is an understatement. Its centerpiece is the Burj Al Arab, the seven-star hotel shaped like a sailboat and overlooking the tranquil gulf waters; it's even equipped with its own heliport. Imaginative projects, such as the Palm Islands and the World Islands, set Dubai apart from its neighbors. Both feats of engineering sit off the coast of Dubai and contain luxury homes, hotels, and resorts, many owned by Hollywood stars.

Dubai may have embraced the luxurious lifestyle of the coast, but the desert beckons right at the city's doorstep. Find out just how miraculous this city by the sea really is with a trek into the magnificent sand dunes that press against it. Take a ride on camel or ATV deep into the seemingly barren wilderness, and watch the hills shift beneath the gaze of an unforgettable sunset. Eat delicious barbecued meats in a Bedouin camp, and then drift to sleep under stars to the sounds of traditional Arab music.

■ **PLANNING Dubai** www.dubaitourism.ae. **Burj Khalifa** www.burjkhalifa.ae. **Burj Al Arab** www.jumeirah.com. **Palm Islands** www.thepalm.ae. **The World Islands** www.theworld.ae. **Desert Treks** www.travelindubai.com.

## ∾ IN THE KNOW ∾
### BASTAKIYA

Dubai might be best known for its glitzy shopping malls and mile-high skyline, but history can still be found within this new kingdom. Bastakiya is the historical center of Dubai, with the 18th-century Al Fahidi Fort now housing the Dubai Museum. Many of the tiny lanes and adobe buildings here have roofs specially designed to create drafts of air in the long, hot days before air-conditioning. The area abounds with art galleries and little cafés, and you'll find the city's gold market nearby. There is a fee to enter the museum, which has limited opening hours on Fridays.

In Dubai, it's just steps to go from luxury shopping to the beach.

The fertile fields of the Constantia Valley are just a 20-minute drive from the center of Cape Town.

# CAPE TOWN

Throw yourself into the capital city's natural wonders and rich history

There's little reason to disagree with Sir Francis Drake: "This Cape is a most stately thing, and the fairest Cape we saw in the whole circumference of the earth."

Table Mountain's flat top and nearly ever-present layer of clouds are instantly recognizable. Buildings stretch back to the mid-17th century's Castle of Good Hope, built by the Dutch East India Company. The city has a modern-day melding of flavors brought to the area by a diverse population made up of the local Bushman and Hottentot tribes, the Bantu from the north, and settlers including Indonesians, French, Dutch, British, and Germans. Cape Town is stately, elegant, and swirling with constant, yet somehow relaxing, activity. Even the penguins—always dressed in their formal attire at nearby Boulders Beach—add a stately (and, yes, amusing) twist on what otherwise would be just another beautiful beach.

But to wander Cape Town in nothing but a happy daze of beauty and flavors would be a mistake. Inject a difficult but necessary dose of South Africa's turbulent past with visits to the District Six Museum, which stands as a powerful reminder of the days of apartheid, and Robben Island, where Nelson Mandela was imprisoned for 18 of the 27 years he spent in jail.

■ **PLANNING** **Cape Town** www.tourismcapetown.co.za, www.capetown.travel. **Castle of Good Hope** www.castleofgoodhope.co.za. Guided tours Mon.–Sat. **District Six Museum** www.districtsix.co.za. **Robben Island Museum** www.robben-island.org.za. Ferries to Robben Island often sell out; book online before you visit.

## ～ IN THE KNOW ～
### KIRSTENBOSCH NATIONAL BOTANICAL GARDEN

Each spring, fields and mountains of the Western Cape erupt into colorful blankets of wildflowers. But even if a tour of the west (including the wonderfully named town of Nababeep, which gets blanketed in a bright orange flower) isn't on your itinerary, work Kirstenbosch National Botanical Garden (www.sanbi.org/gardens/kirstenbosch) into your trip. On the eastern slope of Table Mountain, plants both familiar and otherworldly show off among Kirstenbosch's 4,700 varieties of flora. Even those in your group most focused on large safari game may, even if just for a few hours, think the alien-like pincushion flowers are the most fascinating things they've ever seen.

# DELHI

Witness modern chaos and ancient elegance co-existing in this 5,000-year-old megalopolis.

Modern and massive, India's capital city is a hotbed of think tanks and politicians and ground zero for the country's rapidly climbing bourgeoisie. Built and destroyed 11 times, Delhi is home to 14 million people squeezed into 580 square miles (1,500 sq km)—one of the world's densest and most frenzied cities. It is also strewn with dozens of glimmering gems, many of which continue to evade visitors.

Important sites like Qutub Minar Tower, erected in 1199 to commemorate a victory by the Turks, the beautiful Jama Masjid mosque, and Humayun's octagonal tomb should not be missed. But to delve into Delhi's hidden life, visit the sacred tomb of a 14th-century Sufi saint, Sheikh Nizamuddin Aulia. Air-conditioned malls abound, but Delhi's bustling street markets have much more ambience. Buy flowers at Phool Mandi in the morning, or browse fabrics at the hectic Lajpat Nagar. The narrow-laned bazaars of Chandni Chowk sell, well, just about everything.

For a sensory break, head to Raj Ghat, the busy but reflective Mahatma Gandhi memorial, or to the less visited Lodi Gardens, where you stroll past 15th-century tombs crumbling into the spacious lawns, a reminder that everything in India is reborn.

■ **PLANNING** **Delhi** www.delhitourism.nic.in. **Qutub Minar Tower** www.qutubminar.org. **Phool Mandi** The flower sellers start packing up around 8:30 a.m., so arrive early in the morning for the best selection.

## ~ IN THE KNOW ~
### GREENING DELHI

NGOs and grassroots environmental organizations have begun teaming with the government and everyday citizens to clean up Delhi. Together they have instituted new green policies, embedded watchdog agencies, and empowered and educated individuals. Grassroots projects like Mission Green Delhi and Green Leap Delhi call upon individuals to help make change, while blogs like Delhi Greens and conferences like the annual Delhi Sustainable Development Summit spread awareness of the acute problem. Change is sluggish, and often rife with setbacks, but, as Mahatma Gandhi once said, "You must be the change you want to see in the world."

Delhi's expansive Jama Masjid mosque was commissioned in the 17th century by Mughal emperor Shah Jahan, who also built the Taj Mahal.

# HONG KONG

*It is the rise and fall of empires you are seeing here, the shifting of continents and the tides of power. . . . No other city is quite like this. Hong Kong is perpetually on the go, deafeningly energetic, smelling of oil and duckmess, a city of many cultures poised between the present and the future, but seldom bothering with the past.*

JAN MORRIS, AUTHOR OF *AMONG THE CITIES* & OTHER BOOKS

Hong Kong is most
famous for its hustle
and bustle, but a hike
along one of Hong Kong
Island's mountain trails
offers a far more serene
view of the city below.

# EXOTIC FARMERS & STREET MARKETS

Shop where the locals do and embrace the rhythms of daily life.

## 1 PIKE PLACE MARKET
### Seattle, Washington

You'll forget Washington State is known for its coffee when you see brilliant red cherries, strawberries, and peppers, not to mention all of the handcrafts, fresh fish, fine dining, and wine on offer at this must-see institution.

www.pikeplacemarket.org

## 2 EASTERN MARKET
### Washington, D.C.

These days the capital of the United States is known just as well for its eclectic neighborhoods and antiquing as for its policymakers. Historic Eastern Market is more than just a weekday fresh food lunch stop for movers and shakers; it is also a weekend farmers market and crafty shopping haven for those in the know.

www.easternmarket-dc.org

## 3 FISH FRIDAY
### Grenada

Grenada is known not only for its nutmeg and cinnamon from the central spice market in Grand Anse Bay, but also for Fish Friday. In Gouyave, ultracheap street food and beer and Caribbean music lead to street dancing at this weekend celebration—phenomenon, really.

www.caribbean-guide.info/activities/events.and.festivals

## 4 FLOATING MARKET
### Curaçao

Standing in stark contrast to the high-end jewelry and clothing shops in Willemstad on this Dutch Caribbean island are rickety, colorfully painted wooden boats sitting stern to stem in this mobile market. Mostly from Venezuela, these merchants sail in each morning with pungent fruits and vegetables for sale.

www.curacao.com

## 5 FISH MARKET
### Marseille, France

In southern France, where lunch is a serious undertaking, fishermen arrive each day in the wee hours of the morning to prepare for the haggling over the morning's catch. Several dozen boats fill the Vieux Port, a bustling trading center in the heart of town.

www.marseille-tourisme.com

## 6 ALBERT CUYP MARKET
### Amsterdam, Netherlands

From tulips to truffles, and neckties to tilapia, Albert Cuyp Market is one-stop reality shopping. But this market is just one of many in Amsterdam, which seems to be the outdoor market mecca of Europe.

www.goamsterdam.com

## 7 SCHÖNBRUNN PALACE CHRISTMAS MARKET
### Vienna, Austria

This outdoor market, backlit by Schönbrunn Palace, displays affordable and exquisite Austrian artwork, from Christmas tree decorations to wooden and tin toys. It is open from mid-November through Christmas before it turns into a New Year's market. Strolling in the snow among the vendors with food on a stick, wine, and chocolates is an experience you'll remember.

www.christmasmarket.at

## 8 SPICE BAZAAR
### Istanbul, Turkey

In a city known for its endless Grand Bazaar and rug merchants, this market—located in the Old City near the shores of the Golden Horn—is the most manageable. Enter grand gates into vaulted ceiling–enclosed alleyways filled with mounds of saffron, curry, paprika, teas, and of course, the confection Turkish delight. Don't be afraid to haggle; it's expected.

www.deliciousIstanbul.com

## 9 MEDICINE SHOPS
### Cape Town, South Africa

These local "drug stores," or medicinal markets, are filled from the doorway to the dimly lit back walls with animal skins hanging from strings, herbs and roots in dusty jars, and an expert waiting to mix a cocktail to fix whatever ails you. The hardship endured by the citizens of surrounding townships is obvious as you pass through.

www.tourismcapetown.co.za

## 10 BANG RAK MORNING MARKET
### Bangkok, Thailand

Sift through aromatic Thai spices and learn how to use coconut milk before stepping out of the way of flying fish guts and shouting, meat cleaver–wielding sellers. It is but a short Skytrain ride from the Blue Elephant Cooking School, where chefs help students expertly navigate the market by teaching their tricks of the market-buying trade.

www.blueelephant.com

At the south end of
Galata Bridge you will find
Istanbul's Spice Bazaar,
where locals flock for
spices, nuts, sweets, and
traditional remedies.

A booming shopping district and thriving nightlife make the Shinjuku area Tokyo's center for business—and pleasure.

## JAPAN

# TOKYO

Absorb the urban enigma of Tokyo's traditions among the towers.

One of the world's most densely packed cities, Tokyo confounds, confuses, and enchants, achieving what should be an impossible combination of delicacy and restraint, neon and plastic. Perhaps admitting that you cannot fathom Tokyo is the beginning of understanding it. What other metropolis collectively swoons during the annual cherry blossom festival while proudly flaunting an ultramodern consumer culture? It's easy to find sleek, futuristic Tokyo. But shrines, villages, and traditions abound in Tokyo's districts and markets—if you know where to look.

Make your way past the modern-day punks, Goths, and Lolitas of the Harajuku district to the Meiji Jingu Shrine, dedicated to Japan's late 19th-century imperial rulers. Or explore Asakusa, a village within the city that author Karin Muller calls the "heart of old Tokyo." At Kumon, visitors can take workshops in Japanese arts like ikebana (flower arranging), calligraphy, kimono wearing, and the tea ceremony. For traditional treats like fine sushi, soba, and tempura, locals frequent the food stalls of Jogai, near the bustling Tsukiji Market. Or wander off the teeming, neon-lit boulevards of the city's Shibuya district into Drunkard's Alley (Nonbei Yokocho), a hidden lane lined with tiny wood-paneled restaurants, red lanterns glowing above their doors.

## PLACES THAT CHANGED ME

*Ceil Miller Bouchet,* National Geographic Traveler *writer*

From shrines with goldfish ponds and scarlet maple leaves to high-tech metro trains and window-shopping, Tokyo is a great city for kids. I first discovered Tokyo with my three-year-old son, a cute little blond guy in a stroller. Although that was 14 years ago, he still clearly recalls his fascination with the conveyor belts of sushi sliding by at the neighborhood joint where we'd have dinner. The menu was in Japanese, so the locals, perched on stools next to us, helped me choose delicacies for him. That's how I experienced the warm heart of this teeming city, on the first of many mother-son travel adventures.

■ **PLANNING Tokyo** www.tourism.metro.tokyo.jp. **Meiji Jingu Shrine** www.meijijingu.or.jp. **Asakusa** www.asakusajinja.jp. **Tsukiji Market** www.tsukiji-market.or.jp. Open 24 hours a day.

CHINA

# SHANGHAI

Say hello to the future.

One of the world's most sophisticated, cosmopolitan cities, Shanghai is a place where each moment is lived to its most intense, condensed, and forward-looking essence. Since the mid-1800s, when Shanghai was the first Chinese city to accept foreign trade, Shanghai's city slickers—Chanel-clad rich, pajama-clad poor, and everything in between—have had one thing in common: the certainty that their city is the best, the brashest, and some would say the bossiest in the Middle Kingdom. The city's 20 million residents even have their own language, a dialect called—what else?—Shanghainese.

A walk along the Bund puts Shanghai into perspective. Across the river sparkles Pudong, with its futuristic Oriental Pearl Tower and forest of skyscrapers. Only 20 years ago, Pudong was a vast expanse of rice paddies and small farms. North and then east, past the Bund's turn-of-the-20th-century banks and trading houses (which today are chic malls, hotels, restaurants, and bars), you'll find Suzhou Creek, where old warehouses now operate as contemporary art galleries. Locals still take food just as seriously as they take art and business. In Shanghai's Old

Town, skip the long lines outside the ground floor of Nanxiang Mantu Dian Restaurant, across from Yu Garden's Bridge of Nine Turns, and head up to the third floor to slurp a bowl of Shanghai's famous *xiaolongbao,* or pork dumplings.

■ **PLANNING** **Shanghai** www.meet-in-shanghai.net. **Pudong** http://english.pudong.gov.cn.

## ∾ IN THE KNOW ∾
### THE FRENCH CONCESSION

Patrick Cranley, longtime Shanghai resident and president of Historic Shanghai, never tires of the French Concession. "Any direction within three or four blocks of the Shanghai Library, on the corner of Huaihai Middle Road and Gao An Road, is a great way to discover the area," he says. Wander through the concession for views of early and mid-20th-century mansions, apartment buildings ranging from art deco to Bauhaus, and shops that cover centuries of tradition and the latest trends. And don't be afraid to engage the residents. No matter where you venture in the city, the Shanghainese are friendly and open.

Traditional arts provide a break from Shanghai's intense pace.

# KYOTO

*I stepped into Kyoto for the first time in August 1984, during the three-day festival, Obon, when lights are set along the eastern hills to lead departed souls back to their earthly homes.*

*I followed the lights up white-gravel pathways and realized I knew this place; I had arrived home. I left my comfortable job in New York to live in Kyoto and now, more than 25 years on, I'm still there.*

—PICO IYER, AUTHOR OF *THE GLOBAL SOUL* & OTHER BOOKS

A mountaintop bonfire casts a glow over Kyoto's pagodas, *ryokans*, and temples.

Wat Arun—Temple of the Dawn—lords over the Chao Phraya river, a respite of peace in the bustling Thai capital.

# THAILAND
# BANGKOK

Embrace the spiritual life in the bustling Buddhist capital.

Visitors to Thailand's capital cannot help being overwhelmed by it all. The city is daunting—a steamy, modern sprawl that seems to carry on endlessly. The traffic is maddening, the din endless, and the crowds irritating. Most can't wait to escape to the beaches of the south or the jungles and mountains in the north. Those who stop for a moment, however, can easily discover the essence of the gentle Thai spirit. Limned in gilt and scented with incense, more than 400 Buddhist temples behind high walls, for example, offer beautiful oases of greenery, ponds, and silence. Honor the local tradition by making merit—perhaps by giving alms to the saffron-robed monks who carry their empty bowls through the city. At Wat Phra Kaew, the vast Temple of the Emerald Buddha, wander among the graceful and brilliant Ramayana murals. "The paintings here have provided spiritual and stylistic inspiration for temple murals around the country," says artist Thamnu Haribhitak. "Their influence extends even to contemporary Thai art."

An extra-special experience awaits on the network of *khlongs*, or canals, of Thon Buri, off the western banks of the Chao Phraya river. Hail a river taxi or long-tail boat and explore this hidden world of stilted wooden houses and ancient temples set among rice fields, vegetable gardens, and orchards. Guaranteed, you'll forget your need to rush off to quieter places elsewhere anytime soon.

■ **PLANNING** Bangkok www.bangkoktourist.com, www.tour ismthailand.org. Wat Phra Kaew and the Grand Palace are located on Na Phra Lan Road and charge an admission fee.

## ❧ BEST OF THE BEST ❧
### Get a Thai Massage

**Wat Pho,** a 20-acre (8 ha) complex in the heart of Bangkok, blends the sacred and the sensual. Both a temple and the nation's premier massage school, it is the ideal place to be initiated into the art of Thai massage, a vigorous, deeply relaxing kneading of knotted muscles and sore spots. Expect to be bent, pulled, and lifted by your masseuse, who ends the hour-long session (about $15) with a series of musical claps down the spine. The **WATPO Massage School** is located at 2 Sanamchair Road. Visit www.watpomassage.com for more information.

# KUALA LUMPUR

Explore the fusion of cultures in this soaring capital.

Trade winds carried the world to Malacca and Penang on Malaysia's west coast, but today the vaulting skyscrapers of Kuala Lumpur express the country's global ambitions. While the language of business boardrooms may be English, the streets below reflect Kuala Lumpur's ethnic melting pot. Chinese dim sum and Indonesian satay scent the night markets along Jalan Alor, the call to prayer echoes from the ultracontemporary National Mosque, and Hindu deities stand guard at the gate of Sri Mahamariamman Temple. The city's 1.6 million residents share two characteristics: incredible diversity and pride in the city's breakneck modernization.

Islamic culture and traditions abound in the capital, from the minaret-shaped angles of the huge Petronas Twin Towers to the modest head scarves of its young career women. Don't miss the Masjid Jamek mosque, designed not by natives but by a British colonial architect aping the Indian Mughal style. Enjoy the welcome breezes of the city's Lake Gardens from the veranda of the Carcosa Seri Negara, another remnant of the city's colonial British past, where teatime is a cherished ritual. To accompany a cuppa, choose between cool cucumber sandwiches or spicy curry puffs—flavors that define the city's nonchalant balance of cool and hot.

■ **PLANNING** Kuala Lumpur http://visitkualalumpur.com, www.tourism.gov.my. **Masjid Jamek mosque** Avoid visiting during Friday prayers, roughly noon–3 p.m. Women must cover their heads.

## ❧ IN THE KNOW ☙
### CITY VIEWS

The best view of the city's quirky skyscrapers, a wild mix of architectural styles and influences, may be had while floating in your hotel pool. Kuala Lumpur's most luxurious accommodations, such as Traders Hotel, sport rooftop swimming spots that soar above the tropical heat. Or buy tickets in advance to zoom to the 86th floor observation deck of the glittering Petronas Twin Towers (*www.petronastwintowers.com.my*) for a sunset view of the city. Stay for the evening fountain show below. Traders Hotel is located in Kuala Lumpur City Centre. Visit www.shangri-la.com/en/property/kualalumpur/traders for more information.

The Istana Budaya (National Theatre) boasts Langkawi marble, hand-carved doors, and cutting-edge technology.

# SINGAPORE

Feel an island nation's deft blend of cosmopolitan confidence and colonial charm.

Spouting a proud plume of water spray, the Merlion that guards Singapore's harbor suggests at once its ancient name of Singapura, the Lion City, and its majestic history of sea trade. But the dense backdrop of sleek skyscrapers suggests the city's trajectory as Southeast Asia's financial and cultural powerhouse. For British writer Julia Wilkinson, this unique city-state is "where Asian cultures mingle in exuberant diversity, where the colonial past lingers, and the future holds bright promise."

Drifting in the South China Sea just 85 miles (137 km) north of the Equator, Singapore shimmers. Hail a bumboat for a water-taxi tour through the famous quays along the Singapore River; the architectural fashion show includes the Esplanade, the city's culture and theater hub, and the astonishing Marina Bay Sands, a ship-shaped resort that balances on three 55-story pillars.

Board the crisply efficient subway to explore bustling Little India, with its crayon-colored storefronts, or the chic shopping district along Orchard Road. Linger in the city's past at the National Museum of Singapore near the Dhoby Ghaut metro stop. With an ingenious glass addition grafted on a neoclassical Victorian edifice, the museum—like the Merlion—blends contemporary imagery with a storied history.

■ **PLANNING** **Singapore** www.yoursingapore.com. **River cruise** www.rivercruise.com.sg. Board at Boat Quay, Clarke Quay, & Marina Bay. **National Museum of Singapore** www.national museum.sg. The museum charges an admission fee.

## ~ IN THE KNOW ~
### THE ESPLANADE

The Esplanade is more than a double dome on the skyline. Fondly nicknamed "the durian" for its resemblance to the lumpy tropical fruit, this waterfront complex is one of the world's busiest art centers. Two million visitors a year flock to its indoor and outdoor theaters, three levels of restaurants and cafés, art galleries, couture shops, and spas. Savor the evening harbor views from the open roof terrace, a garden oasis. The Esplanade is located at 1 Esplanade Drive; visit www.esplanade.com for a list of shops and restaurants, as well as upcoming events and ticket sales.

Visit in June, when the annual Singapore River Festival brings the waterfront to life with spectacular performances and shows.

## AUSTRALIA
# SYDNEY
The fast track to falling for Sydney? Eat there.

On Australia Day, choose a favorite ferry to win the annual race around the harbor.

Mention Sydney and images jump to mind instantly: Bondi Beach surfers, the architectural marvel that is the Sydney Opera House, the Harbour Bridge at sunrise. But it's Sydney's food scene—no postcard could do it justice—that's turned the coastal beauty into a modern must-visit.

Though there's plenty of 'roo and crocodile on menus around the city, fear not: You can skip the bush tucker. Sydneysiders—as the city's four million residents are called—prefer appetizingly innovative chow, not the tourist-leaning odder eats. Since the mid-1980s, when the Mod Oz movement infused simple, fresh ingredients with Asian spicing and European know-how, cooking stars including Neil Perry, chef-owner of Rockpool & Spice Temple, and Kylie Kwong, chef-owner of Billy Kwong, have been spoiling locals in a big way. Food-focused types who lean green have another reason to kvell over Sydney: Mod Oz chefs are keen on ethical eating.

But don't just go for flavor in the city's "prettier" restaurants. There's plenty to taste in Chinatown, Kings Cross, and Newtown. Feast on Nepalese *momos,* Indian *pakoras,* and Vietnamese *pho,* and wash them down with a Malaysian *kopi ais* (iced coffee). Of course, overindulgence comes at a weighty price. But penance here is its own reward: A walk along the city's coastline provides a stunning way to ready yourself for the next meal.

■ **PLANNING** Sydney www.sydney.com. **Rockpool & Spice Temple** www.rockpool.com. Neil Perry also has restaurants in Melbourne and Perth. **Billy Kwong** www.kyliekwong.org/billy kwongs.aspx. Closed Sun.

# PARADISE FOUND

## A Perfect Mix of Only the Most Blissful Elements

Remote and little frequented, the places that we call heaven on Earth boast breathtaking vistas and a timeless beauty. The soul of any paradise, however, are its people. Locals know the land's history, give color to its present, and safeguard its magic when the rest of us have gone home.

A day trip to One Foot Island in the Cook Islands Archipelago delivers solitude and never-ending views of the aqua lagoon.

## HAWAII
# HAWAIIAN ISLANDS

Experience the islands' steaming volcanic craters, monster waves, and spiritually imbued parks.

Farther from a landmass than any other place on Earth, the Hawaiian Islands rise as green beacons of life in the middle of the vast Pacific Ocean. From the very beginning, isolation has defined the Hawaiian Archipelago of 137 islands, islets, and atolls strung like uneven pearls across the Tropic of Cancer in a 1,523-mile (2,451 km) line. Each island is different, not only in appearance but also in personality. Oahu is schizophrenic, busy, sophisticated, and urbane, with a surprisingly rural twin personality. Maui is the dreamer. The Big Island, Hawaii, is raw, with plenty of room to spare. Kauai is ancient, wise, and green. On Moloka'i, the pace of life is as steady and unhurried as the beating heart of the surf. Lanai is rugged: a single volcanic mountain

eroded into deep, red gorges that end in cliffs at the sea or taper into lonely beaches.

## THE BIG ISLAND'S FIERY, LAVA-LAPPED HEART

Kilauea (4,078 feet/1,243 m), the world's only drive-up—and most active—volcano, is the red-hot heart of Hawai'i Volca-

noes National Park. The 397-square-mile (1,028 sq km) park was founded in 1916 to protect the amazing natural wonders of Kilauea and its simmering neighbor, Mauna Loa. Pele, the goddess of fire and volcanoes, is said to have sailed in a canoe to Hawaii from a land in the far reaches of the ocean. According to local legend, she settled in Kilauea's crater, where she dwells to

Hawaii remains one of the world's premier surfing destinations, with waves that challenge novices and experts alike.

three events held between late November and Christmas Day," says National Geographic contributor John Seaton Callahan. Surfing remains the symbol of Hawaii, and there's no better place to catch a beginner's wave than in a protected North Shore cove. The laid-back and local North Shore Surf Girls can teach anyone to surf in a single lesson. Watch for gentle-giant sea turtles paddling below the surface.

## MOLOKAI'S SPIRITUAL SIDE

Earthy, real, and unspoiled, Molokai is a place of extraordinary natural beauty: uncrowded white beaches, the world's highest sea cliffs (3,900 feet/1,188 m), and raging surf. It is also a place of supernatural beauty. To best uncover the island's spiritual dimension, head to Kalaupapa Peninsula, the site of the leprosy settlement made famous by Father (now St.) Damien. On one side of a narrow road, a serene little village sits at the foot of 2,000-foot-high (610 m) cliffs; on the other, hundreds of granite headstones solemnly face the shore, each a ghost of Kalaupapa's past. To experience Molokai, book a guided tour of Kalaupapa National Historic Park. "Hawaiians believe that places like this hold mana—power, sacred power. That's what I believe, too. Molokai has mana," says Alan Brennert, author of the best-selling historical novels *Honolulu* and *Moloka'i*.

■ **PLANNING** Hawai'i Volcanoes National Park www.nps.gov/havo. Open 24 hours a day, year-round; road and area closures due to periodic volcanic activity. Check website for updates. **North Shore of Oahu** Find information about dates and tickets for the Triple Crown of Surfing at www.triplecrownofsurfing.com. **North Shore Surf Girls** Rates and online reservations are available at northshoresurfgirls.com. **Molokai** www.gohawaii.com/molokai.

this day. "Madame Pele willing, enter one of the Kilauea volcano wilderness runs held every year in later July and experience landscape and flora that are out of this world," says Michael Pietrusewsky, National Geographic field scientist. Wend your way around Crater Rim Drive, the road encircling Kilauea's oval summit caldera. Make frequent stops to discover the park on foot: lush rain forests with tree ferns; raw, steaming craters; and an eerie, walk-through, 450-foot-long (137 m) lava tube.

## SURF'S UP: OAHU'S NORTH SHORE

This is Oahu as it was: plantation-era architecture, cattle grazing in oceanfront meadows, roadside garlic-shrimp trucks, and sweet papaya stands. Sunsets sear the soul along ragged coves and long sweeps of sand scoured by wind. The celebrated North Shore beaches begin at funky Haleiwa town and stretch to the Turtle Bay Resort. The ideal time to take to the white-caps is winter—surf season—when monster waves sometimes roll in at 30 feet (9 m) high. "To see the best waves and professional surfers, catch the Triple Crown of Surfing—a series of

## PLACES THAT CHANGED ME
*Paul Theroux, author of The Mosquito Coast & other books*

Cresting the long hill of central Oahu, on my way home from town, the Waianae Range on my left, pineapple fields on my right, and big waves breaking straight ahead on the shore of Haleiwa, "Home of the Frigate Bird," I am always reminded of how lucky I am to live in this beautiful place and how passionate I am for it to remain lovely. My bees buzz and make honey every day of the year; the wind in the ironwoods has the yearning note of a cello; and there is never rain without an accompanying rainbow.

The night sky seems a hypnotic dream as lava light reflects off a steam cloud.

Emerald Bay goes glassy as twilight settles in.

# LAKE TAHOE

Glide across crystal-clear waters in the shadow of snowcapped peaks.

Formed by glacial scouring, earthquake faults, and volcanic flows, 22-mile-long (35 km) and 1,645-foot-deep (501 m) Lake Tahoe is North America's largest mountain lake. Split between California and Nevada and ringed by snowy 9,000- and 10,000-foot (2,743–3,048 m) peaks, this crystal blue subalpine lake is famed for its clarity.

Northern Californians flock to Tahoe's big beaches in sum-mer, even bigger ski resorts in winter, and over-the-top casino hotels (on the Nevada side) year-round. Less traveled is the lake's transparent and true north shore. Here simple lakefront cottages, family-owned restaurants, and tiny arcs of sand, including secluded Moon Dunes Beach (one of the lake's only intact sand dunes), retain the rustic charm and sleepy inno-cence of the 1950s.

The best way to experience some or all of the glimmering, 72-mile (115 km) shoreline is at water level. From the north shore, join a guided paddle trip through the behemoth boulder mazes of Crystal Bay, or rent a kayak, pack a picnic, and chart your own course into hidden coves. The Lake Tahoe Water Trail Committee offers route maps (updated annually) for sale, and the developing Lodge-to-Lodge Network makes it possible to paddle by day and head ashore each night when it's time to eat, recharge, and toast the moonrise over the shad-owed Carson Range.

## ~ IN THE KNOW ~
### MARK TWAIN'S TAHOE

When the Civil War grounded his river-piloting career in 1861, Samuel Clemens briefly served in the Confederate militia before hopping a westbound stagecoach for Nevada. After failing to strike it rich, Clemens became a newspaper reporter, assuming the pseudonym Mark Twain. A partly fictionalized recollection of Twain's timber-scouting visits to Lake Tahoe appears in his 1872 travelogue *Roughing It*. Recalling his initial Tahoe sighting, Twain wrote, "As it lay there with the shadows of the mountains brilliantly photographed upon its still surface I thought it must surely be the fairest picture the whole world affords."

■ **PLANNING** Lake Tahoe Reno-Tahoe International Airport is a 45-minute drive from North Lake Tahoe. North Shore www .gotahoenorth.com. May through Oct., **Tahoe Paddle & Oar** (*www .tahoepaddle.com*) in Kings Beach offers kayak rentals and tours.

# BAJA CALIFORNIA

Paddle in the company of whales, dolphins, and sea lions—with a desert backdrop.

The desert and the sea. They shouldn't exist together in one place, but in Baja California—one of Mexico's 31 states—this unlikely duo provides a magnificent playground for kayakers. However, at times, the playground's waters—whether you call it the Sea of Cortés or the Gulf of California—can be, to put it mildly, rough.

For those with experience kayaking and camping, sign on with an outfitter on a trip along the 90-mile (145 km) route from Loreto to La Paz, which hugs a coastline inaccessible to almost any other kind of travel. You won't even see powerboats most of the time. There are few roads and even fewer people. Sea meets desert, heat battles cold, and you may find yourself soaked by massive swells that dump on kayakers who dare put in.

But the rewards are great. You'll be treated to views of rugged desert mountains and empty beaches for camping or picnic breaks. You're visiting the home of bottlenose dolphins and barking sea lions, nine species of whales, and a rainbow's worth of reef fish that dart in and out of the coral, all easily visible in the brilliantly clear waters. You may curse the waves each time they soak you, but you'll be longing for a return trip as soon as you get home.

■ **PLANNING** Baja California www.discoverbajacalifornia.com. Kayak Tours: **Sea Kayak Adventures** (*www.seakayakadventures.com*), **Sea Quest Expeditions** (*www.sea-quest-kayak.com*), and **Miramar Adventures** (*www.miramar-adventures.com*).

## ∾ IN THE KNOW ∾
### WHALE SHARKS

Whale sharks arrive in the Sea of Cortés each spring, when they are drawn to the water's rich soup of plankton. Though whale sharks look rather intimidating, they are the gentlest of creatures, the largest type of fish found anywhere on Earth. Their bodies can stretch 40 feet (12 m) long and weigh 20 tons or more. They filter plankton through their mouths, which are an impressive 4 feet (1 m) across. Watching these creatures cruise gently through the water stops time. Eco Expeditions (*www.baja-eco-expeditions.com*) and Baja Airventures (*www.bajaairventures.com*) offer whale-watching trips.

California sea lions are some of the most playful Sea of Cortés residents.

# BERMUDA

Search for treasure on a spectacular seabed littered with shipwrecks.

Bermuda is the most civilized of islands, with blush-colored beaches, pastel-painted houses fashioned like dainty cakes with white roofs, afternoon high tea, cricket, ocean-side fairways. But this beautiful isle also has a wicked side: surrounding reefs so treacherous that for many years the island was dubbed the Isle of Devils. Take to the waters here and you can observe not only 4,500 types of marine organisms (like green-eyed, six-gilled sharks and jewel-like squid) but also hundreds of shipwrecks from five centuries and 15 countries.

Named after 16th-century Spanish navigator Juan de Bermúdez, one of many "accidental tourists" to set sight on its pink shores, Bermuda has lured nearly 200 ships to their doom since the days of Christopher Columbus. The ill-fated included Spanish treasure ships like the *San Pedro,* the Confederate blockade-runner *Mary Celestia,* the ocean liner *Cristobal Colon,* and the *Minnie Breslauer,* a steel-hulled freighter that sank on her maiden voyage in 1873. To explore the submerged decks, take a snorkeling or diving tour to some of the island's world-class wrecks. You never know what treasures may lurk.

Renowned treasure diver Teddy Tucker rescued a gold-and-emerald cross from the *San Pedro*—one of the most valuable artifacts ever recovered from the sea.

■ **PLANNING Bermuda** www.bermuda.com. Check www.goto bermuda.com and www.bermudadiving.com for information on Bermuda's shipwrecks and the island's dive operators, their schedules, and their rates.

> ## ☙ BEST OF THE BEST ☙
> ### Dive the Wreck of the *Cristobal Colon*
>
> Launched in 1921, the *Cristobal Colon* was one of the world's fastest, most advanced ocean liners, built to carry wealthy travelers to exotic destinations between New York and South America. On a summer night in 1936, her captain mistook a signal light for that of Bermuda's North Rock lighthouse and ran his ship aground on a reef. There she was left to deteriorate until the U.S. Air Force used her hull as target practice during World War II, scattering her parts over the seafloor. Lying in Bermuda's clearest waters, the wreck provides a ghostly canvas from which to see some of the ocean's greatest splendors. *(Check www.gotobermuda.com.)*

Bermuda's waters aren't always so calm: Hundreds of shipwrecks sit beneath the surface.

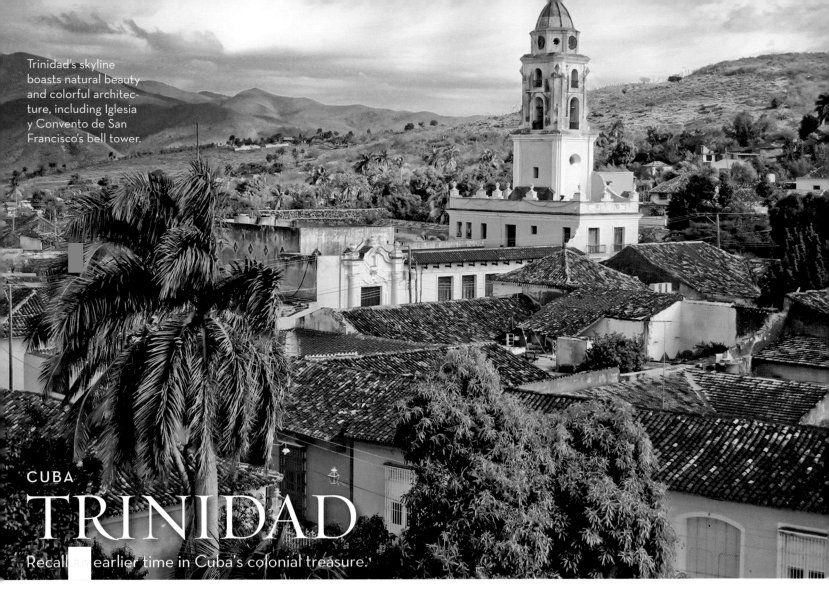

Trinidad's skyline boasts natural beauty and colorful architecture, including Iglesia y Convento de San Francisco's bell tower.

# CUBA
# TRINIDAD
Recall an earlier time in Cuba's colonial treasure.

Tucked between the Sierra del Escambray and the Caribbean Sea, Trinidad's historic core is unequaled for its trove of pastel houses from the isle's golden age. A UNESCO World Heritage site, Trinidad and the Valle de los Ingenios are living monuments to a way of life going back nearly 500 years.

## ∼ IN THE KNOW ∼
### NATIONAL MUSEUM OF THE STRUGGLE AGAINST BANDITS

Trinidad has more museums per capita than any other town in Cuba. One of its odder collections is the Museo Nacional de la Lucha Contra Bandidos, tracing the campaign to eradicate the counterrevolutionary guerillas (Castro called them bandits) based in the Sierra del Escambray from 1959 to 1966. This little-known collection has droves of fascinating photos, maps, uniforms, and weaponry, the greatest prize being the wrinkled fuselage of a U-2 spy plane shot down during the Cuba Missile Crisis in 1962. The museum occupies the pretty 19th-century convent San Francisco de Asís, its signature yellow-and-green bell tower affording a view over town.

Founded by Diego Velázquez in 1514, Trinidad basked in the short-lived glow of a gold mine and its bustling port of Casilda, where conquistador Hernán Cortés set out in 1518 to conquer the Aztec Empire for Spain. Fleets bearing the spoils of Mexico soon filled Trinidad's vaults. But Havana eclipsed the southern city, which became an outpost for smugglers, pirates, and slave traders. Trinidad entered its golden age as the 18th-century sugar boom bankrolled the construction of fine houses, churches, and convents.

The streets fanning out from Plaza Mayor, the old town's compact main square, are replete with colonial gems like the Palacio Cantero, the onetime domain of a powerful plantation owner, Justo Cantero. Stacked with stylish period furnishings, it is today's home of the Museo Histórico Municipal. Be sure to wander the maze of traffic-free lanes at dusk—higgledy-piggledy, to thwart pirates—when sunlight gilds the timeworn, red tile–roofed houses. Look for caged songbirds hung on exterior walls, a centuries-old tradition.

■ **PLANNING** Trinidad http://whc.unesco.org. For general information (in Spanish) on travel in Cuba, visit www.cubatravel.cu.

# TORTOLA

*Unlike other Caribbean isles, Tortola was so much more off the beaten path; we felt as if we had the whole island to ourselves. St. Thomas, St. Barts, and other islands in the area might be more "hip" . . . but my husband and I discovered the true essence of Caribbean island life.*

— MARLEE MATLIN, ACTRESS, AUTHOR, & ACTIVIST

Houses nestled into Tortola's hills look out on the aqua waters of the Caribbean.

Scarlet ibises glide to their roosting sites in Caroni Swamp on Trinidad.

# TRINIDAD

Savor the sweet flavor of mangoes, favorite fruit of this island nation.

Boisterous and multicultural, Trinidad is synonymous with Carnival. The sunbaked streets of its frenetic capital city, Port-of-Spain, teem with Carnival kings and queens, costumed in sequins and plumes and dancing calypso in streets lined with a parade of pompous British colonial architecture, Muslim mosques, West Indian gingerbread houses, and modern office buildings.

Visit once the party's over, when the costumes and sound systems have been packed away for next year, when things slow down enough for you to partake of a different kind of flavor. July promises an especially tasty treat for those in the know: mango season. During this time of year, mangoes drop from the trees and plop to the ground in abundance; the gutters of Port-of-Spain fill with flat, sucked-to-the-last-sweet-drop mango seeds; and the very air smells like you could sink your teeth into it. Explore the fruit markets, an obstacle course of golden pyramids, and haggle alongside the locals for the juiciest "Julies"—heaven after a salty swim at Maracas Beach, the most popular stretch on the north side of Trinidad. Life, indeed, is sweet—but be sure to also try mango chow, a delicious concoction of mango, hot peppers, garlic, and hot sauce that can be had just about everywhere during mango season.

■ **PLANNING** Trinidad www.gotrinidadandtobago.com/trinidad.

## ☙ BEST OF THE BEST ☙
### Birds & Butterflies

Trade the color and noise of Carnival for a well-plumed pageant and orchestra of a different sort. Trinidad is renowned for the kaleidoscopic diversity of its winged denizens (the island claims approximately 400 species of birds and 617 species of butterflies). At the **Asa Wright Nature Centre** (www.asawright .org), perched in the Arima Valley, you can view 170 species of birds. Trails that weave through the 197-acre (80 ha) estate give a ringside seat for the mating dance of the white-bearded manakin. Pause on the veranda as honeycreepers, tanagers, and trogons flit by. To take in the evening flight of the scarlet ibis, visit the 40-acre (16 ha) **Caroni Bird Sanctuary** (www .caronibirdsanctuary.org). About half an hour before sunset, the ibises knife through the sky, crimson darts congregating in the mangrove greenery until it blazes like a Christmas tree.

# LONG CAY

Grab a snorkel and glide through one of the Caribbean's richest marine environments.

A prime spot to play castaway, the tiny, private island of Long Cay belongs to Glovers Reef Atoll, a marine reserve and 90-square-mile (233 sq km) lagoon. With limited electricity, no running water, and a backdrop of brilliant blue Caribbean nothingness, Long Cay is largely unplugged.

Although pirates once used the islet as a lair from which to mount attacks on trophy ships (Glovers Reef takes its name from English pirate John Glover), you may choose rather more pacific pursuits. Slip into a Yucatán hammock and surrender to a timeless existence. Here daily routines center on natural rhythms. Greet the morning by watching ospreys diving for breakfast and porpoises leaping from the water in a synchronized dance. During the new moon, baby turtles erupt from the sand and struggle to get to the ocean.

To embrace island life thoroughly, however, you need to immerse yourself in it, literally. Don a mask and fins and go snorkeling in the so-called Aquarium, a part of Glovers Reef rich with a rainbow of aquatic life. Also well worth a snorkel is the Wall. A two-minute boat ride will take you from Long Cay to a steep, 3,000-foot (914 m) underwater cliff, home to a fluorescent fantasia of tropical fins.

■ **PLANNING Long Cay** www.travelbelize.org. For information about snorkel tours of Glovers Reef Atoll and other underwater expeditions on Long Cay, check www.islandexpeditions.com, www.discoveringbelize.com, www.offthewallbelize.com, and www.splashbelize.com.

## ⚜ BEST OF THE BEST ⚜
### Slickrock

Slickrock is the only resort on Long Cay. When the company moved to Glovers Reef Atoll in 1992, its goal was to create an undeveloped retreat. The result is a private, wind-and-solar-powered collection of rustic thatched-roof cabanas. (A little bit of propane is used only to chill a well-stocked fridge of Fanta and Belize's Belikin Beer.) Luxury at this eco-resort does not come in the form of hot showers, maid service, or air-conditioning; instead, you'll be spoiled with three dozen kayaks, sailboards, surfboards, and a dive shop, as well as sea-greeting verandas, hammocks, and ocean breezes. Consult www.slickrock.com for rates and amenities.

Nestled into Glovers Reef Atoll, Long Cay is a true (mostly unplugged) getaway.

# ROMANTIC GETAWAYS

Fall under the spell of a traditional rose garden or let the lures of history and mystery set your heart aflutter.

## 1 PORTLAND'S GARDENS
### Oregon

Lose yourself for days in the sweet-scented gardens of Portland, especially when the city's famed roses are in bloom from May to October (peaking in June). Portland offers two renowned rose gardens as well as classical Japanese and Chinese gardens. http://web.oregon.com/trips/portland_gardens.cfm

## 2 STONINGTON
### Connecticut

Stroll narrow cobblestone streets lined with 18th-century homes, buy fresh scallops off a boat at the docks, and take in the sunset off the point that juts into the Atlantic. After dusk, settle in for dinner at one of the cozy neighborhood pubs. www.stoningtonboroughct.com/harbor.shtml

## 3 CUMBERLAND ISLAND
### Georgia

Seductive Cumberland, a barrier island larger than Manhattan, is an almost totally undeveloped national seashore. Feral horses, alligators, and wild boar roam the beaches; ruined mansions are scattered through the woods. www.nps.gov/cuis/index.htm

## 4 OURO PRETO
### Brazil

An 18th-century gold-mining boom turned this town at the base of the Espinhaço Mountains, about 210 miles (338 km) north of Rio, into a showplace of baroque architecture. The shops here brim with topaz, emerald, and gold ornaments. www.ouropreto.org.br

## 5 COUNTY SLIGO
### Northwest Ireland

During chilly evenings, sip a pint around a peat fire in a thatched cottage. During the day, hike up the gentler south slope of Ben Bulben. Later, pay your respects to the grave cairn of Queen Maeve and visit Drumcliffe Churchyard, where the body of passionate poet William Butler Yeats lies. www.discoverireland.ie

## 6 SISSINGHURST CASTLE
### England

Sissinghurst's achingly lovely gardens and Elizabethan tower are Vita Sackville-West's tribute to love in its many guises. Visitors can stay at a Victorian farmhouse B&B on the estate grounds or even at the old Priest's House at the edge of the gardens. www.nationaltrust.org.uk/sissinghurst

## 7 REINHARDSWALD FOREST & FAIRY TALE ROAD
### Kassel, Hesse, Germany

You take a slight risk that your lover will fall asleep for a hundred years (or, even worse, turn into a frog), but the mossy allure of the Reinhardswald's oak and beech woods is hard to resist. The dark forest near Kassel, home of the Brothers Grimm, is the site of the restored 12th-century Sababurg Castle, where Sleeping Beauty slumbered. www.cometogermany.com

## 8 TRIESTE
### Italy

Trieste—clinging to the edge of the Adriatic Sea—is a coastal fantasia of Habsburgian palaces (the city was Austria-Hungary's primary seaport), sun-gilded piazzas, and Sacher torte–hawking pastry shops, where indulgence and relaxation are at the top of the list of things to do. www.italia.it

## 9 TANGIER
### Morocco

In the mid-20th century, Tangier was a favorite hideout for expatriate writers with louche tastes in love and intoxicants, but today the old city, which has been occupied by Vandals, Byzantines, and Berbers—among others—retains its seductive power. www.tourisme.gov.ma

## 10 SHIRAZ
### Iran

Unattainable love and loss are themes of the *ghazal,* a genre of Arabic poetry dating from the sixth century. The poet Hafez, master of the ghazal, is honored in Shiraz by an elegant pavilion mausoleum with an intricate mosaic ceiling. Known as the city of nightingales, poets, and roses, Shiraz reveals the ardent heart of Iran. www.itto.org

At the Habsburg Miramar Palace near Trieste, Italy, on the Adriatic Sea, there's no rush to go anywhere.

# OSA PENINSULA

*It was 1965, and I was returning to Costa Rica from the United States . . .
From the air, Osa was as impressive then as it is today. The area that is
now Corcovado National Park was absolutely pristine, with abundant birds,
tapirs, pumas, and monkeys . . . My connection with Osa began right then.*

—ALVARO UGALDE, CONSERVATIONIST & ONE OF THE FOUNDERS
  OF THE COSTA RICAN NATIONAL PARK SYSTEM

The sky seems to stretch on forever over a lagoon within Costa Rica's Corcovado National Park.

# TORRES DEL PAINE

Hike a mountain range that bubbled up from molten granite.

There's no way to avoid the wind in this park in far southwestern Chile, though it does lessen its sting in June, July, and August. But even at its fiercest 51°-south-latitude-with-an-attitude weather, the views here—of Lago Pehoé's glacial blue waters and the impossibly steep Torres del Paine—will, somewhat, mute the wind's effect. Here granite pillars seem to poke the sky, wildlife flourishes, and ice caps spill over into waterfalls.

Hire a van to take you through the park, but keep your camera at the ready. A guanaco, the wild cousin of the llama, could dash across the road at any second. Ask the guide to pull over for a photo shoot, and your next visitor could be a Patagonian red fox.

Don't spend the entire visit off your feet. Hiking is the thing here. The 19-mile-long (30.5 km) range, the Cordillera del Paine, is an upthrusted batholith, a giant bubble of once molten granite that rose from the earth and later was covered with glaciers. As the glaciers retreated, they left behind deep gashes and an uproar of wild peaks. Paths through the park are clearly marked. One of the most popular, the W, zigzags through the cordillera and takes about five to seven days to complete. A shorter, one-day trek will take you to the towers.

■ **PLANNING** **Torres del Paine National Park** www.torresdelpaine .com. Horseback riding and sailing are also available. It's easiest to get to the park via a flight into the town of Punta Arenas. For general information about travel in Chile, consult www.tourismchile.com.

## ~ IN THE KNOW ~
### GUANACOS

Cousins to the llama—and to the camel, too—guanacos are the largest land vertebrates in Patagonia. They look far more delicate than the story their weight tells: They can grow to 300 pounds (135 kg). Social beasts, guanacos live in groups of up to ten females along with their young and one adult male, the harem leader, and they can be seen wandering through Torres del Paine National Park. Male guanacos that haven't corralled a female pack of their own roam in packs of 50 or more. Then, at five years old, they head off solo to start their own breeding lives. (Don't ever annoy a guanaco: They spit when angry.)

A guanaco takes a rare solo rest within Torres del Paine National Park.

## BRAZIL
# FERNANDO DE NORONHA

Dive into an island paradise that even most of the locals don't know about.

A delicate world, Fernando de Noronha's waters are deepest blue, and indigenous birds and blooms provide colorful counterpoints to the area's stark rock formations. The 21-island archipelago sits about 100 miles (160 km) off Brazil's mainland. These islands are blessedly less trampled and more exotic than better-known go-to paradises like Tahiti and Hawaii.

Talk about a transformation. In the 1800s, Noronha functioned as a penal colony. But when environmentalists and biologists discovered them in the late 20th century, the islands were reborn as a sustainable-development locale. Named a UNESCO World Heritage site in 2001 for its diversity of sea animals, the archipelago is the only destination in Brazil that imposes a visitor limit in order to maintain the place's untouched essence.

Mornings here are for diving into the waves of the always warm waters. Try secluded Sancho Bay or the beautiful stretch of Conceicao Beach. Or head out early for Dolphin Bay if you want to see dolphins. Afternoons are for hiking up a mountain and then staying put for the water views and the sunset. Sometimes magic happens, with birds and dolphins gathering at the same time, all beings seemingly knowing that there is no better place on Earth.

### ∼ IN THE KNOW ∼
#### SEA TURTLES

The archipelago's beaches play an important role: From Dec.-July, they're a spawning ground for the green turtle and the hawksbill turtle. After birth, the juvenile turtles call the area home until they're strong enough to take off. In 1984 Project TAMAR (*www.tamar.org.br*) set up shop on the islands to help protect and monitor the sea turtles. Whether you visit in high spawning season or not, stop into TAMAR's visitor center to learn about the sea turtle's life cycle, threats to the species, and TAMAR's conservation efforts.

■ **PLANNING** Fernando de Noronha www.braziltour.com. There are four flights per day to Noronha, two from Recife and two from Natal. You can also book a cruise to the islands from Oct.-Feb. For information on accommodation and tours, visit www.noronha.travel.

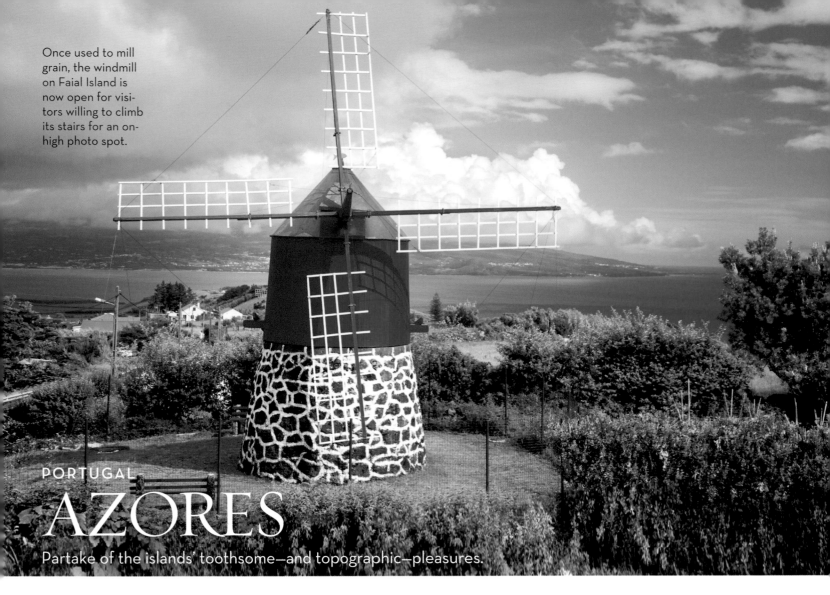

Once used to mill grain, the windmill on Faial Island is now open for visitors willing to climb its stairs for an on-high photo spot.

# PORTUGAL
# AZORES

Partake of the islands' toothsome—and topographic—pleasures.

It is hard not to think of lost mythical worlds while visiting the Azores, an archipelago of nine volcanic islands scattered out in the Atlantic, 870 miles (1,400 km) west of Lisbon. Commentators link the Azores with Plato's lost kingdom of Atlantis, and in *Paradise Lost,* Milton has the far-seeing angel Uriel slide down a beam toward the "sun now fall'n / Beneath the Azores." As the islands were not "discovered" until the 15th century, by Portuguese mariners under Prince Henry the Navigator, Milton's 17th-century poem uses their poetic name to conjure the image of the farthest horizon of the known world.

Today, the islands abound as much in botanic, zoological, and geographic treasures as they do in gastronomic delights. Among the most memorable, and delectable, ways to partake of the Azores is with a spoon. On the largest island, São Miguel, dig in to a subterranean variation on the boiled dinner: *cozida,* a savory stew brewed by the heat of the earth, in a vat submerged in one of the many bubbling steam vents along the shores of Furnas Lake. Humans are not the only visitors who find the Azores a pleasing gastronomic capital: Twenty-eight species of dolphins and whales, 25 percent of the world's known species, favor the feeding grounds along its shores.

■ **PLANNING** **Azores** www.azores.com. International airports operate on three of the islands: Faial, São Miguel, and Terceira. Travel between islands is by local airline or ferry. Rental cars are available on most of the islands.

## ❧ BEST OF THE BEST ❧
### Mid-Atlantic Stratovolcano

Climbing a mountain is always a point of pride, but climbing a stratovolcano in the middle of the Atlantic? The island of Pico is home to a stratovolcano, also called Pico, a conical dormant volcano, looming at 7,713 feet (2,351 m). Climbing its slopes, tamed by a carpet of thyme and the dancing tiny bells of Azorean heath, makes for an epic journey, indeed, but one that can be accomplished in less than five hours. Follow the marked trails to the camp in Pico Alto, the crater near the top. At dawn, be ready to scale Pico Pequeño, a volcanic cone that marks the true summit, and be rewarded with a panoramic view. Visit azores.com for more information.

# COSTA BRAVA

Explore a palette of bold Catalonian color.

The yellow, crimson, and white boats that bob in the water could belong to any craggy Mediterranean coast. The polar bear that guards them, however, means only one thing: Salvador Dalí's home in Costa Brava.

One of art's greatest eccentrics, Dalí took inspiration here. So did other modern masters, including Joan Miró, Marc Chagall, Man Ray, and Pablo Picasso. Towns along the serrated and sun-drenched Catalonian shoreline reflect these artists' free-spirited aesthetic. The medieval city of Girona bursts into bloom during its annual spring festival, the Temps de Flors. Surprising floral creations spill down cathedral steps, and art installations bloom in city squares and stone-walled courtyards.

Though visited by northern European package tours for decades, Costa Brava's inlets shelter its natural charms. Venture across the rocky promontory and nature reserve of Cap de Creus to the whitewashed fishing port of Cadaqués. Dotted with seafood cafés and art galleries, the village was Dalí's home for 50 years. Make sure to visit his labyrinthine house museum, where windows of every size and shape frame the sensuous view of his beloved harbor, Portlligat Bay.

■ **PLANNING** **Costa Brava** www.costabrava.org. **Casa-Museu Salvador Dalí** Dalí's house and museum are located in Portlligat in Cadaqués, www.salvador-dali.org/museus/portlligat. There is an admission fee, and group tours are available. The house and museum are closed most Mondays.

## ⚜ BEST OF THE BEST ⚜
### Prehistoric Empuries

Stroll the beachfront path from the lovely village of L'Escala to Empuries—a route to the sea that has served local residents for several millennia. Empuries (Ampurias) was the site of a Greek and Roman settlement that held sway over the region for more than seven centuries, starting in 600 B.C. Its stone ruins and statues face the sea, with sweeping views of the Golf de Roses and a fine beach. The dramatic audiovisual show at the nearby Museu d'Arqueologia delves into the classical roots of Catalonian history. The museum, which is open year-round, charges an admission fee. Learn more at www.mac.cat/eng/Branches/Empuries.

A medieval castle overlooks the relaxing beaches of Tossa de Mar.

# RELIGIOUS PILGRIMAGES

Steep in the sanctity of spiritual devotion and renew inner peace.

## 1 OUR LADY OF APARECIDA
São Paolo, Brazil

In May 2007, Pope Benedict XVI himself made a pilgrimage to this Marian shrine, the largest basilica in the world, built to commemorate a 16th-century miracle. Three fishermen embraced a statue of Mary that they had removed from a river, whereupon their nets miraculously filled with fish.

## 2 TÓCHAR PHÁDRAIG
County Mayo, Ireland

Tóchar Phádraig (Patrick's Causeway) melds ancient pagan sites with early tales of St. Patrick. On the last Sunday in July, thousands of pilgrims gather at Ballintubber Abbey to climb the Reek, or Croagh Patrick, where Patrick is said to have battled the devil's mother and a flock of demon birds.
www.ballintubberabbey.ie

## 3 LITTLE WALSINGHAM
Norfolk, England

Since 1061, when Richeldis de Faverches experienced a Marian vision in this village, pilgrims (including Henry VIII and Elizabeth I) have meandered Walsingham's lanes, winding through water meadows along the River Stiffkey toward the restored 14th-century Slipper Chapel. Tradition dictates that pilgrims walk the mile (1.6 km) between chapel and village barefoot.
www.walsingham.org.uk/

## 4 NIDAROS CATHEDRAL
Trondheim, Norway

In 1030, Olav, the first Christian king of Norway, died in the battle of Stiklestad. Where he fell, miracles were reported. In 1070, a shrine was established at Olav's burial site in Nidaros. Today, numerous marked pilgrimage routes span Norway's rugged countryside and lead toward the rebuilt cathedral.
www.pilegrim.info

## 5 LOURDES
France

Lourdes was a quiet town at the picturesque foot of the Pyrenees until 1858, when a 14-year-old peasant girl enjoyed a Marian vision in a grotto. Today, the Sanctuary of Our Lady of Lourdes attracts some five million Roman Catholic pilgrims every year, many who come seeking miraculous healings. www.lourdes-france.org

## 6 CASTLE CHURCH
Wittenberg, Germany

In 1517, an Augustinian monk named Martin Luther posted 95 theses protesting the ubiquitous trade in indulgences (writs promising salvation in exchange for cash) on the door of Castle Church, thus sparking the Reformation. Luther sites in Wittenberg include Luther's home and the home of the Reformation's premier scholar, Melanchthon.
www.schlosskirche-wittenberg.de

## 7 JASNA GÓRA MONASTERY
Czestochowa, Poland

Two scars rake the cheek of the icon of the Black Madonna of Czestochowa. Said to have been inflicted by the saber of a Hussite horseman, the wounds symbolize centuries of conflict endured by Poles, who revere this icon that legend states was painted by St. Luke on a tabletop from the home of the Holy Family.
www.thecatholictravelguide.com/Czestochowa.html

## 8 MOSQUE OF UQBA
Kairouan, Tunisia

Kairouan's chief site is the Mosque of Uqba—the first site of Muslim prayer in North Africa and an important pilgrimage site. Here, a three-story minaret dates from 728, and massively buttressed outer walls protect a hidden inner courtyard colonnaded by graceful arches supported by columns of marble and porphyry.

## 9 IVOLGINSKY DATSAN
Ulan-Ude, Siberia, Russia

A bit of Tibet nestled in Siberia, 18.6 miles (30 km) west of Ulan Ude, the monastery of Ivolginsky Datsan was one of the only Russian Buddhist centers to survive Stalin. Today this center of Buryat Buddhist culture is the home of the miraculously uncorrupted body of the 12th Pandido Khambo Lama, who died in 1927. This peaceful Siberian lamasery also serves as the home of rare manuscripts.

## 10 KUMBH MELA
India

Every three years, millions attend the Hindu pilgrimage and bathing festival of Kumbh Mela (Festival of the Pot of Nectar of Immortality), held at a location along the Ganges River determined by the astrological positions of Jupiter and the sun.
www.kumbhamela.net

Religious pilgrims have their choice of routes to get to Nidaros Cathedral in Norway. Don't miss the shrine, built in 1070 to mark King Olav's burial site.

# AMALFI COAST

Find artistic inspiration or just while away the day, a glass of *limoncello* in hand.

Driving here is not for the timid. The road that runs south from Naples and down the Amalfi Coast is famously steep and narrow and kinked with hairpin turns. It winds up cliffs and down into deep gorges. On Italy's most scenic stretch of coastline, the colors thrill, a living kaleidoscope that swirls and changes with every turn: pastel-hued villages terraced into the hillside, deep green gardens blanketed with brilliant blooms, the sunny yellow of the local lemons, and the turquoise waters of the Mediterranean (your near-constant companion).

The Amalfi Coast is a wonderland of winding roads, seaside cafés, colorful buildings stacked high along the hills, and water so blue it looks fake.

Peppered with towns somewhat small and that much smaller, the Amalfi Coast's most famous spots include the namesake Amalfi, Positano, and Ravello. They have inspired writers and artists for centuries, from 14th-century writer Giovanni Boccaccio to 19th-century composer Richard Wagner and 20th-century playwright Tennessee Williams. John Steinbeck described it as a "dream place that isn't quite real when you are there . . . and beckoningly real after you have gone."

When author Elizabeth Berg visited, she found such a place that "[e]verywhere I look—land or sea or sky—I see a

## CULINARY ARTS

Even people who are usually of the I'll-have-whatever philosophy when dining at home will find their culinary center on the Amalfi Coast. A week of cooking classes in and around Positano is, quite possibly, one of the fastest routes to making the area your own. Settle into a B&B, where a gift bag waits on your fridge, and celebrate your arrival with a glass of prosecco. Then, for the next week, there will be visits to fish shops; tastes of *ruta,* an herbal grappa, after a lunch of smoked provolone grilled on lemon leaves; chopping and cooking to turn simple ingredients into simply spectacular final dishes; trips into the hills to make cheese and pizza; and much more. You will be "proven utterly wrong," as Berg was, if you dare think that "simple preparations with so few ingredients" won't render impressive results.

## DAY TRIP TO CAPRI

Here, on Capri, a ferry ride away from Positano, the roads make those on the coastline look like superhighways. Take a chairlift to the top of Monte Solaro and take in the views of cliffs and seas so dramatic that the hair will stand up on the back of your neck. Stop at Villa San Michele, home of the Swedish physician who wrote the 1929 best seller *The Story of San Michele.* Then it's off to the Church of St. Michael, known for its 18th-century majolica floor depicting the expulsion of Adam and Eve from the Garden of Eden.

■ **PLANNING** Amalfi Coast www.amalfitouristoffice.it. **Culinary Arts** cooking-vacations.com/tour/one-week-cooking-on-the-amalfi-coast. **Day Trip to Capri** www.capritourism.com.

A day on the Amalfi Coast is incomplete without at least a taste of house-made limoncello, featuring the local citrus crop.

natural beauty I cannot quite take in: It's too much to comprehend. There is nothing to do but sip an espresso and just feel it all."

## SIP LIMONCELLO

The Amalfi Coast's rocky landscape isn't kind to most crops. But here, against the backdrop of the Mediterranean Sea, lemon trees often scent the air. The fruit turns up in many local dishes, but it is the limoncello you'll crave after a day of touring. With both lemons and pottery in abundance in the area, cold glasses of limoncello—made of lemon peels, water, sugar, and grain alcohol—are often served up after dinner. It's a way to help settle the system after a meal and, as you'll see, to make the experience last just that much longer.

---

## PLACES THAT CHANGED ME
### Gore Vidal, novelist, playwright, & essayist

Sixty-four years ago, just out of the army, I was looking for a place to write until at least the end of the century. I came to Ravello on a bright, cold day in March where I stood on a limestone cliff overlooking the Gulf of Salerno, Paestum opposite me, and I thought—and think—this is the most beautiful spot on Earth and so, in due course, I made it my own, and so it will remain until the next lucky visitor takes my place among the cypresses, the lemons, the vineyards of Magna Graecia where the sea-sky are so intensely blue that you cannot tell where one begins and the other leaves off.

Treat after visual treat—like this bell tower in Sorrento—reveals itself on a walk through the Amalfi's many coastal villages.

# ADRIATIC ISLANDS

Island-hop amid the blue waters of Croatia's Dalmatian coast.

Savvy European travelers have long known the charms of Croatia's long, rocky coastline, which stretches some 800 miles (1,290 km) along the Adriatic Sea and boasts nearly 1,500 islands. In addition to obvious summer pursuits like swimming and diving in crystal-clear, aquamarine water, the hilly islands offer myriad opportunities to hike and bike along sun-warmed rocks and lavender-scented trails.

Each island offers something a little different. Brac, just off the central coast, has a well-deserved reputation for beach life and parties. Long, slender Hvar, next door, is considered the more chic of the two—the ultimate blend of beautiful Venetian-influenced architecture, endless sun, and high fashion. The island's main settlement, Hvar town, would not be amiss along the French Riviera. Smaller, more remote islands like Vis and Mljet offer an easy escape from the crowds. For years, Vis was a restricted naval base, which prevented large-scale development. Lovely Mljet, to the south, is a protected national park.

The coastal city of Split, with its big ferry port as well as excellent road, rail, and air access, makes for a convenient starting point for exploring the islands. Choose from big car and passenger ferries or speedier catamarans.

■ **PLANNING** Adriatic Islands The official website of the Croatian National Tourist Board, www.croatia.hr, is a good first stop for planning an island getaway. Book passenger and car ferries online through the state-run Jadrolinija lines (*www.jadrolinija.hr*).

## ⚜ BEST OF THE BEST ⚜
### Magical Korcula Island

Visitors to Croatia's Adriatic coast are spoiled for choice. Catch a passenger ferry and catamaran (you can get on board in Split and Dubrovnik) to the beautiful, south-central island of Korcula, the alleged birthplace of Marco Polo. The main settlement, Korcula town, is a magical place girdled by massive medieval walls, which surround a perfect herringbone pattern of narrow streets running off the main axis. A short bus ride from Korcula town escorts beach lovers past vineyards, olive groves, and pine forests toward the lovely shores of Lumbarda, a fishing village on the island's southeastern end. Find out more at www.korculainfo.com.

Rumor has it that Marco Polo himself was born on Korcula.

St. Peter's Castle stands sentinel over the harbor at Bodrum.

# TURKEY
# AZURE COAST

Sail from island to island in search of old seaside haunts and new gems.

Turkey's sun-kissed Azure Coast unfurls along the country's Aegean shore. Sometimes called the Turquoise Coast, and definitely deserving of both names, this jagged and primordial seafront runs from Bodrum south and east to the city of Antalya. Although the coast is only 373 miles (600 km) long, its silver groves of olive trees have stood witness to several thousand years of history, and the region even encompasses the mythical birthplace of gods like Apollo. This area was also once home to the Lycian League, an ancient urban cooperative of democratic cities.

Today the Azure Coast, with its coves and bays long kept secret by sailors both ancient and modern, has transformed itself into a sunny alternative to the harried beach scenes in France's Côte d'Azur and Costa Blanca, Spain. Skip the fast-developing, already-too-busy beaches of Bodrum and Fethiye for the still quiet shores of Yalikavak, once the area's chief sponge-fishing port. Plot a springtime visit, when the village's surrounding hills turn into picnic-ready wildflower carpets. Chase your lounging time with visits to the Bodrum Museum of Underwater Archaeology, the carved cliffside tombs at Xanthos, and the scattered ruins of the Halicarnassus Mausoleum—one of the world's original seven wonders.

■ **PLANNING** Azure Coast www.goturkey.com. Azure Odysseys offers gulets (double-masted wooden sailboats) with full crews; visit www.azureodyssey.com to begin charting your own itinerary.

## ⚜ BEST OF THE BEST ⚜
### Lycian Way

Established in 168 B.C., the Lycian League was one of the world's earliest federations founded on democratic principles. The league's principal cities, many of them now in ruins, included Xanthos, Patara, Myra, Pinara, Olympos, and occasionally Telmessos (modern-day Fethiye) and Krya. The region, then called Anatolia and subsequently a Roman province before falling into obscurity, is now located in the provinces of Antalya and Mugla. Today it is also home to Turkey's first long-distance hiking path, the breathtaking 311-mile-long (500 km) Lycian Way (www.lycianway.com). Opened in 1999, the path follows the historic coast past wooded mountains, yawning canyons, abandoned Greek ghost towns, sunken ruins, lighthouse B&Bs, and ancient Hittite routes.

# BEST OF THE WORLD

## SPAS & BATHS

Turn muscles to jelly and skin to silk.

## 1 BANFF NATIONAL PARK
Alberta, Canada

Banff, Canada's first national park, was formed in 1885 as a hot-springs reserve. Now, travelers can hike up Sulphur Mountain to the Upper Hot Springs, which have a 1930s heritage bathhouse and views of Mount Rundle and the Canadian Rockies. www.pc.gc.ca

## 2 HOT SPRINGS NATIONAL PARK
Arkansas

Nearly 50 protected springs produce almost one million gallons of water a day in this area known by Native Americans as the Valley of the Vapors. The healing thermal water supplies the historic Bathhouse Row in the city of Hot Springs and is even available to drink from public fountains. www.nps.gov/hosp

## 3 LA FORTUNA DE SAN CARLOS
Costa Rica

Magma deep beneath Arenal Volcano, one of the country's most active volcanoes, heats the many springs near this northern Costa Rica town. Thermal pools rich in minerals and surrounded by verdant rain forest provide magnificent views of spurting ash and glowing red rocks tumbling down Arenal's sides. www.visitcostarica.com

## 4 BLUE LAGOON
Iceland

Iceland's Blue Lagoon stands out even in a country full of natural wonders: The vividly blue pool holds more than 1.5 million gallons (5.6 million L) of geothermal seawater. Located less than an hour from Reykjavik, the lagoon's silica-heavy water draws more than 400,000 visitors annually from around the world. www.bluelagoon.com

## 5 EDIPSOS
Greece

Aristotle once wrote about the healing properties of these warm mineral springs, located on the northwest coast of Evia, one of Greece's largest islands. The ancient spa town of Edipsos remains a popular rejuvenation spot for Greeks today, with more than 80 thermal baths. www.visitgreece.gr

## 6 SANDUNOVSKY BANYA
Moscow, Russia

This 19th-century Russian *banya* has been called the "czar of bathhouses." The palace-like structure's saunas and bathing pools are uniquely decorated in styles ranging from Renaissance to rococo, with marble staircases and gold frescoes in soaring halls. Attendants provide guests with besoms made from fir or eucalyptus, used in a traditional treatment. www.moscow.ru

## 7 PAMUKKALE
Turkey

Over the millennia, natural spring water has formed Pamukkale, the "cotton castle"—a series of white travertine terraces that cascade down a 600-foot (183 m) cliff in southeastern Anatolia. Visitors can swim over fragments of ancient marble columns that litter the bottom of the Sacred Pool. www.goturkey.com

## 8 MOULAY YACOUB
Morocco

Moroccans have made pilgrimages to Moulay Yacoub, located in the midst of the Atlas Mountains 12 miles (19 km) west of Fès, for centuries. The area's premier spa boasts a variety of healing benefits from its 129°F (54°C) sulfurous hyperthermal water, which comes from nearly 5,000 feet (1,524 m) belowground. www.moulayyacoub.com

## 9 YANGMINGSHAN NATIONAL PARK
Taiwan

Hot-springs spas are scattered throughout the volcanic mountains of this Taiwanese national park just outside Taipei. Bright yellow sulfur crystals can be seen at 2,600 feet (792 m) in elevation at Hsiaoyukeng, while a popular landmark in the Lengshueikeng area is Milk Lake, turned whitish yellow due to sulfur fumes vented from the lake bed. www.ymsnp.gov.tw

## 10 ROTORUA
New Zealand

The impossible-to-miss scent of sulfur suffuses the air of Rotorua, the "geothermal wonderland" of New Zealand's North Island that bubbles and hisses with geysers, mud pools, and hot springs. The Waimangu Volcanic Valley showcases brilliantly colored silica terraces, rocks that billow steam, and Frying Pan Lake, the world's largest hot-water spring. www.rotoruanz.com

More than 400,000 annual visitors to Iceland seek the therapeutic benefits of the Blue Lagoon's silica-heavy geothermal seawater.

After a relaxing boat ride to Santorini, take a donkey ride up the cliff face for a thrilling view of the island.

# AEGEAN ISLANDS

Go beneath the surface to discover what really makes the islands tick.

The Greek Islands are like musical instruments that form an orchestra in their seas—each has an individual timbre and signature tune," muses author Patricia Storace. Not all of these islands mirror the country's blue-and-white flag, nor are they all rocky and bare in summer. Almost every Greek island possesses some vestige of ancient civilization, however. After all, they've been inhabited forever. But some sites are so inspiring that they even lure dedicated sun worshippers off the beach. The few islands formed by volcanic activity have additional drama and fascination.

## ISLE-HOPPING ODYSSEY

Off the country's west coast, seven islands bob like emeralds in a sapphire sea. Venetians ruled these isles for

400 years, the British for 45. But before either set their sights on this Ionian archipelago, Odysseus lived here (on the peaceful isle of Ithaca). The Greek king spent ten years battling his way back to his Ionian address from Troy; visit the islands' beaches, and you'll see why. Begin at Corfu's north and west beaches, then hop to tiny Paxos, a yachts-man's haven covered in olive trees, and its uninhabited twin, Antípaxos. Follow the islands' spectacular chalk cliffs to Lefkáda, a favorite with sailors and windsurfers. From there, it's a stone's throw to Odysseus's Ithaca, a mountain-ous sliver of an island, and across to Kefallonia, the biggest of the group, known not only for its beaches but also for its magical caves, castles, and forests. Before setting sail again, partake of the island's superb Robola wines. Last comes

A fresco of a priest-king from Knossos, the capital of ancient Crete's Minoan civilization

Zákynthos, famous for its poets, currants, loggerhead turtles, Shipwreck Bay, and Blue Caves.

## ARCHAEOLOGICAL WONDERS

Among the oldest sites in the Greek islands are the Minoan palaces of Crete, which had running water, sublime frescoes, and stupendous views. From there, visit the acropolis of Lindos on Rhodes, and walk up a marble stairway with only the sky in sight until you reach the top. Here, the Aegean spreading beneath you, find the Temple of Athena Polias, dating from 300 B.C. Lush Kos, next to Rhodes, is home to the Asclepio, a healing center where Hippocrates taught medicine. Apollo's island, Delos, reached by boat in 20 minutes from Mykonos, is still sacred—no one may spend the night—but you can fill your day exploring houses with mosaic floors, the theater, the Terrace of the Lions, and the phallic effigy near the sanctuary of Dionysus.

The lesser known northern islands of Thasos, Limnos, and Samothrace should be on any antiquity lover's list—the first for its tree-filled agora and theater; the second for the low stone walls of Poliochni, perhaps the oldest city (ca 5000 B.C.) in Europe; and the third for the sanctuary of the mysterious pre-Greek great gods, where the Winged Victory once stood.

## THE VOLCANIC ARC

On Santorini, white villages cling to the caldera's rim. Arrive by ship and see the cliffs from below. Then ride a donkey up the cliff face and gasp at the view from other angles. For a real thrill, take a boat to the crater on Nea Kameni, where chthonic rumblings, Hades-like temperatures, and sulfurous fumes warn that Hephaestus is only sleeping. During the day cruise around Milos, marvel as the scenery changes from towering crimson rocks to cliffs that shift from smooth, galactic white to dark brown smeared with tomato-paste red to erect ebony rods surrounded by aquamarine pools. Mining has scarred the inland into surreal ziggurats and quarries, while the town exudes Cycladic charm and the beaches are to die for. Tiny Nisyros has the Aegean's other active volcano. Walk up to the largest of its five craters. The black-stone path passes Greece's only classical fort made of perfectly hewn massive black blocks.

■ **PLANNING** **Ionian Islands** www.ionian-islands.com, www.ionian islandholidays.com, and www.greeka.com/ionian. You can fly to Corfu, Kefallonia, and Zákynthos, reach Ithaca and Paxos by boat, and drive to Lefkáda over a bridge. **Archaeological Wonders** www .explorecrete.com, www.greeka.com/dodecanese (for Rhodes and Kos), and www.greeka.com/eastern_aegean (for Limnos, Samothrace, and Thasos). **The Volcanic Arc** Santorini and Milos can be reached by plane or boat, Nisyros by boat only. **Santorini** www.santorini.net. **Milos** www.milostravel.com. **Nisyros** www.nisyros.gr.

Climb the pedestrian path in jewel-like Oia, on the north end of Santorini, for spectacular sunsets.

The exclusive Bom Bom Island Resort, on Príncipe, is famous for big-game fishing.

# SÃO TOMÉ & PRÍNCIPE

Make an escape to Eden.

Called the "last island paradise," the tiny archipelago nation of São Tomé and Príncipe is a Portuguese-Creole–flavored Eden in the equatorial Atlantic off Africa. In the 15th century, Portuguese navigators discovered these two volcanic islands in the Gulf of Guinea, and in recent years, oil discoveries have inspired geotourism efforts to protect the parrot-filled rain forest and pristine beaches from overdevelopment.

Jan Hartman, who lived in São Tomé and Príncipe for five years as in-country coordinator for the Earth Institute, discovered "STP" when she was a U.S. State Department official in Gabon. "It was like Bali Hai, the mountain in the mist. Empty volcanic beaches, lush vegetation. A place caught in time, with charming local people."

São Tomé, the larger (and more developed) island and capital, once was an important entrepôt for the slave trade. Most of the population and signs of civilization are located here. For a more authentic tropical paradise experience, similar to what the first Portuguese explorers encountered, escape to Príncipe—a lush locale with spectacular, often empty beaches and forests that harbor a number of unique bird species. Spend the day swimming, snorkeling, kayaking, bird-watching, and visiting the island's tiny, sleepy capital, Santo António.

■ PLANNING São Tomé & Príncipe www.saotome.st.

## ～ IN THE KNOW ～
### CLAUDIO CORALLO CHOCOLATE

São Tomé and Príncipe is cacao bean country. Cacao trees, introduced in the 1800s, flourish in the rich volcanic soil. In 1997, Italian coffee plantation owner turned chocolatier Claudio Corallo and his family restored the abandoned Terreiro Velho cacao plantation in the Príncipe rain forest. The heirloom beans grown here are harvested, dried, and bagged before traveling via small boats to São Tomé and the family's small factory, Nova Moca, where the cacao is meticulously transformed into luxury chocolate. Claudio Corallo chocolate is pure, pricey, and packaged minimally to reduce waste. **Nova Moca tours** (samples included) are available upon request. Visit www.claudiocorallo.com for more information.

# LAKE MALAWI

Search for new constellations in this underwater universe.

Although Malawi occupies just a tiny strip of southeastern Africa, this landlocked country named itself "the warm heart of Africa." At its touristy and peaceful heart lies Lake Malawi, the continent's third largest lake, which occupies about one-fifth of the area of Malawi. Explorer David Livingstone dubbed this clear cobalt water the Lake of Stars because the lanterns from Malawi fishermen cast the impression of a limpid galaxy.

Situated at the southern end of Africa's Great Rift Valley, Lake Malawi dazzles visitors with its neon Neptunian galaxies. It is a sanctuary to thousands of tropical cichlids, and there are more species of fish here than in any other lake on the planet.

It also boasts the first freshwater marine reserve on Earth, Lake Malawi National Park, which lies at the lake's southern tip. Now a UNESCO World Heritage site, the park is also rich in other animal life, including hippos, baboons, crocodiles, and cormorants.

The most colorful and memorable way to navigate Lake Malawi is with a snorkel or a scuba tank. Start your underwater explorations from the brown-sugar beaches of Sunbird Livingstonia Beach, a lakeside hotel and resort with thatch-roofed chalets and private beach access.

■ **PLANNING** Lake Malawi www.malawitourism.com. **Sunbird Livingstonia Beach** For information about rooms, rates, and amenities, consult www.sunbirdmalawi.

## ⚶ BEST OF THE BEST ⚶
### Mumbo & Domwe Islands

The tropical islands of Domwe and Mumbo in Lake Malawi National Park coax visitors with secluded beaches, electric green waters, and a psychedelic marine underworld. Best reached by kayak, **Mumbo Island**—dressed in *miombo* woodlands and ancient fig and baobab trees—has only seven tents, each equipped with hammocks and hot-bucket showers. Playful spotted-necked otters, the island's only mammals, like to join guests for a swim. On larger **Domwe Island,** you will find a self-catering camp, where all lighting comes courtesy of the sun, paraffin lamps, and flashlights. Local *chitenje* fabric adorns tents of timber, canvas, and thatch. For more information, visit www.kayakafrica.net.

Sunset casts a pink glow over Africa's third largest lake.

# ZANZIBAR

Spend your summer like the dolphins and giant humpback whales visiting East Africa's Swahili Coast.

Few places are—or even sound—as exotic as Zanzibar. Mystique, along with the heady perfume of clove trees, seems to hang over this Indian Ocean archipelago along East Africa's Swahili Coast. Sultans, sailors, slaves, and spice traders have all passed through here, as did legendary explorer David Livingstone. In 1866, Livingstone stayed in what has been renamed Livingstone House, as a starting point for his exploration of Africa.

Time your own exploration for July, after the monsoon rains of earlier months have washed away the summer's sweltering heat. This is the ideal time to stroll Zanzibar's palm-shaded beaches, when they are newborn and fresh as flower buds. Coral sand, burning white in the equatorial sun, feels as soft underfoot as fine talc. At noon the sea is blood warm; at dusk, the falling sun sets taffeta highlights on the waves.

You won't be the only traveler to summer here: Giant humpback whales journey from their chilly feeding grounds in the Antarctic to the warm, narrow channel between Zanzibar and the private island of Mnemba. They know a good thing:

Mnemba is haloed by a dolphin-rich sea as crystalline as liquid tanzanite. You can see the dolphins from shore (and perhaps even be lucky enough to swim with them), but you'll have to hire a boat to see the whales.

■ **PLANNING Zanzibar** www.zanzibartourism.net. **Mnemba** The island is private but open to tourists. Inquire about accommodation at www.mnemba.com and www.mnemba-island.com.

## ⚜ BEST OF THE BEST ⚜
### Stone Town

The narrow, winding streets of Stone Town, a UNESCO World Heritage site, focus on commerce, with exotic treasures lurking in just about every tiny shop. You might find intricate jewelry fashioned from 15th-century coins or blue trade beads from Bohemia. Check out the market's formidable selection of vibrantly colored *khangas* (garments), or wander through winding alleys lined with grand (if dilapidated) Arab homes and intricately carved wooden doors. One home particularly worth a peek is Livingstone House, built around 1860 and occupied by many missionaries and explorers on their way to the African mainland.

Fishermen have worked Zanzibar's waters for centuries.

Coconut palm trees stand tall over Quirimbas National Park.

# MOZAMBIQUE
# QUIRIMBAS ARCHIPELAGO

Hop from one tropical island to another.

Slender, rustic, thin-hulled dhows, with ropes of coconut husk, have been fashioned from the rock-hard trunks of mangroves for the best part of a thousand years. On board there's no Wi-Fi, cabin service, or even padded seats, but you won't care. Your gaze will be fixed on the beaches of the Quirimbas, a sparkling necklace of 32 islands so beautiful you'll forget your name.

In the coastal village of Tandanhangue, catch a dhow and head for Ilha de Ibo, the crown jewel of the archipelago. The ruins of Ibo's stone town, the island's main settlement, echo its heyday as a trading post for silks, cotton, ivory, and, tragically, slave trafficking.

En route you'll glimpse many of the same sea creatures Jacques Cousteau admired—humpback whales, hawksbill turtles, bottlenose dolphins—whetting your appetite for the wild menagerie in Quirimbas National Park, where elephants, leopards, and crocodiles all vie for a piece of the naturalist's binoculars.

With 1,500 miles (2,414 km) of unsullied Indian Ocean sand on the doorstep, you can let more than your mind wander. At low tide you can often stroll from one island to the next. Days revolve around beach bumming, diving pristine coral reefs, and eating shockingly fresh lobster. The locals are dark, lean creatures with Arabic features, without a doubt some of the most handsome people on Earth.

■ **PLANNING** Quirimbas Archipelago http://mozambique tourism.co.za. **UNESCO** http://whc.unesco.org.

The Seychelles feature tiny villages, a national park that harbors rare trees and flowers, and some of the world's only remaining giant tortoises.

# SEYCHELLES

Behold islands rich in marvels—many of which you will not find anywhere else in the world.

The Seychellois like to tell the story of how their islands came to be: After God finished creating the world, he was left with a handful of diamonds. So he came to East Africa, resolved to create something marvelous, and scattered the jewels in the Indian Ocean. With that, the Seychelles were born.

This remote, beautiful necklace of precisely 115 islands stretches across the turquoise Indian Ocean, 994 miles (1,600 km) off the coast of East Africa. Writer and editor George Plimpton felt the magic: "The sands, white and soft underfoot, stretch spotless to the sea. The islands are so remote that nothing seems to come ashore on the waves except the sea itself."

## THE ORIGINAL GARDEN OF EDEN & SURREAL BIRD-WATCHING PARADISE

The Vallée de Mai on the island of Praslin is a lustrous forest of giant palms, with monstrous leaves and trunks towering to 100 feet (30.4 m). (Many regard this tropical green swath to be the original Garden of Eden.) The female palms bear a huge seed, a *coco de mer* (coconut of the sea), erotic in shape and weighing up to 40 pounds (about 18 kg)—the largest seed in the plant kingdom.

Follow a hiking trail through this surreal Brobdingnagian palm forest, a UNESCO World Heritage site, and keep your binoculars poised to spot other endemic residents: three

Vallée de Mai Nature Reserve's palms—rising up to 100 feet (30.5 m) tall—make visitors look like miniatures.

and reclaim his throne. He must have felt he was going into exile instead of returning from it. As his boat pulled away, the king reportedly put his hands over his eyes as if to capture and retain his last sight of the islands.

When you must, like Prempeh, sail away from Seychelles, one sight that you would be wise to savor and hold tight is of Mornes Seychellois National Park, a mountainous wonderland of rare trees and flowers. The park is navigable only by a hiking trail, which leads you past thick, emerald jungle, toward panoramic views of Victoria and Ste. Anne Marine National Park. Alpinists should consider climbing the 2,188-foot (667 m) Morne Blanc. A view of the west coast makes for a satisfying finale—and Prempeh-style keepsake—to the steep ascent.

## BEACH RESIDENTS

A granite islet 1 mile (1.6 km) off Praslin's north coast, Curieuse, which served as a leper colony from 1833 to 1965, is a picturesque home to a colony of giant Aldabra tortoises. A national mascot (the tortoise figures into the Seychelles coat of arms), this giant tortoise is found only in Seychelles and on the Galápagos Islands. Any worthwhile tour of the Seychelles demands an audience with one of the islands' ancient creatures. Disembark at Baie Laraie, and expect to be greeted by schools of humphead parrotfish, as well as tortoises, which will be lounging, lumbering, or sunning their shells nearby.

■ PLANNING Vallée de Mai and Mornes Seychellois National Park www.seychelles.travel.

species of bronze gecko, blue pigeons, bulbuls, Seychelles warblers, and the black parrot. Serious birders, however, would be wise to head to the plainly named Bird Island. With only one hotel (Bird Island Lodge), the coralline Bird Island is a giant nest to sooty terns, fairy terns, flame-plumed Madagascar fodies, and common noddies, as well as hawksbill turtles.

## VIEW FROM THE TOP

There appear to be as many stories about the enchantment of the Seychelles as there are waves in the surrounding ocean. One of them involves a young African king named Prempeh (ruler of the Ashanti nation, now part of Ghana) who was kicked off his throne and exiled to the Seychelles. He came to love the islands and traded his leopard skin raiment for baggy trousers and a silk hat. After 25 years he was allowed to leave

### ⚜ BEST OF THE BEST ⚜
#### Château de Feuilles

A sensible, islands-wide edict forbids building a structure higher than the highest palm. Thus the hotels, while luxurious, are spread out, their lobbies the size of football fields. The most exclusive is the intimate, ten-room Château de Feuilles (www.chateaude feuilles.com), where the air is sweet with the smell of gardenias and frangipani. This eminently civilized hotel hides amid a tangle of palms, orchids, and birds of paradise. Nineteenth-century British explorer Charles Gordon declared Praslin and its Vallée de Mai the original Garden of Eden. Spend the night here, waking up to birdsong and panoramic views of almost objectionable splendor, and you'll be hard-pressed to disagree.

The area's clear
waters make
it easy to spot
marine life.

# NATIVE HEALTH TREATMENTS TO EXPERIENCE OR LEARN

Consult the wisdom of the ages for what ails you.

## 1 POLYNESIAN *LOMILOMI*
Kailua, Hawaii

Master practitioners (*kahuna*) and elders (*kupuna*) kept the Hawaiian traditions of this Polynesian massage form alive despite being forced underground, from the 1890s to 1970s. Lomilomi is traditionally administered at home, although versions are offered at places like the Lomilomi Hana Lima Healing Center & Day Spa.
www.lomilomihanalima.com

## 2 SAGE SMUDGING
Sedona, Arizona

According to some Native American traditions, the cleansing smoke of burning desert sage attaches to negative energy and forces it to dissipate. Several spas offer this popularized ritual, which often involves prayers or chants to dispel negative thoughts and bad spirits, but you can also buy sage bundles and try it yourself.
www.visitsedona.com

## 3 CURANDERISMO HEALING
Cuernavaca, Mexico

This holistic folk tradition with Maya and Aztec roots combines prayer, herbal remedies, massage, and healing techniques. Most practitioners learn the craft from relatives or in apprenticeships with experienced *curanderos,* like those at La Tranca Institute of Healing.

## 4 SWEDISH MASSAGE
Stockholm, Sweden

While the eponymous chopping and smoothing techniques are simply called traditional or classic massage in Sweden, it was likely a Dutch physician who systemized its modern form. Still, spas throughout the country—like the elite Grand Hôtel in Stockholm—have embraced and refined the craft.
www.grandhotel.se/en/explore/spa

## 5 NORWEGIAN SAUNAS
Oslo, Norway

These hothouses have kept away Nordic cold for centuries, but their purpose is actually to promote blood flow by alternating temperatures—traditional saunas are located near water for quick dashes between hot and cold. Try the Nordtvet Public Baths outside Oslo.
www.visitoslo.com

## 6 TURKISH BATHS
Istanbul, Turkey

Melding Greek and Roman social bathing practices with the importance of cleanliness to Islam, hammams are architectural mainstays from antiquity. The bathing process leads you through three rooms of varying temperatures and humidity, where attendants use coarse mitts to exfoliate before applying soap or administering massage. Visit Galatasaray Hamami in Beyoglu.
www.galatasarayhamami.com

## 7 DEAD SEA SALT SCRUB THERAPIES
Ein Gedi, Israel

Perhaps because of its ancient past, Dead Sea salt is said to have healing properties. At the Ein Gedi Sea of Spa, visitors can relax in thermo-mineral pools, slather on therapeutic black mud, or enjoy a massage with coarse salt crystals from the sea. A swim offers the sensation of levitating.
http://eingediseaofspa.com/massage.php

## 8 AYURVEDA
Kerala, India

Incorporating preventive and curative measures, this holistic medical system is still used by a majority of the Indian population. At the Kerala Ayurveda Academy, students and workshop participants learn the techniques of herbal remedies, yoga, and diet in the place where the practice originated some 3,000 years ago.
wwww.ayurvedaacademy.com

## 9 BALINESE *LULUR*
Bali, Indonesia

Rice, fragrant spices, yogurt, and frangipani are crushed to create a warm body mask applied during massage. Traditionally lulur is a series of exfoliating masks lasting 40 days and reserved for royal brides-to-be. Fortunately for visitors, condensed versions are available. Consider the one-hour treatment at Tunjung Sari Spa.
www.balispacentre.com

## 10 ACUPUNCTURE
Beijing, China

Two thousand years ago, ancient Chinese used sharpened rocks or pottery to drain abscesses and ward off disease, but modern students at the China Beijing International Acupuncture Training Center learn a less rudimentary practice. Thin metal needles inserted at key points on the body are said to promote the flow of energy that can lessen or eliminate pain.
www.cbiatc.com

On Hawaii, a masseuse's expert technique ratchets up relaxation provided by the natural surroundings.

Hakone Ginyu is one of more than 2,000 onsen resorts devoted to the Japanese ritual of "naked communion."

# HOT SPRINGS

Soak in hot springs in the foothills of Mount Fuji.

An *onsen,* or traditional Japanese bathhouse, is fed by the intense geothermal activity that underpins much of Japan and that accounts for more than 2,000 onsen resorts across the country. Bathing in such springs is to experience what the Japanese call the "naked communion of the onsen,"

## ~❧ IN THE KNOW ❧~
### SENTŌ

While onsen are a mostly rural phenomenon, sentō are public bathhouses usually found in cities—Tokyo alone has well over a thousand. Like onsen, sentō have long been an intrinsic part of Japanese culture. They are rooted in the religious bathing traditions associated with Buddhist temples in India, whence the practice spread via China and arrived in Japan in the eighth century. Recently, however, their number has been in decline as more Japanese homes are built with tubs and as young people become more self-conscious about shared nakedness. Older Japanese still use sentō (foreigners are welcome) and fret that in missing the presumed emotional intimacy created by physical proximity—known as "skinship" in Japan—the young are failing to be socialized properly.

and it is considered a vital way of breaking down barriers in a hierarchical society of ritual and formality. Naked, all are equal.

At Tenzan Tohji-kyô, two hours from Tokyo, you slip gently into natural hot springs, surrounded by trees, birdsong, and moss-covered rocks. Steam rises into a sun-dappled glade as you revel in the tranquillity of the moment, the mountain air icy fresh, the pools deliciously warm, your handful of fellow bathers quiet and lost in thought. Tenzan Tohji-kyô is traditionally built, its wood and stone buildings blending perfectly with its natural surroundings. You undress in the simple interior, wander outdoors, and sit on a low stool in front of handheld showers to give yourself the wash that etiquette demands. Then you dip into one of the six pools, each of a different temperature. Within minutes, the onsen's spell—the water, the muscle-soothing heat, and the beauty and calm of your surroundings—will have worked its magic.

■ **PLANNING** Tenzan Tohji-Kyô www.tenzan.jp. By train from Tokyo, take the JR Tokaido line to Odawara and change for Hakone-Yumoto. Free shuttles run from the station to the onsen, which is quieter Mon.–Fri. Spring (April–May), when the blossoms are out, is a good time to visit. Bathing suits are not allowed.

# THAILAND
# KOH LIPE

Plunge into the pristine undersea reefs of the Andaman Sea.

A sun-drenched jewel off Thailand's west coast, Koh Lipe has risen to the top of intrepid beach lovers' A-list of island paradises. Unlike nearby Phuket and Koh Phi Phi, Koh Lipe has avoided the perils of rapid development by a simple stratagem: Visitors can arrive only by boat. The island was largely spared the destruction that engulfed the southern peninsula's coastline during the 2004 tsunami.

One-quarter of all the tropical fish species in the world are found here in Tarutao National Marine Park, a 51-island archipelago that is one of the country's first ocean preserves. Dolphins, manta rays, sharks, and sperm whales patrol the deeper waters, while clown fish, angelfish, lionfish, and brilliant coral make the area a snorkeling favorite. At Hin Chabang, a ten-minute sail from shore, species mingle at a cleaning station, where parasite fish clean their larger brethren.

On land, snorkelers and divers make their base near Pattaya Beach, the most developed tourist spot; others prefer the seclusion of Sunrise and Sunset Beaches. Take an hour to stroll or kayak the island's perimeter and savor the iridescent pastels of the shallows, or hail a traditional long-tail boat to journey to neighboring islands.

■ PLANNING Koh Lipe www.kohlipethailand.com. **Tarutao National Marine Park** There is an admission fee to enter the park. For information on scuba diving and snorkeling in the region, consult www.asiadivesite.com/thailand-dive-sites.

## ～ IN THE KNOW ～
### THE CHAO LEI

Koh Lipe is home to about 500 Chao Lei, or sea gypsies, a small ethnic community whose language is a curious hybrid of Malay and Thai. The Chao Lei hold claim to half the island and live in small villages, predominantly around the far eastern side of the island near Sunrise Beach. Package tours will not take you to their settlements, but the area is not restricted and you can visit by touring boat. The origins of the Chao Lei are a mystery. Some have converted to Buddhism, but most Chao Lei follow animistic beliefs. The name Koh Lipe means "paper island" in Chao Lei, which has no written language.

An arrival-by-boats-only policy keeps the island from getting crowded.

# CAMBODIA
# SIHANOUKVILLE

Feast on prawns, privacy, and priceless views on the Cambodian coast.

A haven for backpackers and budget travelers, Victory Beach lies at the northern end of Sihanoukville.

A sunset on a pristine beach overlooking the Gulf of Thailand, lit by flaring torches and accompanied by a guitar: This is what peace means in Sihanoukville, Cambodia, as the country rebuilds after years of strife. Named for King-Father Norodom Sihanouk, this seaside enclave was a favorite retreat for the Cambodian royal family in the 1960s. The Vietnam War and the Khmer Rouge's reign of terror intervened, and a grim reputation followed the town into the 1990s. Now, adventurous sun lovers are spurning crowded Thai island resorts for this tropical port town's white-sand beaches, just 115 miles (184 km) southwest of Phnom Penh. You may well end up echoing the thoughts of National Geographic writer and photographer Kris LeBoutillier, who describes his favorite local beaches as "deserted, lush, and ringed with sapphire blue water . . . and they seem to be mine." Choose a sunning spot among a half dozen beaches, edged with bungalows and bars for the backpacker set. At open-air cafés, cooks sizzle the catch of the day—which might be barracuda—and beach vendors hawk succulent barbecued prawns, which they balance atop broad-brimmed straw hats. At the new town market, Psar Leu, counters glisten with vats of sea eel and urchins.

## GO FISH

Fishing has been the livelihood of Sihanoukville for centuries. Commercial ships and, more recently, cruise liners line the town's busy docks. Charter fishing boats also anchor here. The dry-season months of late November to May present the Gulf of Thailand's best season for sportfishing. Though local commercial fishermen notoriously use dynamite and cyanide to harvest their catches, amateurs can rent reels and rods to hook snapper, barracuda, and even a few black marlin. .

## UNDERWATER ADVENTURES

A day of fishing always includes a communal feast featuring the group's catch. And often, your captain will invite you to jump in a sheltered bay for some leisurely snorkeling. Scuba divers find a handful of operators offering PADI certification

---

### ⌁ IN THE KNOW ⌁
#### SAILING THE CAMBODIAN COAST

With 61 islands dotting the coast from Kep to Koh Kong, Cambodia is a sailor's dream. On Sihanoukville's Otres Beach, Otres Nautica is an ideal place to rent a catamaran or small sailboat to zip along the shore. Larger boats and kayaks are also available. You may also explore on leisurely day trips and overnight sailing charters with Sail Cambodia's 45-foot (14 m) boat. For a map of Sihanoukville and information on boat rentals, visit www.sihanoukville-cambodia.com. For longer and chartered sailing trips, consult www.sailcambodia.info.

and fun dives; more than 25 dive sites have been established off the Cambodian coast, and the area's coral reefs are dotted with seahorses and nudibranchs—brilliantly colored toxic slugs that seem outfitted for an undersea carnival. Choose live-aboard options to venture on longer expeditions among the region's 61 islands. Return to Sihanoukville at sunset for its Full Moon Parties—raucous beachfront celebrations that include rock-and-roll, fire shows, and cocktails for all.

■ **PLANNING** **Cambodia** www.tourismcambodia.org. **Fishing** Fisherman's Den and Sankeor offer daily fishing trips. For contact details, see www.sihanoukville-cambodia.com/about-sihanoukville/activities/boating-and-fishing.html. Water sports and pleasure boat rides are also available. **Diving** Visit www.divecambodia.com for information about diving excursions and certification classes.

Ochheuteal Beach puts on the best early evening show around town.

# PALAWAN

Absorb the rich biodiversity and sugary white, sandy beaches of the "last frontier" of the Philippines.

As befits its remote location, the Philippine coastal province of Palawan shelters one of Asia's most biodiverse land-and-sea environments. Palawan's roughly 1,200 miles (2,000 km) of irregular coastline, dotted with thousands of islets, rocky coves, and sugary white-sand beaches, are a nature explorer's dream. In fact, many coastal villages are accessible only by boats that deposit visitors in the shallow, clear sea to walk ashore. Designated a fish and wildlife sanctuary in 1967, the province's extensive coral reefs, mangrove forests, and limestone cliffs offer almost endless discovery.

Fantasy Island surely exists among the hundreds of coral-fringed islets up and down the archipelago. Powdery sand beaches slip into turquoise waters teeming with fish. On the main island, hike the 3-mile (5 km) Monkey Trail to experience a mountain-to-sea ecosystem that culminates in the Puerto Princesca Subterranean River National Park's navigable underground river, a UNESCO World Heritage site. Aboveground, the 5-mile (8 km) coastal rain-forest route is home to long-tailed macaques, blue-naped parrots, and hundreds of other species. In the province's northern Calamianes islands a World War II–vintage wreck rests in calm, crystalline waters off Coron Island. Nearby Culion Island, a former leper colony surrounded by sea grass beds and coral reefs, is an emerging ecotourism destination.

■ **PLANNING** **Palawan** www.visitpalawan.com. For accommodations, consult www.palawan.com. **Puerto Princesa Subterranean River National Park** www.puerto-undergroundriver.com; admission fee.

## ⚓ BEST OF THE BEST ⚓
### El Nido Marine Reserve Park

In 1984, the lush tropical region at the northern tip of Palawan was declared a turtle sanctuary. Today the 139-square-mile (360 sq km) El Nido Marine Reserve Park is home to several endangered species of turtles and more than 800 species of fish. Its forests shelter such rare birds as the Palawan peacock pheasant and the Palawan hornbill. The park takes its name from the Spanish word for "nest." Here skillful climbers scramble up limestone walls to collect the nests built by swiftlets in the crags and crevices. The edible nests are unfortunately destined for bird's nest soup, often considered a delicacy in China.

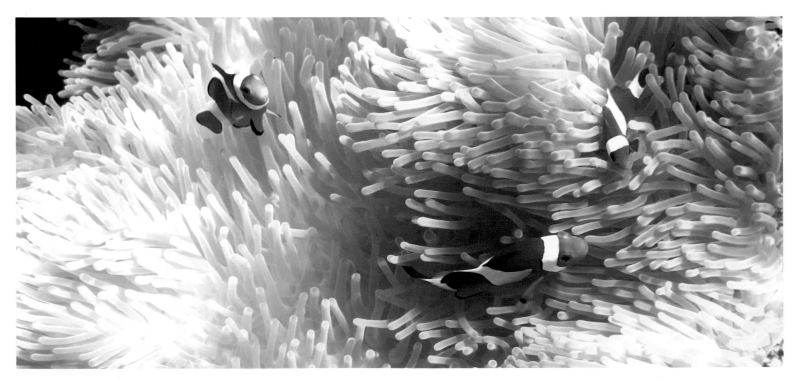

Palawan's 1,200-mile (2,000 km) coastline is home to countless colorful species of fish and other sea life.

Snorkeling excursions off Yap provide great sights and solitude.

# YAP'S OUTER ISLANDS

Enjoy the simple life in a far-out way.

Only a few outsiders travel to these sun-bleached, low-lying coral atolls in any given year. Of the 14 islands, just a few are populated permanently.

Make your way here and you'll dive unsullied reefs alive with sharks, nudibranchs, and brightly striped mandarin fish. In the area's lagoons, dive guides will help you search out manta rays. Later, you'll deep-sea fish for wahoo, mahimahi, and red snapper.

You'll get the chance to settle into a simpler, more sustainable lifestyle. Travelers often find it surprising how the islanders use a few local staples for such a wide variety of needs. The coconut tree, for instance, can provide everything from baby food to building material.

And you can sail off in traditional Yapese style: The Yap Traditional Navigation Society and its school, the Yap Traditional Maritime Institute, founded in 2006, have helped revitalize the art of Yapese boatmaking. A few hours in one of the hand-carved canoes, sails aloft, allows you to dream, if only for a little while, that you can stay here forever.

■ PLANNING Yap www.visityap.com. Continental Air Micronesia makes three flights to Yap each week. You can also get to Yap by private boat. The island uses U.S. currency. **Yap Traditional Navigation Society** www.yapnavigation.com.

## ∼ IN THE KNOW ∼
### FALUBWA

At some point (probably on your first night in town), somebody will hand you some *falubwa*, aka *tuba*, a locally made fermented toddy of coconut sap. The scarcity of visitors and the cultural esteem placed on hospitality add up to the certainty that you will be well taken care of while in town—and falubwa will definitely play a role. As the sun goes down, groups of men form drinking circles, pass around a cup of tuba, and recount their exploits of the day. All visitors to the island—male and female—are encouraged to join in.

Fiji's privately owned Wakaya Island is now home to an eco-friendly resort.

SOUTH PACIFIC

# FIJI

*Yesterday we passed close to an island or so, and recognized the published Fiji characteristics: a broad belt of clean white coral sand around the island; back of it a graceful fringe of leaning palms, with native huts nestling cosily among the shrubbery at their bases; back of these a stretch of level land clothed in tropic vegetation; back of that, rugged and picturesque mountains.*

—MARK TWAIN, *FOLLOWING THE EQUATOR*, 1897

INDONESIA

# LOMBOK

Climb above the clouds east of Bali.

Lombok's landscape features rice fields and a volcano.

Breathing deeply in the thin air, a climber's first view of Gunung Rinjani is otherworldly deep gorges, hot springs, waterfalls, a turquoise lake, and a perfect volcanic cone.

At 12,221 feet (3,725 m), Indonesia's second highest volcano is sacred to the local Muslim Sasak and Hindu Balinese, who manage treks into Rinjani National Park. En route to the summit, often wreathed in smoke and mist, visitors may glimpse the rare black ebony leaf monkey, gray macaques, crested cockatoos, and shy civet cats.

Sustainable tourism projects provide a livelihood for many locals. Rinjani received the National Geographic Society's World Legacy Award in 2004 for its effort to nurture cultural shows, village tours, religious festivals, oral histories, and mountain lore, adding depth to a rigorous climbing experience. The classic three-day trek aims not for the steep summit, but for the jade-colored Segara Anak, or Child of the Sea, a crescent-shaped lake amid volcanic debris 1,968 feet (600 m) below the rim. More adventurous hikers tackle the edge of the caldera, which affords vast views of the Java Sea.

Twice a year thousands of Sasak and Balinese pilgrims make offerings of rice, fish, and betel nuts to the deities of the lake and mountain. They regard the ascent of Rinjani as a spiritual adventure as much as a physical one.

■ **PLANNING Lombok** www.indonesia.travel. **Gunung Ranjani National Park** www.lombokrinjanitrek.org. The park charges a modest entrance fee. Closed Jan.–March during monsoon season.

## ☙ BEST OF THE BEST ☙
### Mount Krakatoa

The islands of Indonesia are among the youngest spots on Earth, formed only 15 million years ago. Thus the country—particularly Bali and Java—is home to the largest collection of active volcanoes in the world. More than 150 centers of volcanism are found throughout the archipelago, with eruptions that have catastrophic consequences. With the equivalent impact of several hydrogen bombs, the 1883 eruption of Java's Mount Krakatoa killed 36,000 people. Subsequent 20th-century eruptions at the volcano built a new island, called the child of Krakatoa, Anak Krakatau. Java Rhino offers Mount Krakatoa ecotours that last from one to five days. Visit www.krakatoatour.com for itineraries.

# AITUTAKI

Float above cobalt blue sea stars in a palm-fringed, turquoise lagoon.

Aitutaki is everything you ever imagined the South Pacific to be: emerald waters filled with coral gardens and striped and speckled fish, perfect tangerine- and fuchsia-striped sunsets. Captain William Bligh and his *Bounty* crew were the first Europeans to visit the 7.1-square-mile (18 sq km), comma-shaped islet in 1789. Today, a turquoise lagoon fringed by palm trees and beaches teeming with pure open space help make Aitutaki the second most visited island in the Cook archipelago, after Rarotonga.

Nirvana for snorkelers, Aitutaki's lagoon shelters blue chromis, masked butterfly fish, and other colorful marine species. Motus, or tiny islets, line the perimeter and protect the translucent triangle of calm seas from the surrounding fierce and endless ocean. Etu Moana (blue starfish), a cluster of eight Polynesian-style boutique villas—all with elevated king-size beds facing the water, thatched roofs, and private gardens with outdoor showers—provides guests with bicycles, snorkeling equipment, and kayaks for unlimited exploration.

Start the day in your paradise found with fresh star fruit and pawpaws by the pool, and then hop into a kayak and paddle into the reef-splotched, 7-mile-long (11 km) lagoon. Glide ashore on a deserted stretch of white sand, beach the kayak on the shore, and then snorkel above cobalt blue sea stars, giant clams, and yellow barrel sponges.

■ **PLANNING** Aitutaki www.aitutaki.com. **Etu Moana** www .etumoana.com. Getting to Etu Moana requires flying in a small prop plane from Rarotonga. A lei greeting at the Aitutaki airport and transfers to and from the resort are included.

## ∼ IN THE KNOW ∼
### TIVAEVAE

Perhaps the most famous of Cook Islands handicrafts are *tivaevae (tivaivai)*: brightly colored, intricately embroidered ceremonial cloths, pieced together by small groups of women using a native technique similar to quilting. Because of the social significance of crafting tivaevae and the number of months required to make one, they are considered prized family heirlooms and typically are not available for sale. You can commission a custom tivaevae through the Atiu Fibre Arts Studio *(www.atiu-fibrearts .com)*, which also offers five-day tivaevae workshops. Atiu is accessible by short flight from both Rarotonga and Aitutaki.

Brilliant sunsets cap days of snorkeling and kayaking.

Tuscany's famed cypress trees dot Val d'Orcia, an agricultural region where visitors can enjoy farmhouse stays and peaceful drives.

# COUNTRY UNBOUND

*Finding renewal of the mind, body, and spirit*

In some places man and nature exist in perfect harmony. These are places where traditions have shaped the landscape—and have been shaped by nature in their turn. Villages nestle at the feet of protective peaks. Centuries-old farms flourish among meadows of wildflowers. Hiking trails lace rocky, sparsely inhabited coasts. The balance is delicate, the charm irresistible.

Take a boat on the Gulf of St. Lawrence for a close-up of the Percé Rock and a visit to a massive (and noisy) gannet seabird colony.

## QUEBEC, CANADA
# GASPÉ PENINSULA

Find out how seabirds summer on Bonaventure Island.

Jutting into the vast Gulf of St. Lawrence, the eastern tip of Quebec is the perfect mix of isolation and civilization. The 11,714-square-mile (30,340 sq km) Gaspé Peninsula—or Land's End in native Micmac—is Quebec's wind- and sea-sculpted continuation of the Appalachian Mountains. Divided into five natural areas—the Coast, Land's End, the Bay of Chaleur, the Valley, and the Upper Gaspé—the peninsula contains six wildlife sanctuaries, 25 of Quebec's highest peaks, and four national parks.

During the summer months, pack a picnic and board an early boat from Percé for a tour of Bonaventure Island and Percé Rock National Park (Le parc national de l'Île-Bonaventure-et-du-Rocher-Percé). Boats cruise past Rocher-Percé, an offshore sphinx of limestone that rises from the Gulf of St. Lawrence. Disembark on Bonaventure Island for a visit with the island's seasonal residents. Guides will lead you to a fairly easy trail that winds along in relative quiet—wind in trees, the chatter of other visitors—until the squawking (and, yes, stink) filters through. When the trail ends, the great reveal: 250,000 migratory birds—including the continent's largest colony of northern gannet seabirds.

After hiking back down, tour the island's historical buildings. Or settle into the post-gannet quiet with your lunch and a view of the gulf, before boarding a boat back to Percé.

■ **PLANNING Gaspé Peninsula** www.infogaspesie.com. **Bonaventure Island and Percé Rock National Park** www.sepaq .com/pq/bon. Boat tours leave from the Percé town pier May–Sept.; prime bird-watching is in June and July.

### ∽ IN THE KNOW ∾
#### "LE GRAND RASSEMBLEMENT"

In Ste.-Flavie, a gateway to the Gaspé Peninsula, life-size concrete sculptures appear to move with the tides near the Centre d'Art Marcel Gagnon. Inspired by nature, self-taught artist and painter Gagnon began "Le Grand Rassemblement" in 1986 by installing 80 reinforced concrete sculptures (each weighing 1,510 lb/685 kg) in the St. Lawrence River. In 1992 he added wooden rafts, which seemingly float at high tide, and in 2003 he expanded the gathering to more than a hundred creatures that appear to be walking out of the water toward a half-buried globe. Shifting tides and shadows create an optical illusion of movement.

# CAPE BRETON

Voyage between the sea and the sky.

With its salt-tanged fishing villages and mountainous interior cloaked in dense woods, Cape Breton is the prize of Nova Scotia, a green getaway splashed with lakes and lapped by the blue waters of the Gulf of St. Lawrence and the Atlantic Ocean.

Famous resident Alexander Graham Bell proclaimed, "I have seen the Canadian and American Rockies, the Andes, the Alps and the Highlands of Scotland, but for simple beauty, Cape Breton outrivals them all."

It's easy to sample the best of Cape Breton, since the Cabot Trail makes a 184-mile (296 km) loop around a sizable chunk of the island, passing through Cape Breton Highlands National Park at its northernmost point. The land is rugged, built on some of the oldest visible rock on Earth. The park alone, reason enough to make the drive, offers hiking trails, camping, austere mountains, and sheltered beaches. Along the way, you'll witness creatures great and small of both land and sea. Pilot whales cruise through the Gulf of St. Lawrence from May until November. Minkes, finbacks, and humpacks, too. Sharing the trail with you: moose and black bear, red fox and coyote, and more. Seabirds and shorebirds abound, too.

■ **PLANNING** **Nova Scotia** www.novascotia.com. **Cape Breton** http://cbisland.com. **Cape Breton Highlands National Park** www.pc.gc.ca.

---

### ⚜ BEST OF THE BEST ⚜
#### Keltic Lodge Resort & Spa

Surrounded by cottages on a spit of land so narrow it feels like an island, this majestic hotel has pampered guests for more than 60 years. This elegant, Tudor-style resort (with impeccable service) is perched high on a cliff within Cape Breton Highlands National Park and provides breathtaking views of Cape Smokey Provincial Park rising out of the sea across the gulf. When you're not unwinding in the luxurious spa, dining on Maritime crustaceans, or taming the 18-hole Highlands Links course, you can explore a gorgeous hiking trail on the property. Open June to mid-October. For details, see http://kelticlodge.ca.

The 184-mile (296 km) Cabot Trail has few rivals for sheer spectacle, weaving past timeless fishing villages, moody highlands, and plentiful wildlife.

TEXAS

# HILL COUNTRY

Scale the lunar summit of a billion-year-old granite dome.

Texas' famed Hill Country is a rumpled terrain marked by wooded canyons cut by spring-fed rivers, endless miles of appealing two-lane blacktop, and quirky locales like Bandera, which still considers itself the hell-raising Cowboy Capital of the World. Come spring, blooming bluebonnets and scarlet Indian paintbrush transform stream banks and meadows into a living Impressionist landscape.

The bucolic backdrop begins just north of Austin, continues south to San Antonio, and sweeps west some 200 miles (320 km) before the land begins to flatten out. Old-timers still refer to the area as German Hill Country, a nod to the first non-native settlers, German immigrants who'd purchased millions of acres sight unseen.

You almost can see it all—oak woodlands, mesquite grasslands, and gravelly slopes—from the rosy, lunar summit of Enchanted Rock. Located north of Fredericksburg, the 425-foot-tall (129.5 m), dome-shaped mountain of pink granite is about a billion years old and covers 640 acres (260 ha). Climb to the bare rock top, where thousands of years of weathering have created patches of vegetation called vernal pools. Lie back against the sun-warmed rock and gaze into the clear blue sky curving brilliantly just beyond your outstretched hand.

■ **PLANNING** **Enchanted Rock State Natural Area** www.tpwd.state.tx.us. The park is open year-round (entrance fee) yet frequently closes before noon on weekends due to limited parking. Arrive before 9 a.m. or after 5 p.m.

Picnic tables in this region are good for sitting—but even better for feasting on barbecue.

# CALIFORNIA
# BIG SUR

Absorb the primordial essence of a wind- and wave-sculpted reserve.

Along Big Sur's fabled coastline, redwood groves reach skyward, the Santa Lucia Range plunges into the Pacific Ocean, and waves are beaten to froth on ragged rocks. Stark, remote, and sparsely populated, this 90-mile (145 km) stretch of California's Highway 1 snakes slowly and daringly along a cliff-hanging course from Carmel to San Simeon. It is a brooding place of elemental power that can make human affairs seem inconsequential.

"When the sun is fierce on Big Sur's high ridges, the redwood canyons are cool and dark, and there is a wintry salt spray on the rocky beaches. Such contrast evokes a wide range of moods, expanding our sense of both outer and inner space," says Michael Murphy, who co-founded the Esalen Institute here in 1962.

Civilization exists in pockets, yet it is sufficiently tucked away for the coast to retain its primordial essence. Absorb it all—pungent salt air, relentless surf, migrating gray whales, undersea kelp forests, and towering rock cliffs—at the eye-bending Point Lobos State Natural Reserve just south of Carmel, a 550-acre (222 ha) park with another 750 acres (303 ha) underwater. While you wander trails through pines and wind-sculpted cypress, listen for barking sea lions sunning below on shores lapped by blue waves iced in the meringue of white foam.

## PLACES THAT CHANGED ME

*James Fallows, author of* Postcards From Tomorrow Square

The drama of visible geography is available wherever the mountains are new enough and the climate is dry enough to prevent a veil of green. But to me its glory is California's Big Sur . . . In 1967, on a visit home to California after my first year in college, I camped for weeks with a high school friend in Big Sur. We pitched tents under the soaring Bixby and Limekiln bridges. We lay on our backs and looked to the top of redwoods . . . The glory of Big Sur made us feel restored, excited, and alive. It does the same now.

■ **PLANNING Big Sur** www.seemonterey.com/big-sur-california. **Point Lobos State Natural Reserve** www.parks.ca.gov. The park is a day-use area that closes a half hour after sunset. Diving is permitted at Whalers and Bluefish Coves with proof of certification.

# LOUISIANA
# PLANTATION COUNTRY

Fuel your drive with music, food, and eye-catching antebellum architecture.

It takes just a few minutes to settle into the pace of southern Louisiana. Unless you're lured onto a dance floor to swirl to some zydeco or swamp pop, there will be no rushing. The air, the curvy roads, and the Cajun and Creole cuisines that demand a post-lunch nap don't allow hurrying along.

You'll stop endless times along this 150-mile (241 km) stretch of Louisiana's River Road—the Mississippi River is your constant (though often coy) companion along the route from New Orleans to St. Francisville—to photograph oaks draped with Spanish moss and stately plantation mansions built in the years before the Civil War by the wealthy men who ran the sugar trade. The names of the plantations, many of them National Historic Landmarks, conjure up images straight out of a Hollywood film: Oak Alley Plantation, Judge Felix Poche Plantation, and St. Emma Plantation, whose sugarhouses were a temporary home to Confederate troops in 1862.

At Rosedown Plantation, in West Feliciana Parish, the remaining 371 acres (150 ha)—one-tenth of its peak size—have been transformed back to the vision of the house's original owners, Daniel and Martha Turnbull, who used slave labor to create gardens inspired by their honeymoon in Europe.

■ **PLANNING** Louisiana www.louisianatravel.com. **River Road** www.nps.gov/nr/travel/louisiana/riverroad.htm. Many of the plantation houses are open only by appointment. Call ahead to schedule tours. **Oak Alley Plantation** www.oakalleyplantation .com. **Judge Felix Poche Plantation** www.pocheplantation.com. **Rosedown Plantation State Historic Site** www.crt.state.la.us/ parks/irosedown.aspx.

---

## ∾ IN THE KNOW ∾
### DINE AROUND BATON ROUGE

Slow food indeed. From the time it takes to make a proper roux to the realization that it's best to sit awhile after the latest over-indulgence, the area's cuisine demands slow. While there's an abundant supply of tasty food to be had along the River Road (you'll be a crawfish-eating expert by trip's end), the city of Baton Rouge provides a concentrated dose of marvelous. Three to try: **Juban's** (www.jubans.com), for upscale, Creole-inspired meals; the giant **Ralph & Kacoo's** (www.ralphandkacoos.com), for a family-friendly meal of New Orleans-style treats; and **The Chimes** (www .thechimes.com), for fine po'boys and a good beer selection.

# COTTAGE COUNTRY

Slow down, kick back, and let the iconic Muskoka chair work its magic.

Muskoka—the heart of Ontario cottage country—hovers around Lakes Muskoka, Rosseau, and Joseph. If these deep, cold lakes are memories of glacial meltwater, the region—mapped with open-rock ridges; beaver ponds; waterfalls; and forests of pine, oak, and hemlock—is also a throwback to another, slower time. In Muskoka, a recreational paradise since the 19th century, maintaining tradition is in itself a time-honored tradition.

A present-day Muskoka to-do list is much as it was a century ago: jump off rock faces, eat s'mores over an open fire, and watch early morning sun burn off mist over a glassy lake. But nothing in Muskoka qualifies as the choice activity. After all, this is the motherland of the so-called Muskoka chair. Crafted from Ontario pine and cedar, and perfectly fashioned for dockside daydreaming, this iconic symbol of rest and relaxation serves not only as requisite perch, but also as regional (and ideological) mascot. Take your cue from the 1.5 million summertime visitors: Just set your chair down anywhere along the 8,700 miles (14,000 km) of wooded shoreline—where you are now as likely to spot a yacht as you are to spot a family of loons—sit down, and settle back.

■ **PLANNING Muskoka** www.discovermuskoka.ca. Reach Muskoka by car (2 hrs. from Toronto), bus *(www.hammondtransportation.com)*, or train *(www.northlander.ca)*. The area is framed by Algonquin Provincial Park to the east and Georgian Bay Islands National Park to the west.

---

## ≱ BEST OF THE BEST ≰
### A Taste of Yesteryear

The upside of nostalgia is the spirit of preservation, and Muskoka has it mastered. Nearly every town and village has a general store harking back to bygone days, and many, like **Rosseau General Store,** built in 1874, are more than a hundred years old. Also redolent of yesteryear is **Don's Bakery** *(www.donsbakery .ca)* in Bala, a darling village where Lake Muskoka meets the Moon River. Appearing virtually unchanged since it opened in 1947, Don's offers lemon-meringue tartlets, éclairs, scones, and Old World charm. But for the best bite of nostalgia, you must stop at **Webers** *(www.webers.com)*. This roadside hamburger stand on the edge of Highway 11, halfway between Toronto and Muskoka, has been slinging patties to cottagers since 1963.

In Muskoka, the only must-do is taking it easy.

# SPORTING WAYS

With every paddle, kick, or toss, these competitors add another link to history.

## 1 OUTRIGGER CANOE RACING
### Hawaii

The outrigger canoe is as central to Hawaii's identity as the philosophy of aloha. During June and July, races take place almost every weekend somewhere in the state. The biggest is from Moloka'i to Oahu, a 40-mile (64.3 km) haul through the treacherous Kaiwi Channel.
www.visitmolokai.com

## 2 CURLING
### Canada

The centuries-old Scottish sport in which people slide smooth granite stones down a 146-foot-long (45 m) sheet of ice toward a bull's-eye (trying to knock their opponents' stones out of the way in the process) is particularly popular in Canada. From November to March, Canadian Curling Association championship events are held nationwide.
www.curling.ca

## 3 GAELIC FOOTBALL
### Dublin, Ireland

Fast and furious Gaelic football is a heartfelt Irish passion and a physical celebration of ancient traditions and culture. The modern game is a rough soccer-rugby hybrid. Winners play in the All-Ireland series in August and September for a spot in the mid-September finals at Croke Park Dublin.
www.gaa.ie

## 4 HIGHLAND GAMES
### Scotland

To experience traditional sports like caber toss, tug-of-war, and stone and hammer throws, as well as piping and dancing competitions, cheer on the tartan-clad participants during Highland Games, held throughout the region from May to mid-September.
www.shga.co.uk

## 5 JAI ALAI
### San Sebastián, Spain

Jai alai, or *zesta punta,* is billed as one of the fastest ball games on Earth. Nimble players use curved wicker scoops to hurl and catch hard rubber balls (pelotas) in high-walled courts (frontons). Tournaments are held from June to August in San Sebastián and other Basque country locales.
www.spain.info

## 6 BANDY
### Stockholm, Sweden

Bandy, or Russian hockey, is ball hockey on a frozen football field—lightning fast, lots of goals, no fights, and outdoors. Developed in Russia and refined in England, bandy is a cultural obsession in Stockholm. In winter, join raucous hometown Hammarby fans (wear green and white) at the Zinkensdamm sporting ground in the district of Södermalm.
www.worldbandy.com

## 7 CAMEL RACING
### Abu Dhabi, United Arab Emirates

A dusty chaos of men, camels, and SUVs, this grunting spectacle takes place on weekends between October and April throughout the emirate. Trainers lead colorfully adorned camels across the desert to long, sand oval tracks where, since 2002, racing robots (with mechanical whips) have replaced the sport's traditional child jockeys.
www.visitabudhabi.ae

## 8 KOKPAR
### Kazakhstan

Born out of the nomadic lifestyle of the steppe, *kokpar* is played throughout Central Asia. In this hectic, dust-raising game, two teams of players on horseback compete to carry a headless goat carcass to their goals. During Nauryz, a region-wide spring holiday, matches are played throughout Kazakhstan's southern cities, including Taraz and Shymkent.
http://visitkazakhstan.kz

## 9 MONGOLIAN WRESTLING
### Ulaanbaatar, Mongolia

Each July, Mongolians gather in the capital city for Nadaam, a festival nearly as old as the Olympics. The marquee event is traditional wrestling, or *bökh,* featuring more than 500 grapplers and no weight classes or time limits. Prematch, wrestlers perform a traditional eagle dance to show off their physiques.
www.mongoliatourism.gov.mn

## 10 MUAY THAI
### Bangkok, Thailand

Revered as a sort of religion, traditional kickboxing, or *muay thai,* once was used to decide the fate of kings—ritual and ceremony surrounds this most respected of bloody battles. Champions become national heroes. Multiple bouts of this quintessential Bangkok spectator sport are held at stadiums, including Lumpini Stadium, throughout the week.
www.muaythialumpini.com

A competitor's kilt goes for a swirl during the 26-pound (12 kg) ball competition at Scotland's Highland Games. Other events include tug-of-war and hammer throws.

# VERMONT

Savor the intimate charms of the Northeast Kingdom or embark on a border-to-border ramble.

Leaf peepers find there's more to love about Vermont than the fall foliage.

Amid ancient mountains gentled by time, farm families work the same tilted acres their ancestors did. Sleek Holsteins graze green meadows, and slender church spires beckon the traveler toward bucolic villages. "Vermont is an incredibly beautiful place, but beyond that there is an extraordinary sense of community that permeates the state," says Jerry Greenfield, co-founder of Ben & Jerry's Ice Cream. Tranquil village greens, classic inns, covered bridges, and striking country vistas lure millions of visitors to this relatively small (9,609 square mile/24,885 sq km) and resplendently lush slice of New England each year, especially in early October when the state's dense cover of deciduous trees flares into a spice box of colors.

## EAT WHERE THE DAY TAKES YOU

The uncrowded hiking-biking-canoeing corner known as the Northeast Kingdom is the Vermonters' Vermont. Anchored by the gateway town of St. Johnsbury, the National Geographic geotourism partner encompasses Caledonia, Orleans, and Essex Counties. "The Kingdom's charms are intimate," says Tom Slayton, former editor of *Vermont Life,* "to be savored at a gentle pace." Forgo detailed planning; instead, allow each day to unfold as naturally as the maple tree sap tapped during March to mid-April sugaring season at local Maple Grove Farms. Learn about the process at the farm's Sugar House Museum in St. Johnsbury, and then head to cheese-churning Cabot Creamery in Cabot Village to see how the farmers' cooperative's award-winning cheddars are made. End the day at the Wildflower Inn, a family farm turned family-friendly "village" in Lyndonville, with cozy, country-style accommodations and 570 acres (230 ha) of pure Vermont meadows, gardens, and woods.

## INN-HOP THROUGH CURRIER & IVES COUNTRY

From the Massachusetts border, just south of Jacksonville, Vermont's Route 100 dips and twists north through New England villages and countryside some 200 miles (320 km). The narrow, two-lane strip of asphalt—more country lane than highway—hugs the east side of the Green Mountains as it heads up through the center of the state until it's within sight of Canada. When snow blankets the route, the Currier & Ives Scenic Byway beckons skiers and snowshoers for a wintertime ramble. Most picture-perfect villages along the route have an

## PLACES THAT CHANGED ME

*David Mamet, award-winning playwright & author*

My Vermont is not gentle. It is beautiful and various and changes valley to valley—old farm homes, fascinating to watch the way builders accommodated the land, the exposure to the sun, protection from the winds and snow. Much of the charm of these houses lies in their rational situation, their active relationship with the geography. They have the human beauty of an act of understanding, the beauty of a tool. They are a testament to endeavor and a recognition of human limitation.

inn or two with blazing fires and warm welcomes. About 50 miles (80 km) north of Stowe and its dark-timbered Trapp Family Lodge (founded by Maria and the other *Sound of Music* von Trapps), Route 100 abruptly ends just south of Lake Memphremagog. Like a winter-toughened, speech-chary Vermonter, it says goodbye without a lot of sentiment or fanfare. You have to respect a road with character like that.

■ **PLANNING Vermont** www.vermontvacation.com. **The Northeast Kingdom** www.travelthekingdom.com. **Maple Grove Farms** www.maplegrove.com; open year-round. **Wildflower Inn** www .wildflowerinn.com. Breakfast included; book the renovated one-room schoolhouse for a romantic getaway. **Route 100 Trapp Family Lodge** www.trappfamily.com.

Plan extra time for drives around Vermont: Great photo opportunities abound.

# MARTHA'S VINEYARD

Ferry to a postcard world of character-filled towns best explored on two wheels.

Beware: Both the year-rounders and the longtime summer regulars will try to convince you that their way to experience Martha's Vineyard is *the* way to experience Martha's Vineyard. Feel free to smile, nod, and go find your own version of the island. Though Martha's Vineyard is just over 20 miles (32 km) long, its towns, from Tisbury to Aquinnah, have distinct characters.

Author Bebe Moore Campbell discovered this for herself: "I was pulled by wanderlust from the tony 'up island' town of Chilmark to the fishing village of Menemsha," she wrote, "past the quintessential New England houses of Edgartown, with their shiny white clapboards and black shutters, down Main Street in Vineyard Haven, up to Oak Bluff's funky Circuit Avenue with its ice-cream parlors and T-shirt stores, to way past the glass factory in West Tisbury."

Though people do ferry their cars over to the island, it's far easier to park yours at the ferry terminal at Woods Hole and explore by bicycle. There are plenty of bike rental shops on the island and miles and miles of flat-enough roads. Should you find yourself feeling weak and in need of refueling, Mad Martha's Ice Cream in Vineyard Haven has long had a rep as the island's best scoop stop.

■ **PLANNING Martha's Vineyard** www.mvy.com. **The Steamship Authority** www.steamshipauthority.com. The ferry ride from Woods Hole Terminal to either Vineyard Haven or Oak Bluffs takes 45 minutes. If you plan to bring a vehicle on the ferry, reserve ahead.

## ❦ BEST OF THE BEST ❦
### Farming Around

After days at the beach, you might need a break. Or, at least, any kids in your company might. (*Another* sand castle?) That's where Martha's Vineyard's small but thriving agritourism industry comes in handy. Yes, there are farms on the island—and, as is the case with other aspects of the island, some of the farms are just that much more interesting than those on the mainland. A favorite, **Island Alpaca Company** (*www.islandalpaca.com),* gives kids the chance to go nose to nose with the furry beasts. Come August, the island's ag community goes hog wild for the Martha's Vineyard Agricultural Society Fair.

Each of the Vineyard's towns has its own personality.

No matter the season, Longwood Gardens puts on a show for visitors.

# BRANDYWINE VALLEY

Experience the opulent du Pont way of life.

The narrow roads of the Brandywine Valley meander through meadows and woodlands, over covered bridges, and past the former and current country mansions of the ultrarich. In this bucolic corner where Delaware and Pennsylvania meet, the du Pont family—the closest thing America has to an aristocracy—built estates graced by lovely gardens and filled with world-class art.

Indulge in the *richesse* with a visit to Longwood Gardens, the beloved, decades-long project of Pierre S. du Pont. In the early 1900s, at the same time he was heading General Motors, this über-businessman devoted his free time to planting different exotic gardens across 1,000 acres (404 ha)—Italian, topiary, and formal rose to name a few. His conservatory has been expanded to cover 4.5 acres (1.8 ha) of endless bloom; wander among jewel-like orchids, nodding birds of paradise, and hanging bougainvillea. Outside, evergreen yews are sculpted into cones and spirals.

You can get a sense of what it must have been like to partake in the du Pont way of life at the spectacular Main Fountain Garden. On a warm summer evening, stand on the balcony in front of the conservatory and watch the ponds below come alive with hundreds of uniquely choreographed fountains that dance, swirl, and gyrate in a spectacular show. Colored lights spotlight different water movements, and you can't help but to be awed by the finale, punctuated with fireworks.

■ **PLANNING** **Brandywine Valley** www.brandywinevalley.com. **Longwood Gardens** The gardens are located near Kennett Square, about 30 miles (48 km) southwest of Philadelphia; www .longwoodgardens.org.

## ⌁ IN THE KNOW ⌁
### BRANDYWINE RIVER MUSEUM

Housed inside a 19th-century gristmill, the Brandywine River Museum *(www.brandywinemuseum.org)* features a vast collection of works by the Wyeth family. Illustrator N. C. Wyeth became captivated by the Brandywine Valley upon moving there in 1908. See his paintings of local scenes and illustrations for *Treasure Island* and *The Last of the Mohicans* at the museum, along with landscapes and portraits by his son, watercolorist Andrew Wyeth, and grandson, American realist painter Jamie Wyeth. From April through mid-Nov. you can also visit N. C. Wyeth's house and studio and Kuerner Farm, made famous in Andrew's watercolors.

Visitors who fall in love with the area's textiles can take some of the hand-woven goods home.

## GUATEMALA
# SANTIAGO ATITLÁN
Visit Maximón, the deity who is both saint and devil.

Santiago Atitlán sits on the shores of Lake Atitlán, a flooded caldera ringed by perfect volcanic cones. In this town in Guatemala's highlands, women still dress in colored smocks, men wear traditional striped pants, and the staccato whispers of the Tzutujil language still flow through the jumble of square buildings and narrow streets. About 500 years ago, the conquered Maya were forced to use stones from their temples to build the local Catholic church.

But indigenous beliefs live on in the worship of Maximón, a deity who is both saint and devil, somehow a mixture of Christianity and the old Maya ways. Represented by a wooden statue wearing a dark suit topped with cowboy hats and colorful scarves, the drinking and smoking saint is said to cure disease, remove curses, resolve disputes, and otherwise answer prayers. You'll find Maximón at an unassuming shrine, where you might wander through a cloud of incense and watch someone push a lit cigar into the saint's frowning mouth. To truly immerse yourself in his world, puff a cigar, light a candle, sprinkle *quetzalteca* cane liquor before him, and share your desires with the deity beneath the cowboy hats. Like travel writer Carl Hoffman, you may feel "I'm in the moment, and somehow it all makes sense."

■ PLANNING **Santiago Atitlán** www.santiagoatitlan.com. **Statue of Maximón** In Santiago Atitlán, ask a villager to direct you to Maximón (and expect to pay a small fee for the service). It's customary to bring cigars or alcohol as an offering.

### ～ IN THE KNOW ～
#### THE LANGUAGE OF HANDWOVEN CLOTH

The brightly patterned skirts and intricately handwoven blouses that some Guatemalan women wear make them as colorful as tropical fish around a reef. Even today, their outfits—called *trajes*—are often made on backstrap looms, which women tie to a tree or post and then loop around their backs. The colors and symbols they use—ranging from Guatemala's ceiba tree to geometric designs—can explain where the woman is from, what language she speaks, and whether or not she's married. Santiago Atitlán is known for purple stripes. Visit the local **Cojolya Association Weaving Center & Museum** (*www.cojolya.org*) to see demonstrations and to sign up for classes.

# MASAYA

Leave Granada to the masses. Make your way to Masaya, where both a volcano and the arts glow hot.

Masaya Volcano, the most active volcano in Nicaragua, belches away just a half hour from Augusto C. Sandino International Airport in Managua. The neighboring town of Masaya, alive with art and culture, is firmly rooted in the country's folklore traditions.

But that volcano. You can drive right up to its lip—just park with your front wheels facing out in case a quick retreat is necessary. She doesn't speak up often, having blown her stack about 20 times since the early 16th century with the last go-round in 2003, but she's far from dormant. A peek inside her crater—you can get that close—douses visitors with the scents of smoke and sulfuric gases. Visit around sunset and you may hear thousands of parakeets singing from their unlikely homes in Masaya's crater walls, a seemingly incongruous occurrence considering the heat and the volcano's pungent excretions.

The only experience that could chase the thoughts of the parakeets' song away is a guided walk to the nearby Tzinaconostoc Cave, where hundreds of bats are hanging around and seeming to wait for visitors. The guided trails leading to the cave vary from 0.9 mile (1.4 km) to 3.7 miles (5.9 km) in length.

■ **PLANNING** **Masaya Volcano National Park** www.masaya nicaragua.com/volcanonationalpark.php. The volcano rises in the middle of the park, and the visitor center is located about halfway up the volcano. To reach the rim, you can drive (recommended) or hike the steep trail. A small fee is charged for the guided walk to Tzinaconostoc Cave.

---

### ✹ BEST OF THE BEST ✹
#### Mercado de Artesanías

Don't let the exterior of the fortresslike Mercado de Artesanías turn you away. The interior is stocked full with crafts and souvenirs—some pieces are of much higher quality than others—waiting for buyers to fall in love with them and whisk them away. Inside you'll find woven hammocks (a local specialty), woodcrafts, and embroidered blouses. Located next to the central bus station in the town of Masaya, the market also hosts Thursday night folk-dancing exhibitions called Noches Verbenas, turning the market into part shopping experience, part giant party with plenty of traditional Nicaraguan food for sale.

---

An active volcano, Masaya is visible from just about everywhere in the surrounding area.

# OUT-OF-THE-ORDINARY STAYS

Instead of settling in at just another hotel, find the home of your dreams.

## 1 ABBEY ROAD FARM BED & BREAKFAST
Carlton, Oregon

A fabulous base for exploring Oregon wine country, Abbey Road Farm is set in converted grain silos. The circular rooms are furnished with Jacuzzi tubs, king-size beds, and floor heating, and each has a sweeping view over the English gardens. Guests are treated to award-winning Pinot Noirs and concerts on the lawn pavilion.
www.abbeyroadfarm.com

## 2 HALL GREEN
Lifford, County Donegal, Ireland

Set among verdant hills, this jaw-dropping 17th-century farmhouse slows the pace of life to a standstill. The McKeans pour their hearts into this home, and the tastefully appointed, antique-filled rooms verge on the palatial.
www.thehallgreen.co.uk

## 3 HUNTSTILE ORGANIC FARM
Near Bridgwater, Somerset, England

Huntstile offers the charming yet ordinary experiences one would expect from a farm stay. Or you can take the modern-day owners of this ancient farmhouse up on the chance to go from farm stay to farm enthusiast. Take a course in beekeeping or sausage making. Or explore the on-property stone circle; it has been blessed by Druids.
www.huntstileorganicfarm.co.uk

## 4 SOLE E TERRA
Sardinia, Italy

Culinary delight is writ large in Gallura, an area known for the protected Arcipelago della Maddalena, fabulous beaches, and ancient megalithic outposts. Enjoy freshly picked strawberries at breakfast and five- to seven-course dinners made by Petra, a skilled chef and devotee of *agriturismo*. There's local music, too—cricket concerts at bedtime, birdsong in the morning.
www.soleeterra.it

## 5 MILIA MOUNTAIN RETREAT
Crete, Greece

After hiking the surrounding peaks, Milia's guests dawdle over local wines and learn to cook dishes like grape leaves stuffed with rice and herbs grown in the organic garden. The 16 unique rooms are outfitted with wood-burning stoves, candles, and handwoven blankets.
www.milia.gr

## 6 SANDAI HOMESTAY & COTTAGES
Mount Kenya, Kenya

At this self-sustaining ranch in the rugged foothills of Mount Kenya, electricity is available only in the evenings, but with canopy beds and fabulous views into the Aberdare National Park, you can experience the charm of old Africa without exactly roughing it. Safaris are organized on request.
www.africanfootprints.de

## 7 HERITAGE INN
Old Delhi, India

The interiors of this stately former residence of the maharajah of Sirohi evoke the heyday of the old Raj, with chandeliers, embellished fireplaces, intricately carved hardwoods, and pieces of Hindu temple. The guest rooms are stacked with colorful Indian handicrafts.
www.heritageinn.in

## 8 YURTS
Mongolia

On the steppes of Mongolia most herders live in traditional *gers,* the white, felt-lined yurts that are the most valuable possessions of nomadic tribes. Supported by a lattice frame and heated by a central stove fueled by firewood or dried animal dung, some gers also boast modern facilities, such as a windmill generator and a satellite dish.
www.gertoger.org

## 9 STONEHAVEN VINEYARD HOMESTAY
Marlborough, New Zealand

Flanked by beautiful gardens and acres of vines, Stonehaven is a little piece of Kiwi paradise. This comfy stone-and-timber homestay is close to mountain paths for tramping (hiking) and seeing the local wildlife in action. Delicious dinners are prepared with homegrown vegetables and vintages from the owner's cellar.
www.stonehavenhomestay.co.nz

## 10 WWOOF FARM STAY
In the Andes between Loja & Cuenca, Ecuador

It's a simple exchange: You provide volunteer time in the local community and, in return, your local Quechuan farm hosts will feed you and give you a temporary space to call your own in a rustic house on an organic farm in the Andes.
http://wwoofinternational.org

A home away from home adds structure to a trip. In Inner Mongolia, guests experience the yurt way of life.

It's a short walk across
one of the man-made
Uros Islands on Lake
Titicaca, yet each feels
like a world of its own.

# LAKE TITICACA

*Lake Titicaca, at almost 13,000 feet (3,960 m), is the highest navigable lake in the world. It is vast and mysterious, more so than any other lake I have swum in; I will never forget its transparent and icy waters. And it is home to many different cultures—one of the most extraordinary being the Uros people, who live on groups of floating islands made from bundles of reeds, as they have since the time of the Incas.*

—OLIVER SACKS, NEUROLOGIST & AUTHOR OF *THE MIND'S EYE*

# THE COFFEE TRIANGLE

Take a deep dive into coffee.

No matter a coffee lover's heritage, a visit to the Triángulo del Café, or Coffee Triangle, in the northwest of Colombia is, to a great degree, a return to the homeland. Three of Colombia's departments—similar to the states of other countries—make up the Coffee Triangle: Quindío, Caldas, and Risaralda.

Devotion to the bean infuses the entire area. There's even a theme park dedicated to the wonders of coffee: Parque Nacional del Café, which features a full coffee farm and exhibits that walk visitors through the coffee-production process. Roller coasters, bumper cars, horseback riding, and other rides and activities provide a buzz for those too young to sip the liquid gold.

But don't just look; dig in. Immerse yourself in the backstory of your beloved beverage with a stay at a hacienda that doesn't just serve guests its coffee, but also allows them to get their hands dirty in the production process. A turn as a *chapolera*—coffee picker—deepens the appreciation for the work that goes into your morning brew. And, as it should, the workday comes to a close with a food tour of local shops that rely on coffee-drenched recipes. Sleep could be a problem.

■ **PLANNING** **Triángulo del Café** For a listing of hotels, restaurants, and shops in the Coffee Triangle, as well as airlines that serve the region, consult www.triangulodelcafe.travel. **Parque Nacional del Café** www.parquenacionaldelcafe.com.

---

### ⌁ IN THE KNOW ⌁
#### COFFEE BEANS

That bean you grind in the a.m.? It's a seed, and if it hadn't found its way to your kitchen, it could have kicked off the coffee-production process. Three to four years after planting, coffee trees bear fruit—coffee cherries. After a *chapolera* picks the bright red, ripe coffee cherry, the berry is removed from the bean. Then the beans rest before being dried in the sun and packed in sisal bags, ready to be shipped to roasters the world over.

Typical of the region, the brightly colored houses are a photographer's delight.

Weavers take six weeks to a year to finish one Panama hat.

## ECUADOR

# WEAVING VILLAGES

Cap off your look with one of Ecuador's greatest style innovations.

Traffic willing, the town of Montecristi sits just 20 minutes down the road from the fishing city of Manta in Manabi Province. Tell friends you're visiting Montecristi to buy one of its signature products—a Panama hat—and they're sure to do a double take. Despite their name, Panama hats originated in Ecuador, and there's no denying that Montecristi makes some of the world's finest specimens.

The town, 230 miles (370 km) north of Cuenca, which also boasts a large and prominent hat industry, is home to weavers, or *tejedores,* who have been working the hair-thin strands of straw into hats since the Spanish conquest. Though the town once boasted 2,000 master weavers, there are now fewer than 50. It's a dying art. In Montecristi, you can do no better than to wander down Chimborazo Street, where the Pachay family's shop awaits. In certain sartorial circles, the Pachays are famous. Even casual hat lovers will take a detour from Ecuador's beaches to make a pilgrimage. After choosing your hat, just pop on the black band that's been popular since 1901, the year of Queen Victoria's death, and head out, protected, into the sun.

■ **PLANNING Montecristi** www.ecuador.com. You can find the Pachay family shop on Chimborazo St. (near the intersection of 23 de Octubre) in Montecristi. The town serves as a good base for exploring Ecuador's coast.

## ~ IN THE KNOW ~
### ORIGIN OF THE "PANAMA HAT"

The "Panama hats" misnomer took hold in the early 20th century, when the headgear became a must-have for blocking the brutal tropical sun during the digging of Panama's Big Ditch. These fedoras are not only the most stylish but also among the lightest and most breathable summer hats in the world. And they are among the most venerable, as Ecuador's *toquilla* straw and the weaving technique—though not the styling, of course—date to Inca times. Each hat takes six weeks to a year to make, with hundreds of wispy pieces of straw woven together into a seamless golden fabric.

A hike around Patagonia's Paine Massif may pass over glaciers, through bogs, and along lakes.

CHILE

# LAKE DISTRICT

Bundle up for a cooler cruise to the home of Magellanic penguins and elephant seals.

When viewed on a map, the rugged world of Chile's Lake District looks remote and far from civilization, but it is surprisingly accessible. You'll fly three hours from Chile's capital city, Santiago, to Punta Arenas. Here, don the warm clothing you've packed and hop aboard your ship for a cruise through the glacier-laden fjords that edge into the Pacific. Five-day cruises from Punta Arenas to Ushuaia, Argentina, sail through bays and past glaciers, making stops to visit Magellanic penguins, the expert swimmers that call the region home.

"In Chile's Lake District, a combination of natural wonders gather to provide a unique travel experience," says Jorge Rodriguez of Adventure Latin America. "Here, lakes and volcanoes mark the beginning of the Chilean Patagonia, heading south."

Along the way, the boat winds down Beagle Channel, the islands of Tierra del Fuego on either side. But there are more than just islands here. Beagle Channel, named for the ship that Charles Darwin sailed on through those same waters, is home to glaciers large and larger. As you gaze out on the glaciers, you'll see why Darwin, who sailed that way in 1833, wrote in *The Voyage of the Beagle:* "It is scarcely possible to imagine anything more beautiful than the beryl-like blue of these glaciers, and especially as contrasted with the dead white of the upper expanse of snow."

■ **PLANNING Chile** www.chile.travel. **Cruceros Australis** www .australis. **Adventure Latin America** www.adventurelatinamerica.net.

## ❦ BEST OF THE BEST ❦
### Outdoor Adventures

No matter what kind of adventure you're after, Chile's Lake District can provide. The white-water paradise of the **Futaleufú region** (www.allsouthernchile.com/futaleufu-chile.html) offers 60 miles (97 km) of top-class rapids along the Río Futaleufú. Even the most expert mountaineers know better than to underestimate the three jagged peaks of **Parque Nacional Torres del Paine** (www.parque torresdelpaine.cl), separating Argentina and Chile. For those who seek thrills that require no expertise, the hinterland wonder of **Parque Nacional Vicente Pérez Rosales** (www.chile.travel), Chile's first national park, features a zip line through the canopy of trees.

# MENDOZA

Raise a glass to the area's most famous crop.

Mendoza is tucked at the foot of the prodigious Andes in a region furrowed by great riverbeds and mapped with vast plains and sparkling lakes. Mendocinos, spoiled with more than 300 days of sunshine a year, sum up their home as "land of sun and good wine," a line from the region's state song, "Hymn of the Grape Harvest."

The award-winning vineyards of central-west Argentina can trace their roots to the 16th century, when Spanish colonialists began to travel and settle here. Capture the essence of the region with a visit to the outlying vineyards and orchards. But don't rush off. The area's inns make for a perfect place to lay your head after a day and evening tasting the region's most famous varietal, Malbec. Though Malbec will be your go-to wine while in the area, don't ignore its tasty local cousin. Torrontés, Argentina's lesser known white wine, dates from the Spanish missionaries of the 1600s. The refreshing and highly aromatic varietal (with tropical fruit and honeysuckle flavors) is best sipped chilled and young.

Like the sunshine, the wine flows year-round. If you have a choice (and don't mind crowds), visit in March for Vendimia, the month-long festival that celebrates the grape harvest. After the Archbishop of Mendoza blesses the season's first grapes with holy water, everybody takes to the streets to watch parades and get a glimpse of the beauty queens hoping to be named the year's Harvest Queen.

■ **PLANNING** Mendoza www.mendoza.travel. From Buenos Aires, the journey to Mendoza takes about 1.5 hours by air or 12 to 14 hours by bus.

---

## ⚜ BEST OF THE BEST ⚜
### One Perfect Day

Though the Malbec may draw you to the province, its capital city, also named Mendoza, may put you in the mood for a move there. The city, with its wide, tree-lined boulevards, shaded plazas, and open-air cafés, has an inviting laid-back vibe. Stroll along the **Sarmiento** pedestrian mall, sipping a *cortado* (espresso cut with milk). Follow with a jog or hang glide in **Parque General San Martín** (*www.parques.mendoza.gov.ar*), and then head off to buy handcrafted leather goods at **Plaza Independencia.** Follow with a wine tasting at The Vines Wine Bar & Vinoteca at the Park Hyatt Mendoza (*mendoza.park.hyatt.com*).

Lots of sun and a winemaking heritage add up to an oenophile's dream.

# LAKE DISTRICT

*Standing alone, as from a rampart's edge,*
*I overlooked the bed of Windermere,*
*Like a vast river, stretching in the sun.*
*With exultation, at my feet I saw*
*Lake, islands, promontories, gleaming bays,*
*A universe of Nature's fairest forms*
*Proudly revealed with instantaneous burst,*
*Magnificent, and beautiful, and gay.*
— WILLIAM WORDSWORTH, *THE PRELUDE*

In a region known for its lakes, Windermere takes the size prize. On warm days, the 10.5-mile-long (17 km) lake beckons to boaters.

# LOIRE VALLEY

Sleep like a king or stroll through noble gardens.

Wander the cobblestones of the medieval village of Beaugency.

Sprinkled throughout the Loire Valley, about 80 miles (129 km) south of Paris, more than 300 castles encapsulate the tremendous flowering of French Renaissance culture. Among them, grandiose Chambord is the valley's largest castle, with a maze of 440 rooms and 365 chimneys; Chenonceau spans gracefully over the swan-dotted River Cher; and turreted Azay-le-Rideau was famously described by Balzac as "a many-faceted diamond set in the Indre." For an extra special experience, spend a luxurious night in one of the castles, or immerse yourself in the exquisite elements of their French Renaissance gardens.

## La Vie en Château

"A château-to-château horseback riding trip sits at the top of my list when it comes to experiencing the storybook-charming Loire Valley," says Sheila Buckmaster, editor at large of *National Geographic Traveler* magazine. At the small, elegant Château de la Barre in the Loire region, you'll be the guests of Count and Countess de Vanssay, who invite you to listen to chamber music in the Grand Salon (surrounded by portraits of their ancestors), to dine on family silver and porcelain in the vast 17th-century dining room, and to sleep in a luxurious bedroom amid sumptuous, museum-quality furnishings. Flanked by the Loire River and Château de Chambord, Château de Colliers falls within UNESCO's Loire Valley World Heritage site and is another fairy tale option. Constructed for his mistress by Chevalier de Bela—Louis XV's secret agent—Colliers has been the de Gélis family home since 1783. Be sure to check out the Empire guest room, which has a hidden stairwell leading to a private roof terrace with a view of the wild river landscape.

## Garden Life

"The Loire Valley, awash in gardens, is paradise for those who love artfully planted flowers and shrubs," says Buckmaster. One of the most famous château gardens in the Loire Valley, created by master landscaper André Le Nôtre, the grounds of the Château de Villandry epitomize the French Renaissance garden: a stylized and beautiful combination of broad avenues and geometric patterns, terraces and clipped hedges, statues and water gardens, and fountains and pools. "To visit these gardens is to be in a museum of botany—a museum where things flourish," says Claude Taittinger, president and director-general of Champagne Taittinger. Seek out Villandry's lovely Jardin d'Ornement, where the theme of love permeates in a confection of geometric box parterres shaped in flames, butterflies, hearts, and daggers. "This quartet of complexly planted boxwood parterres symbolizes the Renaissance view that love has four states: fickle, tender, tragic, and foolish," Taittinger says. The gardens at Chenonceau overflow with aromatic shrubs, orange trees, and climbing roses in a scented tribute to onetime château owners Diane de Poitiers and Catherine de Medici. Submerse yourself in the tricks of the gardening trade at the international garden festival that takes place at Chaumont-sur-Loire every August, or, for true-blue green thumbers, the Garden Design Academy in Chabris offers distance and on-campus courses in garden design, as well as study tours of the Loire Valley gardens.

■ **PLANNING** **Château de la Barre** www.chateaudelabarre.com. **Château de Colliers** www.chateau-colliers.com. **Château de Villandry** www.chateauvillandry.com; closed mid-Nov.–mid-Feb., except Christmas holidays. **Chenonceau** www.chenonceau.com. **Garden festival** www.loirevalleytourism.com. **Garden Design Academy** www.gardendesignacademy.com.

## ⚜ BEST OF THE BEST ⚜
### Hidden Châteaus

While some of the Loire's châteaus steal the limelight, there are lesser known jewels that gleam brighter thanks to their lack of crowds. Blois's opulent château has a great 13th-century Gothic hall and tower from its original fortress. François I established a glittering court life at the elegant **Château d'Amboise;** its late 15th-century Chapelle St.-Hubert, a dazzling example of Flamboyant Gothic, allegedly contains the tomb of Leonardo da Vinci. The **Château d'Ussé** is a truly fairy-tale castle of romantic turrets silhouetted against a dark forest, while the **Château de Saumur** sits above the little, winding streets of its half-timbered town.

Château de Chenonceau holds court over gardens and the River Cher.

# BEST OF THE WORLD

# COOKING LOCAL CUISINE

Explore local culture and learn about agriculture by taking a cooking class.

## 1 THE MADRONES
### Philo, California

The workshops at the Madrones pay homage to tried-and-true locals who've been at it for a while, like Fran Gage and her Old Chatham Ranch olive oil. Workshops include a cooking class, lunch, a takeout meal, and a field experience.
www.themadrones.com

## 2 SAZÓN
### San Miguel de Allende, Mexico

Go on a market tour with Chef Paco, owner of Petit Four Pâtisserie and Confiserie, and then get back into the 18th-century casa's kitchen, where you can learn the secrets of salsa verde, guacamole, and *chilaquiles,* and even perfect the art of the *michelada,* Mexico's famous beer cocktail.
www.sazon.com

## 3 FAMILIA ZUCCARDI VINE-YARD
### Olive Oil Estate & Cooking School, Mendoza, Argentina

Start your visit with the lovely Zuccardi family with an empanada-baking class in the wood-burning *barro* ovens, followed by a tasting of local wines like Malbec and Bonarda, and finish with a visit to the Olive Shed, where youngest brother Miguel recently began producing fragrant oils.
www.familiazuccardi.com

## 4 CATACURIAN
### El Masroig, Catalonia, Spain

This cooking school in a fourth-generation stone house in El Priorat, a region just 100 miles (160 km) southwest of Barce-lona, offers various workshops on regional specialties like charcoal-grilled meats, *bomba* rice and paella, Siurana olive oils, and vibrant Montsant wines.
www.catacurian.com

## 5 L'ATELIER DE LA CUISINE DES FLEURS
### Tourrette-sur-Loup, France

Most cooking classes focus on flavor, but scent is the favored currency at Chef Yves Terrillon's small atelier and floral confectionery. The school's 25-student classes uncover the secrets behind cooking with flowers in dishes like milk chocolate and violet tiramisu, duck fillet stuffed with jasmine confit, and fragrant strawberries and cottage cheese.
www.crea-t-yvesculinaire.com

## 6 CPH GOOD FOOD
### Copenhagen, Denmark

Danish duo Mia Kristensen and Jacob Damgaard share their love of Nordic cuisine in hands-on classes that focus on Nordic food culture and its most popular dishes; Nordic baked goods—the Danes really are fond of making Danish, though they call them *wienerbrod;* and "fruit & veggies of the north," with a focus on black currants, gooseberries, and other in-season local crops.
www.cphgoodfood.dk

## 7 TOSCANA SAPORITA
### Massarosa, Tuscany, Italy

At her school, founded in 1994, chef Sandra Lotti teaches you the secrets of capturing basil's essence and helps you master your gnocchi rolling in a spacious 16th-century villa. She also peppers her instructions with humorous and gossipy tidbits about how the French ripped off Italian cooking during the Renaissance.
www.toscanasaporita.com

## 8 &BEYOND
### Baghvan Pench Jungle Lodge, Madhya Pradesh, India

Chef Manish Tyagi's organic *baghiya* (kitchen garden) teems with custard apples, pawpaws, potatoes, peppers, and bananas. After the tour, he'll show you how to make mint chutneys, toasty naans, and chicken in banana leaves. Finish with a shot of local mahua tree wine.
www.andbeyondindia.com

## 9 CONRAD HOTEL
### Bangkok, Thailand

The ongoing workshops and classes here attract some of Asia's top chefs, who are collaborating with Bangkok's hottest kitchen talent and taking traditional Thai ingredients like galangal, coconut milk, and lotus root to the next level.
http://conradhotels3.hilton.com

## 10 SHERMAY'S COOKING SCHOOL
### Singapore

Although the Culinary Institute of America opened a Singapore branch in 2011, Shermay Lee was teaching students how to cook long before that date. Her classes include everything from the art of Japanese decorative cakes to the secrets of steamed *pau* and are taught by Singapore's best known chefs, including Shermay herself.
www.shermay.com

From the how-to's of mint chutneys to violet tiramisu, cooking classes around the world help students put their at-home kitchens to far better use.

PROVENCE, FRANCE

# LUBERON

Live the Provençal high-society life.

Medieval *villages perchés;* honey-colored farmhouses; vineyards; a bounty of produce; and fragrant fields of scarlet poppies, sunflowers, and lavender: Art enthusiasts will find the Luberon instantly familiar, with landscapes of Cézanne and Matisse at every turn. It's a place "richer than any heart can hold, but no less real; a state of mind as well as a space on the map," writes *National Geographic Traveler* magazine contributor

Tom Mueller. The region's sunny weather, its hills and plains, and the low, oak-covered mountains between Avignon, Cavaillon, Carpentras, and the Luberon Regional Nature Park have attracted settlers since Roman times. The Romans left behind columns, bridges, and triumphal arches, but it was the arrival of the exiled popes in the 14th century that changed the area forever. The pontiffs, ensconced in Avignon's fortresslike Palais

On Tuesdays, wander the impossibly charming streets of Gordes to load up on fabric, soaps, and oils at the weekly market.

des Papes, supported innovation in art, architecture, and theater and built an enduring reputation for the good life that still drifts in the lavender-scented breeze.

Explore it all from your base at a *mas* (that's local lingo for "farmhouse") that any member of Provençal high society would be proud to call her own. You can book a room at a mas that's been converted to a B&B, like Le Mas Perréal or

consider taking over an entire property, like Mas d'Alfred in Cavaillon. Don't rush off to explore; settling in is half the fun. Instead, walk to the nearest village to sip a pastis (the local anisette liquor) or a glass of cool rosé at a café terrace, and take a moment to watch the daily late afternoon game of *pétanque* (a kind of French bocce) unfolding under the shade of gnarly-trunked plane trees.

Named after the Provençal village, Roussillon red is a rich combination of warm red tones.

## TOUR DE PROVENCE

The easiest way to see how varied the area's villages are: a one-day tour that goes from market to monastery. Start in Gordes, with its tumble of restored limestone houses clinging to the side of a cliff. Though at its most crowded on Tuesday market days, it's a wonderful day to see the town at its most vibrant (and get all of your souvenir shopping finished in a flash). The town's winding lanes are lined with stands groaning with piles of Provençal fabric, soaps, and oils. Cap the mayhem with peace and quiet—and a very different Provence: grab a map of local walking trails at the tourist information office and head out of town through stone-wall lanes and across the hilly plateau for the 3.5-hour loop to the 12th-century Sénanque Abbey. The abbey, surrounded with lavender fields, is perhaps one of Provence's most photographed sites. For a true retreat, book a stay with the Cistercians for a few days of silent meditation.

## DIG DEEP INTO THE LOCAL COLOR

Nearby, in picture-perfect Roussillon, the town's vibrant red-ocher color contrasts strikingly with the dark green hill. The town perches on the edge of a dramatically red canyon. This is the heart of one of the world's biggest ocher deposits, where 17 different shades of soil—violet, orange, yellow, and all hues in between—once were worked. You can visit the old ocher quarries via the 0.6-mile (1 km) Sentier des Ocres. To learn more (and maybe even take an ocher painting workshop), stop by the old Mathieu Ocher Works. Time your Roussillon visit for sunset, so you can head to a magnificently restored Provençal mansion, La Maison Tacchella, now a bookstore and jazz café, for a view of the hills and valley from their terrace.

## LOOP THE LUBERON

Feel the wind and hear the cicadas on one of the many hiking paths crisscrossing the Luberon countryside and mountains. Each village tourist information office has a map with plenty of ideas for nearby walks. One of the easiest trails for nature lovers starts above the village of Bonnieux. A broad, smooth path winds along the hillcrests through the shade of a majestic cedar forest planted in 1860. The 1.9-mile (3 km) loop's highest point opens onto a sweeping view of the southern Luberon valley all the way to the foothills of the Alps.

■ **PLANNING** Le Mas Perréal www.masperreal.com. **Mas d'Alfred** www.homestay.com. **Gordes** www.avignon-et-provence.com/luberon/gordes-france. **Mathieu Ocher Works** www.okhra.com; workshops require advance registration. **La Maison Tacchella** www.maisontacchella.fr. **Bonnieux** www.slowtrav.com/france/hiking/bonnieux.htm.

---

## ∽ IN THE KNOW ∽
### THE MISTRAL

The soul of Provence is in the mistral, the wind that swooshes down from the Rhône Valley from the north. The mistral is uniquely Provence, a wind like no other, a living presence swirling and swishing and looping around the trees and through your hair. Rows of tall cypress trees bow away from the mistral. A popular character in Provençal nativity scenes pulls his cap down against the wind whipping his big cape. Like the people and the land, Provençal architecture has adapted as well. Farmhouses often face southeast, their backs to the breeze, and church bell towers have open iron grills to let the wind stream through.

Let the relaxation continue into the evening hours with a leisurely meal at one of the Luberon's charming cafés.

The architecture in and around Stockholm ranges from its impressive city hall to simple cottages, a ferry ride away from the city.

SWEDEN

# STOCKHOLM ARCHIPELAGO

Sample a true smorgasbord as you shuttle from island to island.

While Stockholm has kissing cousins on the devotion to seafood front, Sweden's capital city—a web of 14 islands strung across Lake Mälaren on the country's eastern coast—one ups most by encouraging one rather amusing activity: salmon fishing outside the Royal Palace. Near the Opera House, too. No license required. Whether you opt to catch your own or just choose to see what the locals reel in, the local catch will, most certainly, play a starring role on your trip.

## PLACES THAT CHANGED ME

### Gabriella Le Breton, National Geographic contributor

It was pitch-dark, the stars unable to punch more than pinpricks of light in the velvety night sky. My friend navigated the motorboat expertly through the Stockholm Archipelago's black waters, past grassy islands dotted with timber houses. After an hour, we rounded an island and there they were: eight majestic tall ships anchored in front of us. My friend pulled closer so we could marvel at the ships' intricate sails, ropes, and rigging. We joined the sailors on the beach for a night of tales of sailing derring-do by the open fire. I enrolled in a sailing course the next day.

An easier way to experience Stockholm's seafood—and other local delicacies—is to track down an authentic smorgasbord, the quintessentially Swedish buffet. Appropriately, there's a wide choice of places to tuck in: Ulriksdals Wärdshus's smorgasbord features an impressive 14 varieties of herring; the Grand Hôtel Stockholm's buffet comes complete with a seven-point guide; and tuna in spicy coconut broth is just one of Sturehof's more eclectic offerings.

Steel yourself for the true liquid accompaniment to smorgasbord: aquavit, a clear spirit flavored with countless varieties of herbs, spices, and fruits. A small glass of aquavit complements the various courses of the buffet: dill seed with salmon, fennel with mackerel, lingonberry with meatballs.

Once you're done eating, admire the Royal Palace and Storkyrkan cathedral, or lose yourself in Swedish history in the Skansen open-air museum. Marvel at the restored 17th-century man-of-war *Vasa*, and pick up some genuine Swedish design pieces in the city's countless boutiques.

■ **PLANNING Stockholm** www.visitstockholm.com. **Ulriksdals Wärdshus** www.ulriksdalswardshus.se. **Grand Hôtel Stockholm** www.grandhotel.se. **Sturehof** www.sturehof.com. **Skansen** www.skansen.se. ***Vasa* Museum** www.vasamuseet.se.

# DOURO VALLEY

Take an immersion class—guided or on your own—in the region's bold beverage.

There is something dizzying about Portugal's Douro Valley, and it's not just an aftereffect of drinking too much of the region's famed port wine. As you vineyard hop through the area, you'll wind through a variegated patchwork of terraced vineyards carved into slopes pitched as steep as 70 degrees. The sinuous curves of the Douro—river of gold—unfurl far below.

But drive through you should. (Or, if you prefer to focus on the drink instead of the driving, take a guided tour.) The Douro Valley remains a bit untamed, free from the glitz of more highly traveled wine meccas. Like the landscape, Douro vines are tough; they have learned to survive in soil made by hand. Over centuries, workers broke up the schist of the cliffs and backfilled the miles of dry stone-wall terraces with the crumbled, flaky rock mixed with fertile soil transported from the riverbank. The resulting mineral-rich, free-draining "anthroposoil" forces a grapevine's roots to reach down deep into bedrock for survival. Douro's favored grapes are indigenous, characterful old varieties unknown in the rest of Europe.

The Tintas and Tourigas produce small, intensely flavored berries that are still, at many wineries, trodden by foot to create the must for the region's rich, fortified wines.

■ **PLANNING** Douro Valley www.discoverdourovalley.com. For a private guided tour of the valley, consider www.cellartours.com.

## ∽ IN THE KNOW ∾
### WATCH THEM STOMP

At many of the top vineyards in the Douro Valley, people continue to tread grapes by foot. This centuries-old technique, they claim, allows for the gentle but complete extraction of color and tannins. During treading, the grape skins must be methodically pushed down to the floor of the stone vats, known as *lagares*, a sensitive art that no machine can perform perfectly. Treading is choreographed in two acts: The *corte*, or cut, in which the "chorus" links arms and marches methodically across the vats, is followed by the more passionate *liberdade*, when the treaders dance about while keeping their sensitive soles attuned to any grape skins that dare rise to the surface.

At vineyards all over the valley, grapes are readied to be transformed into port.

## ITALY

# TUSCANY

Take a grand tour of the Italian Renaissance.

Florence, Tuscany's regional capital, offers the most lavish of artistic feasts, but away from the great set pieces of the Uffizi Gallery or the genius of Michelangelo or Botticelli, smaller, jewel-like paintings, such as Benozzo Gozzoli's fresco cycle in the Palazzo Medici Riccardi, bear more humble—but no less eloquent—witness to the glory of the Renaissance. Art conspires with architecture, as well as with landscape, history, and religion, in Tuscany's ancient monasteries, timeless custodians of tradition dotted throughout the region's peerless countryside. Architecture and tradition also inform Tuscany's finest medieval townscape, Siena's Piazza del Campo, or main square, scene of the historic Palio horse race.

Tuscany's delights range from Florence's artistic masterpieces to the goes-on-forever beauty of the countryside.

## FOLLOW THE FLORENTINES

Though Florence's top tourist sites are popular for a reason, take a local's advice to escape the crowds—and to see things everybody else usually misses. "While the tourist hordes flock to Michelangelo's 'David' and the Uffizi," says medieval historian Gloria Papaccio, "we Florentines come to the peace-ful chapel of the Palazzo Medici Riccardi to revel in the ideal vision of the Renaissance." Papaccio means Benozzo Gozzoli's "Journey of the Magi," a three-fresco cycle painted in 1460 and tucked away in the depths of a palace that belonged to the Medici, the powerful banking dynasty that dominated Flor-ence for almost four centuries.

Though nearly 600 years old, the colors of the "Journey of the Magi" in Florence's Palazzo Medici Riccardi remain vibrant.

The cycle ostensibly depicts the journey of the wise men to Bethlehem; in truth, Gozzoli depicts Florentine nobles riding through a glorious Tuscan landscape still recognizable today. But these aren't any Florentine nobles. Gozzoli's wise men are portraits of his Medici patrons.

## STEAL AWAY TO A MONASTIC RETREAT

Some monasteries remain places of devotion, such as the ninth-century Sant'Antimo south of Montalcino, where the Gregorian chants of monks still echo around the honey-colored stones of Tuscany's loveliest Romanesque building. "The harmony of this place brings inner peace," says one of the monks, Brother Emanuele. "The wind, the birds, our church, these ancient melodies—everything reminds us of the Divine." Other monasteries are abandoned—the lonely, eerie San Galgano, for example—while a few, such as Badia a Coltibuono, founded in 1051, have found new purpose after losing their religious raisons d'être.

Napoleon dissolved the Badia in 1810, but it has prospered since, and today it offers a medley of Tuscan seductions: the fine architecture of its almost-thousand-year-old buildings; the beauty of its pastoral setting high in the Chianti hills; the superb food in its stylish restaurant; the excellent wine produced by its owners (the abbey is the headquarters of one of Tuscany's leading wineries); and the lure of faultless hospitality—the oldest parts of the abbey have been converted into a series of charming small apartments where you can retreat, however briefly, from the travails of the wider world.

## GATHER WITH THE COMMUNITY

It is Europe's most dramatic pageant. The spectacle of the Palio, a twice-yearly, three-lap bareback horse race around the main square in Siena, has been played out for hundreds of years as a powerful symbol of continuity and, for all its intense rivalry, of community and civic pride.

Nurse a cappuccino long enough at one of the many cafés on the *campo,* or piazza, in which it takes place—Manganelli at number 53-54 and Il Palio at 46-49 are less expensive than some—and you feel that the city's entire population has passed before you. Not only that, but gazing around the campo and its amphitheater of majestic palaces, you'll see why so many have called it Europe's finest medieval square.

■ **PLANNING** Italy www.italia.it **Palazzo Medici Riccardi** www .firenzeturismo.it. **Sant'Antimo** www.antimo.it. **Badia a Coltibuono** www.coltibuono.com. Near Radda in Chianti; 50-minute cellar tour and tastings daily, April-Oct., 2-5 p.m. Restaurant closed Nov.-early March; apartments available to rent early March-Nov. **Siena** www.terresiena.it. The Palio takes place on July 2 and Aug. 16. Be sure to book accommodation well in advance.

## PLACES THAT CHANGED ME
*Ismail Merchant, producer of* A Room With a View *& other films*

The attraction of Tuscany, and particularly Florence, is that it takes you on a journey—not a short journey but an endless one. Amid all the beautiful views, good food, hospitality, and graciousness you don't feel like a tourist—but, instead, like someone under a spell. When I was in Tuscany filming *A Room With a View,* I remember being in a horse-drawn carriage near Fiesole. I looked down to see wonderful cypress trees in a landscape lit unlike any other I'd ever seen. The spell, the beauty were completely intoxicating. I never wanted to shake that feeling; I wanted it to last.

The Palio is not, by any standard, a tourist gimmick. The horse race around Siena is one of the city's most important traditions.

Glaciers that receded at the end of the last ice age gave Lake Bled its start.

## SLOVENIA
# LAKE BLED
Glide on a gondola over a serene, electric green Alpine lake.

Slovenia packs a lot of beauty into a tiny space. Just half the size of Switzerland, the country is blessed with a Venetian-inspired Adriatic coastline, imposing mountain peaks, and a jewel box of a capital in Ljubljana. But the biggest attraction, arguably, is Bled, an electric green mountain lake, complete with an abbey-topped islet in the middle and an ancient

fortress on its perimeter. The Alpine backdrop is so perfect it would make the set designers for *The Sound of Music* blush.

Bled owes its existence to glaciers that receded at the end of the last ice age. They left behind the pristine water and verdant, free-flowing fields that recede to the snowcapped Alps in the distance.

Man picked up where nature left off. The tiny island's Church of the Assumption dates from the 12th century and was rebuilt several times over the years. From the shoreline, its baroque steeple resembles nothing so much as a punctuation mark as if to say, "Wow." Thousand-year-old Bled Castle dominates a bluff overlooking the northern shore. It houses a chapel and museum and yet another jaw-dropping vantage point. To reach the island, travel in style by *pletna* (a Slovenian-style wooden water taxi that drivers have been rowing across since the 12th century). You can also rent your own rowboat.

■ **PLANNING Lake Bled** www.bled.si. Car traffic is limited around the lake. Opt instead for the well-marked walking trail that follows the perimeter. Plan on around two hours to circle the lake.

### ⚜ BEST OF THE BEST ⚜
Slovenia's Most Beautiful Lake

As gorgeous as Bled is, it may not even be Slovenia's most beautiful body of water. Many would argue that that distinction goes to **Bohinj,** 18 miles (30 km) southwest of Bled and easily reachable by car or bus. Bohinj lies within **Triglav National Park** *(www.tnp.si/national_park)* just below Mount Triglav, Slovenia's highest peak at 9,400 feet (2,860 m). Bohinj offers a more secluded, rural feel than Bled but has the same magical, blue-green water. Agatha Christie, who vacationed on the lake, famously said she could never plot a murder there because it was far too beautiful. See the regional website, www.bohinj.si, for more information.

# TRANSYLVANIA

Spelunk your way to a new understanding of Transylvania.

Bram Stoker's Transylvania, with its sinister count and his remote hilltop castle, bears little resemblance to the modern-day region. Yet Transylvania's beauty will haunt you forever.

Over the centuries, the region's hilly terrain served as a natural border between the principalities of Europe and the Ottoman Empire to the east. Nearly a millennium ago, to fortify the territory, Hungarian kings opened the area to settlers from the Rhine Valley in today's Germany. This inflow of Saxons—the name given to those early pioneers—helped to create what remains a fascinating cultural mosaic of ethnic Germans, Romanians, Hungarians, and Roma.

The Saxons' astonishing architectural legacy of fortified towns and churches remains intact. Though it would be foolish not to spend time visiting the regional capital, Brasov; Sighisoara, with its cobbled citadel and 13th-century clock tower; and Sibiu, with its sweeping central square straight out of the Middle Ages, you must get out of town. More than 400 caves are carved into the Apuseni Mountains, in the western Carpathians. No expert spelunking skills are necessary for a visit to Bears' Cave (named for the bear bones found inside) or Vartop Cave, with its footprint evidence of the Neanderthals who once passed through.

■ **PLANNING** Transylvania www.romaniatourism.com. A car is the best way to get around, especially if you're going to visit the caves, but the region is also well served by an antiquated yet decent network of trains and buses. The tourism office can also provide information about guided trips to the Apuseni caves.

## ⌁ IN THE KNOW ⌁
### VILLAGE-HOP BY HORSE-DRAWN CART

The historic Maramures borderlands stretch north of Transylvania toward Ukraine. Take at least week to explore the region's isolated villages, each boasting its own giant wooden church and string of ancient farmhouses fronted by intricately carved, oversize wooden gates. There are few hotels here, so it's best to arrange a farm stay and explore the area by bike or from the relative comfort of a horse-drawn cart. The tourist office in the region's largest city, Baia Mare, can help with bookings. See www.visitmaramures.ro for details.

Picturesque towns like Deutschkreuz prove that there's more to Transylvania than a certain count.

# BEST OF THE WORLD

## GO TIME TRAVELING

Enchanting places where modern and medieval live side by side.

**1 BRUGES**
Belgium

Fairy-tale towers, canals, and swarms of tourists collide here, but like your first kiss you'd be nuts to miss it. This contender for Europe's best preserved city is stuffed with fine Flemish art, and the cobblestone Markt, 13th-century belfry, and castle-like city hall are swooning material. Many gems, however, are reconstructed.
www.brugge.be

**2 CÓRDOBA**
Spain

Mystical, beguiling Córdoba was the main Roman outpost in Spain and then the capital of the western Islamic empire for three centuries. The Mezquita is the country's grandest mosque while Alcázar de los Reyes Cristianos, a royal fortress with lush gardens, hosted one of the first tribunals of the Spanish Inquisition.
www.cordobaturismo.es

**3 GAMLA STAN**
Stockholm, Sweden

A tightly woven mesh of cobbled lanes, Gamla Stan (meaning "old town") was the site of Sweden's first settlement. These three blobs of island are steeped in history and pomp, the Royal Palace, parliament, and cathedral wreathed in candy-colored baroque and Renaissance buildings.
www.visitstockholm.com

**4 QUEDLINBURG**
Germany

One look at a thousand half-timbered buildings—smiling crookedly up at the tenth-century fortress and cathedral—and you'll agree Quedlinburg does Gothic magic better than a Disney film set. Visitors wander the twisting lanes to admire richly adorned guild houses, Renaissance town hall, and the Domschatz, a glittering religious treasure.
www.quedlinburg.de

**5 CESKÝ KRUMLOV**
Czech Republic

Ceský Krumlov quietly waylays visitors with an unaffected charm. The curiously outsize castle has a sprawling rococo garden, climbable round tower, and gorgeous theater with ingenious 18th-century stage machinery.
www.ckrumlov.info

**6 KRAKÓW**
Poland

Poland's premier city is a jewel box of astonishing beauty, its Gothic steeples and cakelike Renaissance facades miraculously surviving World War II intact. The main square, Rynek Główny, is the largest in medieval Europe, but pride of place goes to its signature castle, Wawel.
www.krakow.pl

**7 TALLINN**
Estonia

Once a linchpin of the Hanseatic trading league, Tallinn is today one of Europe's most coyly attractive cities. Its old merchants' houses have aged well despite the effects of fires, wars, and pillaging, and the core has a scale that is refreshingly walkable. Peter the Great resided at the baroque Kadriorg Palace.
www.tourism.tallinn.ee

**8 FÈS**
Morocco

Oldest of the world's imperial cities, Fès is the cultural and spiritual heart of Morocco. Sitting on a plain overlooking the Middle and High Atlas regions, the patchwork of palaces, mosques, fountains, and madrassas (religious colleges), linked by winding alleyways to clusters of bazaars can be wildly intoxicating. The Moulay Idriss Zawiya is the splendidly carved mausoleum of the city's founder, who died in A.D. 828.
www.visitmorocco.com

**9 MEDINA**
Saudi Arabia

The holiest place in Islam after Mecca, Saudi's "radiant city" was the capital of a burgeoning Arab empire. Although the government razes historic sites to curb "idolatry," the soaring spires of three ancient mosques are mercifully undisturbed. Few spectacles rival sunset over Al-Masjid al-Nabawi, the Prophet's Mosque where Mohammed, the founder of Islam, is buried.
www.sauditourism.com.sa

**10 OLD TOWN OF TBILISI**
Georgia

This melting pot of medieval, classical, and Soviet styles has served as Georgia's capital for nearly 1,500 years. Perched on a hillside next to the rushing Mitkvari River, the old town evokes the ancient Eurasian trading route with its gold-domed Orthodox cathedral, caravanseries (travelers' inns), and stolid walled fortress, the Narikala.
www.georgia.travel

The frozen river provides an alternative walkway to the cobblestones of Stockholm's Gamla Stan. Area highlights include the Royal Palace and Storkyrkan cathedral.

# MONTENEGRO

Keep an eye out for this tiny country's mythical creatures.

Smaller than Connecticut, little Montenegro packs an outsize punch with its spirit of independence and almost mythical allure. Bordering Croatia to the north and surrounded by Bosnia and Herzegovina, Serbia, Macedonia, and Albania, this nation of 625,000 situated 1,000 miles (1,610 km) south of Scandinavia is home to its own fjord and a very Scandinavian-esque claim that fairies fly through its misted hills and among its lake-dotted valleys.

You can search them out in Durmitor National Park, a UNESCO World Heritage site of black lakes and forests that centers on the massif of Mount Durmitor. Hike, climb, or raft the steep-sided Tara River Canyon, the longest such chasm in Europe, where the river water is clean enough to drink. If you're lucky, you might get a glimpse of the mythical Starpanja, the father of all fairies.

For more otherworldly wonders, make a pilgrimage to the Monastery of Ostrog, the resting place of St. Basil. The 17th-century landmark was built right into a mountain cliff. Or, if you prefer a storybook-style ending, head to the tiny tidal island of Sveti Stefan, with its centuries-old red-roofed village, a spot Monetenegrin writer Milisav Popovic describes as a "Lilliputian wonder." Seems the perfect place to spot one of Starpanja's kin.

■ **PLANNING  Montenegro** www.montenegro.travel. **Durmitor National Park** http://whc.unesco.org.

> ### ⚜ BEST OF THE BEST ⚜
> #### Stari Bar Fortress Ruins
>
> In the shadow of Mount Rumija, these monumental ruins throw up archaeological finds going back to 800 B.C. Defended on three sides by natural rock cliffs and framed by a fragment of 17th-century aqueduct, the site holds the fascinating remains of some 240 buildings from 2,000 years of settlement. The Romans razed and then abandoned Stari Bar, but under Byzantine emperor Justinian the town was rebuilt and developed into a thriving cultural center, only to be trashed again by reconquering Montenegrins. Buses depart from the seaport of Bar, just 3.1 miles (5 km) away on Montenegro's spiffy southeastern coast.

The Bay of Kotor spills out into the Adriatic Sea.

# GREECE
# MESSINIA

Picnic near a fortress that sits in the sea.

The only reason tourists haven't beaten a path to Messinia, the southwest "finger" of the Peloponnese, is its distance from Athens. Don't make the same mistake. Messinia's distance from Greece's more touristed areas is to your advantage (and delight). Its white beaches curve around turquoise waters, and it's blessed (or cursed) with just as much history as the Argolid or Delphi. Its hills conceal the ruined palace of Homer's sage Nestor, while at the peninsula's tip the twin castles of Koroni and Modoni, the chief eyes of Venice, monitored sea traffic for 300 years. In the north, newly excavated ancient Messene reveals the order and beauty of postclassical Greece.

Base yourself in Kalamata, the second largest city in the Peloponnese and the capital of Messinia. You should know, it's not Greece's most beautiful city (by any stretch) but it's a convenient home base from which to explore the area. And, as you've probably guessed by the name, it's also home to olive groves that produce what some experts consider the finest oil in the world. Wander the town, and then visit its market to gather a picnic lunch of succulent olives, cured meats, piquant *sfelo* cheese, real country bread, and *lalanges* (fried dough biscuits). Then drive off to Methoni, just over an hour away on the coast. There, after snacking on your picnic lunch, walk down a stone bridge to the 13th-century fortress that sits out in the Ionian sea with views to the islands offshore.

## ~ IN THE KNOW ~
### TREAD SOFTLY BUT LUXURIOUSLY

Messinia's Costa Navarino provides luxury with a conscience. The resort boasts Europe's largest geothermal heating and cooling system—part of a plan that ensures all energy comes from renewable sources. But the resort, which sits on the Ionian Sea, also helps connect guests to nature. Cross the dunes to Yialova Lagoon, which offers refuge to more than 270 bird species. For more information about the resort and its sustainability efforts, visit www.costanavarino.com.

■ **PLANNING** Messinia www.messinia-guide.gr. **Kalamata** www.kalamata.gr.

# CRETE

*The earth is reddish, and as spring advances into summer the vegeta-
tion dries to russet in the fierce sun, and there are colors of orange and
purple in it—fire colors. In evening or morning, when the sun is low in
the sky and falls more obliquely on the hillsides, the scrub glows with a
soft burnish, flame-colored, forming a landscape almost too beautiful
to be quite believed in.*

*—*BARRY UNSWORTH, BOOKER PRIZE–WINNING AUTHOR OF
*CRETE* & OTHER BOOKS

History buffs and sun worshippers alike have plenty of reasons to celebrate on Crete.

A beach-perfect climate and seaside resorts await on the Crimean Black Sea.

## CRIMEA, UKRAINE
# BLACK SEA COAST
Play in the mud along the former "Russian Riviera."

A less crowded alternative to the Mediterranean, the Black Sea coast of Ukraine's Crimean Peninsula remains a mystery to many travelers—and that in itself is a bit of a mystery. The former "Russian Riviera" of the Soviet era boasts a subtropical climate, underwater grottoes, and seaside resorts.

Resorts along the coast offer a recuperative mix of mineral spas, palm trees, vineyards, bike trails, and secluded beaches.

### ∽ IN THE KNOW ∽
#### EXPLORE GREAT MOMENTS IN HISTORY

The coast is a significant cultural crossroads where you can wander by an education's worth of important historical sites from the Greek, Roman, Byzantine, Russian, and Tatar cultures, as well as modern Crimean history and architecture. Visit the terrestrial and underwater ruins at the ancient city of Khersones (12th to 4th century B.C.), the neo-Gothic Swallow's Nest castle perched 130 feet (40 m) above the sea near Yalta, and the Livadia Palace, also near Yalta—home of the last of the Russian tsars and site of the Big Three's (Churchill, Roosevelt, and Stalin's) 1945 Yalta Conference.

Towns like Saki have revived age-old treatments like curative mud baths so you can experience the restorative powers of a 20-minute soak in a giant tub of warmed-over, mineral-rich mud. As writer Cathy Newman poetically puts it, "There is nothing to set our cells to celebrating and our corpuscles to dancing like being mummified in a viscous slurry of mud."

The curative properties of Crimean mud have been known for years. Mud enthusiasts have reported relief from a variety of ailments, including arthritis, rheumatism, psoriasis, and neuralgia. The mud baths are a semi-solo experience. You'll step into a white enamel tub, an attendant wearing a plastic apron and rubber boots looking on. She'll release the mud from the ceiling with a tug of a suspended hose, and then add a layer of brine and a dash of diluted hydrogen sulfide on top (to improve circulation). Don't be surprised if the mud burps like primordial stew.

■ **PLANNING** Black Sea Coast www.traveltoukraine.org. Visa restrictions for foreign visitors have been eased in recent years, and travelers from many countries, including the United States and Canada, can enter the country freely for stays of less than 90 days.

# BRIDGE OF GOD

Hike to the spot where mountains kiss—and land meets sky.

Chefchaouene, an ancient town in the northern Rif, rests in a valley between the twin peaks of Ech Chaoua (meaning "the horns") that give the city its name. It's a perfect starting point for hikes into the Rif Mountains, a place of astonishing tranquillity and stark beauty located just inland from Morocco's Mediterranean coast.

A sweeping postcard view proves just reward after a steep hike to the summit of 5,300-foot-high (1,616 m) Ech Chaoua, where a northward path leads first toward the hamlet of El Kalaa and then to the Bridge of God. Formed by eroding red sandstone that once joined two mountains, this natural archway soars 82 feet (25 m) above the Oued Farda River. The bridge is at its most divine at sunset, when the already ruddy sandstone kindles with hot color.

After your day-long trek, catch a deep breath at the peaceful northern beach town of Oued Laou, bookended to idyllic effect by mountains on one side and a broad, empty beach on the other. With its coves, colorful fishing boats, steep cliffs, and few tourists, lazy Oued Laou seems custom designed for a post-hike rest.

■ **PLANNING** **Bridge of God** The best way to see the Bridge of God is with an experienced outfitter like Journey Beyond Travel. Consult www.journeybeyondtravel.com for itineraries and reservations. **Oued Laou** www.visitmorocco.com.

---

### ✧ BEST OF THE BEST ✧
#### Laid-Back Chefchaouene

This mellow, white-and-blue mountain village lazing at the foot of the Rif's peaks is among the country's most storybook-pretty locations. Chefchaouene is characterized by its Andalusian red-tiled roofs, coil of narrow lanes, and petite and welcoming medina (an excellent place to buy a rug). Pop into one of the town's many shops and watch artisans weaving woolen blankets and rugs in jubilant primary colors. If Moroccan medinas, normally a delirium of color and bustle, are more typically known for their amphetamine-like energy, the market in Chefchaouene seduces with a determinedly more languid vibe.

Celebrate the finish of a day-long trek with an idyllic view of the Mediterranean.

# OMAN

Swim with sea turtles and parrotfish in this desert country.

The mysteries of Oman have long lured travelers. This desert sultanate possesses everything from cosmopolitan cities like Muscat and Nizwa to desert oases and even fantastic beaches—when surrounded by views of pleasure yachts anchored off the coast, says writer Meghan Miner, "it can be easy to forget the sea is Arabian, not Mediterranean."

Much of the country is geared toward the luxury traveler, whether from the West or from neighboring countries in the Persian Gulf. Still, even backpackers, women included, will be amazed at the country's charms and the ease with which you can just hop into a rental car and start exploring.

Much of the country has a sense of abandonment about it, with long desert roads. Now and then, around the bend appears a rocky outpost crowned by a long-decayed, lonely fort. One of Oman's undisputed jewels is the Daymaniyat Islands Nature Reserve, a string of nine uninhabited islands and Oman's sole nature reserve. Here you'll find the peninsula's best diving, just offshore from Muscat. The jagged, moonlike rocks jut above the ocean; within their crags sea turtles and parrotfish abound in iridescent blue shallows and pools. Snorkel or scuba dive in an extraordinary underwater realm of more than 350 types of coral. On land, the park hosts breeding ospreys in winter and thousands of terns in summer.

■ **PLANNING** Daymaniyat Islands Nature Reserve The reserve is closed from May-Oct. For information on travel within Oman, consult www.omantourism.gov.om.

## ～ IN THE KNOW ～
### FRANKINCENSE

Most of us associate frankincense with the story of the three wise men. According to the New Testament, when the Magi traveled to Bethlehem to visit the infant Jesus, they carried gifts of gold, myrrh, and frankincense. Like myrrh, frankincense is a fragrant resin. It comes from the native Boswellia tree, whose unmistakable smell pervades the air throughout the country—and in its markets. Oman, it would seem, is infatuated with frankincense. Buy some and you can burn it as incense; many believe the aroma can help reduce stress and anxiety. Frankincense can also be used to make perfumes and potpourri.

A deep dive reveals Oman's greatest treasures.

Sip the world's best Pinotage a grape's throw from Cape Town.

SOUTH AFRICA

# CAPE WINELANDS

Indulge in wines as complex and big as the country that gave birth to them.

With its storybook mountains and valleys, its dozens of vineyards and fine restaurants, the Winelands region east of Cape Town—including the towns of Paarl, Franschhoek, and 300-year-old Stellenbosch—beckons seductively. It is a temptation no one should resist. The Winelands are also part of the region's history. The area's

Dutch settlers produced South Africa's first (but, the story goes, quite awful) wines in the 1650s.

March is harvest time. Rows of ripened grapes blanket the lowlands. Pickers are hard at work. At the wineries, the heady aroma of fermenting fruit hangs heavy in the air. Fairview, on the slopes of Paarl Mountain, invites the public to its tasting room at nine each morning. Though a glass of the Pinotage—plus a breakfast-worthy pairing with some of the farm's cheese—would be a decadent enough start to the day, there are other wineries ahead. The Boschendal winery, set against the Drakenstein Mountains between Franschhoek and Stellenbosch, produces some of the country's most famous wines—and their legendary status is fully deserved. The list of local wineries worth a visit goes on and on. For your trip to-do list: Hire a driver.

## ✹ BEST OF THE BEST ✹
### South Africa's Must-Sip Varietals

If you're going to study—and by study, we mean drink—your way through the Cape Winelands, **Pinotage** is a good varietal with which to start. The wines produced from the national grape of South Africa are big on berry flavors. To read more about them, visit www.pinotage.co.za. But Pinotage isn't the only varietal in the area. Other must-sips in the Cape Winelands include wines made from the ever-so-finicky **Pinot Noir** grapes, some spicy **Shiraz,** the adult juice from any of a trio of **Chardonnay** grapes, and two **Sauvignon Blancs.**

■ **PLANNING** Cape Winelands www.tourismcapewinelands.co .za. Paarl www.paarlonline.com. Franschhoek www.franschhoek .org.za. Stellenbosch www.stellenboschtourism.co.za. Fairview www.fairview.co.za. Boschendal www.boschendal.com.

# INDIA
# RAJASTHAN

Step back in time in Rajasthan's mystical cities and forts.

The rolling, rusty, dusty landscape of Rajasthan is the ideal antidote to India's urban chaos. Located in the country's remote northwest corner and gently pushing into the vermillion Thar Desert toward Pakistan, Rajasthan has a proud past marked by its sixth-century Maru-Gurjara temples, medieval fort-crowned sites, magnificent palace hotels, and quietly warm hospitality. Here, elegant men in mustaches and turbans, and smiling, bangled women offer a glimpse into a bygone era with a side of modern Rajput pride. To many, Rajasthan defines the word "exotic."

The spectacular ocher-stone forts in Jaipur (the Pink City and capital) and Jodhpur (the Blue City) are excellent examples of Mughal architecture—lavish structures with intact details like *jali* screens and *jharokha* arches originally built for kings. Most are open to the public today, and they are an excellent way to experience the mystical past. Jaisalmer, the Golden City, is on the westernmost frontier and abuts the desert. A safari through its copper-colored sands offers memorable views of the city's massive fort, whose tawny sandstone walls atop Trikuta Hill glow at dusk and dawn. But no city is more popular or beloved than Udaipur, dotted with four medieval palaces and several new palace hotels that hug the banks of Lake Pichola and swell with visitors during autumn and winter's wedding season.

■ PLANNING Rajasthan www.rajasthantourism.gov.in. **Micato Safaris** (*www.micato.com*) offers itineraries that include everything from motorcycle rides through the Thar Desert to Rajasthani weddings, replete with tailored sari fittings.

## ❧ BEST OF THE BEST ❧
### Udaipur's Forts and Palaces

Located in the town of Eklingji, 13.7 miles (22 km) north of Udaipur, on National Highway No. 8, the ancient ruins of **Eklingji** date from 971, when the fort was built in honor of the presiding deity Eklingji, a form of Lord Shiva. Meticulous sculpted marble and granite carvings include erotic depictions and an enormous, and elaborately pillared, two-story hall. In the Aravali Hills, just 30 minutes outside of town, the peaceful and grandiose 18th-century **Devi Garh Palace** in the village of Delwara awaits. Now a five-star hotel, Devi Garh's private dining turrets remain an ideal lunch spot.

# INDIA
# SHIMLA

Keep an eye open for real monkeys as you hike to the temple of the monkey god.

Known for its Victorian architecture and crisp Himalayan air, this 150,000-person city (tiny for India) lies 220 miles (354 km) north of Delhi in Himachal Pradesh near Tibet. Immortalized by Rudyard Kipling in his libidinous potboiler, *Kim,* Shimla has replaced salacious military scandals with concrete condominiums and Bollywood film crews. The city's upper slopes still serve as a cooling-off zone, while upper-crust Delhi weekenders, eager to show off their English acumen, incessantly refer to the city's lower reaches as "downstairs."

Although Shimla's political relevance has long since faded, its weathered charms triumph. Architectural highlights include Christ Church, the Gaiety Theatre, the town hall, and the post office, and reveal the Raj era's taste for all things Anglo. To get a deeper experience of British colonial refinery, check yourself in at the extravagant Wildflower Hall. Just 45 minutes from Shimla, the former home of Lord Kitchener stands adjacent to a virgin cedar forest and is graced with teak floors, four-poster beds, and stupendous views.

Of the seven magical hills of Shimla, Jakhoo Hill, a 1.2-mile (2 km) upward slope from the center of town, is the highest, at 8,051 feet (2,454 m). Its peak is marked by a temple dedicated to the monkey god Hanuman, whose rascally and sometimes thieving primate descendants—rhesus macaque monkeys—can still be found at the site today.

■ **PLANNING** Shimla www.hptdc.nic.in. **Wildflower Hall** www.oberoihotel.com.

## ~ IN THE KNOW ~
### EXPLORE THE WORLDS ABOVE

Many Himalayan hill stations offer extreme beauty and retreat from the world. Rugged **Almora,** in the Kumaon region of Uttarakhand, is a small, U-shaped mountain town with a heritage dating to the 15th century. Considered the holiest of all Hindu pilgrimages, the hill town of **Badrinath,** hidden in the mountains of Nar-Narayan, is dominated by lordly and mystical Neelkanth Peak. Rocky **Zanskar** lies 12.4 miles (20 km) south of Rangdum near the precious Pazila watershed and remains the most isolated of the Himalayan valleys. For a woodsier experience, head to the **Dhanaulti Hills,** where dense virgin oak and rhododendron forests abound. In verdant **Gulmarg,** also known as the Meadow of Flowers, you'll find cows and flowers aplenty.

Scottish in style, the Viceregal Lodge provides fantastic views of the region's mountain ranges.

# DANCE LESSONS

Pick up some impressive moves and harness the true rhythms of a region's soul.

## 1 HULA
### Waikiki Beach, Hawaii

Few dances conjure up white sands, turquoise seas, and palm trees as vividly as the hula, brought to Hawaii by Polynesian settlers. Admire the swishing grass skirts and lush floral headpieces of hula dancers competing at one of Hawaii's regular hula festivals, and pick up free lessons from performers on Waikiki Beach Walk.
www.gohawaii.com

## 2 RUMBA
### Havana, Cuba

Originally brought to Havana by slaves, the rumba has evolved into a complex dance pulsating with African rhythm and Hispanic flair. Learn from the professionals at the Centro Cultural El Gran Palenque before practicing with the locals.
www.cubaabsolutely.com

## 3 DIABLADA
### Oruro, Bolivia

The *diablada* ("devil's dance"), as performed during the ten-day Carnaval de Oruro, is a riot of noise and color, an elaborate seven-act performance with hundreds of dancers sporting elaborate costumes and grotesque painted masks. Each year, before Lent, the surrounding Andean Highlands echo to the sounds of the symbolic dancing battle and accompanying marching bands.
www.adventure-life.com

## 4 TANGO
### Buenos Aires, Argentina

The prestigious Mayoral and Elsa Maria Tango Academy, patronized by Princess Diana and the Clintons, offers an authentic 19th-century *petit palais* setting in which to develop the *gancho* kick. Group and private lessons are offered for students of all ability levels.
www.mayoralyelsamaria.com.ar

## 5 GAELIC CEILIDH
### Loch Ness, Scotland

The Gaelic ceilidh remains true to its origins as a social dance, encouraging courtship in remote Scottish and Irish communities. Gather some friends and reserve the turreted Aldourie Castle, located on the shores of Loch Ness, where you can enjoy private dance lessons with local instructors to the traditional sound of fiddles, accordians, flutes, *bodhráns* (frame drums), and tin whistles.
www.aldouriecastle.co.uk

## 6 WALTZ
### Vienna, Austria

Before braving the polished floors of the Hofburg, perfect your moves at the Elmayer Dance School. Founded in 1919 and located next to the Spanish Riding School, it's where locals learn the original fast-paced and quintessentially Viennese waltz.
www.elmayer.com

## 7 CSÁRDÁS
### Budapest, Hungary

Budapest's heart beats to the rhythm of the Roma violins that accompany this spirited dance. A traditional Hungarian folk dance that starts slow before speeding up to a fast finish, *csárdás,* locals say, isn't as much about learning a routine as it is about learning an idiom. Watch and learn from the Hungarian State Folk Ensemble at the Danube Palace.
www.gotohungary.net

## 8 ADUMU
### Kenya

The *adumu* is an exuberant Maasai dance performed during the coming-of-age ceremony of warriors. The young warriors jump high into the air as their mothers, adorned with intricate, beaded costumes, sing in tribute to their brave sons.
www.maasaimara.com

## 9 KATHAK DANCING
### Udaipur, India

The delicate twisting hands, sinuous neck movements, and sheer drama of *kathak* "storytelling" dances have entertained Indian emperors and maharajas for 1,700 years. The romantic lakeside city of Udaipur is home to the Rajeev Surti Dance Factory, where this celebrated Bollywood choreographer teaches the ancient rituals of kathak with a contemporary twist.
www.rajeevsurtidancefactory.com

## 10 KECAK
### Bali, Indonesia

The *kecak* is better watched than attempted. Not only does it have no musical accompaniment—a 50-man chanting "monkey" chorus provides the rhythm—but it's performed around a blazing fire. The dance rendition of the Hindu epic, the Ramayana, is best appreciated at the cliff-top Uluwatu Temple.
www.bali-dance.com

Though it's doubtful anybody can catch as much air as Maasai warriors can, they'll school willing students in the adumu dance.

# BHUTAN

Celebrate one of Bhutan's most pungent autumn crops: matsutake mushrooms.

Quietly and firmly tucked into the Himalaya between Asia's largest and brashest countries, China and India, Bhutan is home to sharp granite ridges, cliffside monasteries, and dramatic, 4-mile-high (6.4 km) peaks that soar into the sky with ecclesiastical dignity. Somehow this tiny Buddhist nation has remained a serene, selfless, and uncontaminated oasis of self-reflection. In pristine reserves like the geothermal Jigme Dorji National Park Reserve, you may catch sight of red pandas, snow leopards, and rare blue poppies before retiring to the gurgling thermal baths of Gasa Tsachhu to exchange stories with fellow travelers.

But for all the country's grand natural wonders, it's worth timing your visit to a much smaller one: the mid-August arrival of matsutake mushrooms (or, as they're called in Bhutan, *sangay shamu*). While the country's farmers do sell the mushrooms to other countries (and they pull in quite the price for the prized vegetable), there's no beating the experience of eating matsutakes at their freshest, their scent instantly recognizable.

Spend two days dining on a variety of matsutake dishes at one of two Aman Resorts, Amankora Paro or Amankora Thimphu.

■ **PLANNING** Bhutan www.tourism.gov.bt. **Amankora Paro/ Amankora Thimphu** www.amanresorts.com.

## ⌒ IN THE KNOW ⌒
### DEBUNKING THE TRAVEL MYTHS

Many myths continue to plague tourism in Bhutan. Contrary to popular belief, Bhutan is neither exclusionary nor wildly expensive. The government does not limit the number of tourists, but visas are only approved for people who book with a local licensed tour operator. Individuals cannot apply for their own tourist visa. The tariff fee is $200 per day during the low season and $250 per day during high season (March–May, Sept.–Nov.), which can be applied toward taxes, lodging, meals, travel with a licensed guide, camping equipment, and other services. Another myth frequently heard is about when to go: Summer may indeed bring monsoon rains, but it's rarely enough of a deluge to ruin a trip.

Few travelers to Bhutan return home without a prayer flag photo.

Cruise from Guilin down the "green silk belt" of the Li River for back-in-time views of bamboo groves and karst peaks.

# CHINA
# LI RIVER
Sail through dreamy landscapes straight from a Chinese scroll painting.

The perfect antidote to China's megacities, a float down the poetic Li River past a panorama of bamboo groves, sleepy villages, and crumpled karst peaks will send photographers into rapture. Cruises leave from Guilin, a southern Chinese city of three million people that has drawn poets and painters, soldiers and sailors, missionaries and monks for more than 2,000 years. The Li River "forms a green silk belt, the mountains are like blue jade hairpins," reported one Tang dynasty poet. Such words still draw more than half a million overseas visitors to this region yearly—not to mention millions of Chinese tourists.

Yet somehow the Li River remains enchanting, even timeless, as a succession of tour boats slips downstream each day in a well-choreographed routine that takes about five hours. Local sampans scuttle by. Egrets rise placidly from stands of bamboo. Girdles of mist drape the karst peaks and coil above the emerald green rice paddies. Water buffalo labor the fields, and fragrant osmanthus bushes dot the hills. Village life continues on the banks as it has for centuries. And each mountainous vista seems more dramatic than the last, as though you've entered a world of living landscape paintings.

## ∽ IN THE KNOW ∽
### TAKE TO THE WATER BY NIGHT

Cormorants are fish-eating waterbirds with sharp, hooked bills and swanlike necks. When a loose ring around the bird's neck prevents swallowing, cormorants can be trained to drop the fish into a basket. Every seven fish or so, the fisherman lets the bird gulp down its reward. On the Li River, fishing is done at night because a boat's electric lantern light attracts fish to the water's surface, where the cormorant can easily dive for them. On a moonlit eve, the karst hills make a ghostly backdrop. While visitors can watch a fishing demonstration in Guilin, the best experience is from the village of Yangshuo, at the end of the Li River cruise. Visit www.lirivercruise.com for more information.

■ PLANNING Li River Many outfitters offer Li River cruises. See www.guilinchina.net, www.chinahighlights.com, and www.china odysseytours.com for rates and itineraries.

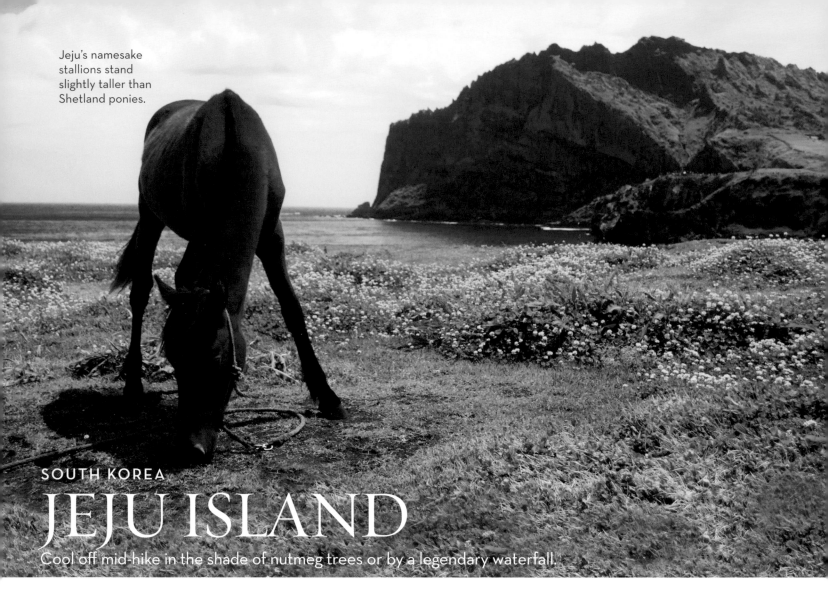

Jeju's namesake stallions stand slightly taller than Shetland ponies.

# JEJU ISLAND

Cool off mid-hike in the shade of nutmeg trees or by a legendary waterfall.

Just an hour's flight from Seoul, the island of immortality's 712 square miles (1,844 km) is an eco-enthusiast's paradise: a UNESCO Biosphere Reserve since 2002, with some 4,500 plant species. It's known as a honeymooners' paradise, but hikers (whether solo or in groups) shouldn't be put off. Leave Jeju's big hotels on the southern coast to the romantically inclined. You can take the rest of the island.

Book a countryside home stay near the Bijarim Forest and use it as a base to hike among the forest's sole species, the *bija* (nutmeg) trees. The coniferous giants, protected in a forest composed entirely of this species, bloom in April. Trails through the park offer shade year-round as well as a chance to contemplate forest "elders" like one 800-year-old tree measuring 20 feet (6 m) in circumference. Other hikes on the forested island will have you crossing paths with wild ponies and landscapes brilliant with oleander and Korea's national flower, the purplish rose of Sharon.

After all that walking, you might be in search of a place to just . . . stop. Consider Jeongbang Falls, where, according to an inscription, a Chinese emissary passed in search of the secret of immortality in the second century B.C.

■ **PLANNING** Jeju Island Access to the island is by airplane or ferry. Most flights to the island's international airport originate in Seoul. For general information on travel in South Korea, consult http://english.visitkorea.or.kr.

## ∾ IN THE KNOW ∾
### VISIT THE GRANDFATHERS

Every place needs a little protection. On Jeju Island, totem statues called *dol hareubang* (stone grandfathers) guard the town entrance, fortresses, and other places. The statues are so funny, though, that it's hard to see how the baddies would be scared away. Carved from local volcanic basalt and standing about the size of a small child, these elfin creatures have bug eyes and big noses that, if rubbed, are said to provide a host of benefits, including enhanced fertility, protection from evil spirits, and heavenly blessings. **Wonderful Bukchon Dol Hareubang Park** (*www.dolharbangpark.com*) brings together 48 of these shamanistic cuties along with an interpretive center.

# JAPAN
# SHIKOKU

Embark on a traditional Buddhist pilgrimage that combines nature and spirituality.

Mountain-ringed Shikoku—the smallest and least visited of Japan's four main islands—is best known for its "walk of life," a pilgrimage to 88 Buddhist temples that retraces the footsteps of the eighth-century monk and scholar Kobo Daishi. Completing the 745-mile-plus (1,200 km), island-wide circuit on foot is an intense physical and spiritual workout that can take a month or more. Shikoku's landscapes provide great company: farming villages against hilly backdrops, fishing villages clinging to rustic coastline, and deserted beaches along the subtropical southern coast. But nobody will blink if you save time—and your knees—by covering the steep route via bus and riding the train up Mount Koya, the pilgrimage's traditional start and end point.

The bus route doesn't mean you have to separate yourself completely from the true pilgrims, known as *o-henro-san*. It's not unusual for Shikoku's locals to help the pilgrims in any way possible, whether it's offering a kind word or a meal. The best way to ensure you meet some of the walkers: Stay at one of the temples that offers them basic lodging. Affordable, traditional accommodations also are available at Shikoku's rustic to luxurious *ryokans*, Japan's traditional, tatami-mat guesthouses.

■ **PLANNING Shikoku** www.tourismshikoku.org. For an overview of the pilgrimage, including a map of the temples and tips on preparing for the journey, visit www.shikokuhenrotrail.com. Trip length depends on your level of fitness and can last 40 to 50 days or more.

---

## ꙮ BEST OF THE BEST ꙮ
### Uchiko

While on Shikoku pause in Uchiko, a lovely rural town preserved as a center for folk arts and traditional trades. Along Yokaichi-Gokoku Street, several white and cream traditional buildings with their black-and-white plasterwork have been designated Important Cultural Properties. Visit the town's magnificent **Japan Wax Museum** and **Kami-Haga Residence,** with artfully arranged displays of domestic furnishings and professional tools. There's also the restored **Uchiko-za Kabuki theater,** built in 1916, as well as a 1920s pharmacy, now the **Business and Livelihood Museum.** Visit www.jnto.go.jp for more information.

The smallest of Japan's main islands, Shikoku has 88 Buddhist temples.

# GET TO KNOW THE LOCALS

These tours of some of the world's most distinct cultures will open your eyes—and your heart.

## 1 THE AMISH EXPERIENCE
### Pennsylvania

Though the Amish of Lancaster County, the country's oldest Amish settlement, tend to stick to themselves, living (and farming) as their forefathers did when they arrived from Europe in the early 18th century, many do interact with outsiders. Visit several Amish farms, see their milking and crafting operations, and learn what it means to live "plain."
www.amishexperience.com

## 2 KLEIN TOURS
### Ecuador

Walk with shepherds and tend local crops in the indigenous Karanki community of Magdalena. Perched 9,842 feet (2,999 m) above sea level on the slopes of Imbabura Volcano, this pristine locale was home to Atahualpa, the last of the Inca emperors.
www.kleintours.com

## 3 GHUIZHO MINORITY TRIBES
### China

Discover one of the most ancient pockets of Chinese culture hidden among the luxuriant landscape of the south-central province of Ghuizho. A stay in the remote villages of the minority Miao and Dong tribes will open even the most experienced eyes to a colorful patina of traditional food, music, dance, and everyday simple pleasures.
www.chinaprofessional.com

## 4 VLČNOV
### Czech Republic

Among the vineyards of rural Moravia, the town of Vlčnov dresses up in colorful folk costumes for the annual Ride of the Kings festival. The fete commemorates a young ruler who escaped from his enemy in women's garb and engages visitors with games, song, processions, and celebrations throughout town and at the local *budy*, or wine cellars.
www.vlcnov.cz

## 5 TRIBEWANTED
### Sierra Leone

Brit Ben Keene founded Tribewanted for "cross-cultural community tourism," planting the seeds of sustainable tourism in beautiful, remote locations like Sierra Leone's John Obey Beach, 20 miles (32 km) south of the capital, Freetown. Visitors spend several weeks working with locals to create solar towers, beach kitchens, and other ventures.
www.tribewanted.com

## 6 MANGO AFRICAN SAFARIS
### Tanzania

Proprietors of this remote camp on the shores of Lake Tanganyika have established a trust to preserve local oral history, as well as the rich habitat of thousands of wild chimpanzees. Observe a thriving colony of these primates close to the Greystoke Mahale Camp.
www.mangoafricansafaris.com

## 7 LADAKH
### India

At an altitude of 11,500 feet (3,500 m) on India's northernmost plateau, Ladakh's geography shelters one of the most intact Tantric Buddhist societies left on Earth. Village-to-village walks with local guides and porters and overnight stays in homes adapted to Western comforts allow visitors to step into rural community life.
www.shaktihimalaya.com

## 8 RINJANI TREK
### Indonesia

At 12,221 feet (3,725 m), Indonesia's second highest volcano is sacred to the Muslim Sasak and Hindu Balinese, who manage treks into Gunung Rinjani National Park. As they ascend, visitors are immersed in village tours, religious festivals, and mountain lore, adding depth to a rigorous climbing experience.
www.lombokrinjanitrek.org

## 9 SINGSING
### Papua New Guinea

Meet participants donning paint, feathers, and pig tusks in preparation for the annual Mount Hagen *singsing*, a gathering of 75 tribes, as part of a tour that includes boating the Sepik River. Visitors contribute to a clean-water project for local communities.
www.wanderlustandlipstick.com

## 10 JUNGALA INDIGENOUS ART & TOURISM
### Alice Springs, Australia

Jungala Kriss preserves and shares the legends and poetry of Mbantua, the Aboriginal name of Australia's Red Centre near Alice Springs. On Jungala's weeklong treks, hikers sample kangaroo meat, bush oranges, and pasion fruit and meet artists and old-timers who illuminate the culture of the bush.
www.jungala.com.au

Seventy-five tribes gather in Papua New Guinea for the annual Mount Hagen Cultural Show.

# HILL COUNTRY

Meet local artisans in the highlands of the Golden Triangle.

The lowland people call them *chao khao,* or "mountain people," the remote ethnic hill tribes that live in the blue-green jungle mountains of northern Thailand. No longer a notorious center of opium production, the peaks of Chiang Rai Province, studded with gold-spired Buddhist stupas, are Thailand's hidden beauty spot. Amid a landscape of mountain valleys, lakes, and rice fields, the rural Karen, Akha, Hmong, and other minorities typically wear their wealth in weighty silver headdresses and vivid, ribbon-embroidered tunics. Their folkways and beliefs, some animist, some Christian, separate them from the Buddhist majority.

To meet gracious craftsmen in their thatch-roofed homes, climb high. Ridgetop roads ascend from valleys along the Mekong River to tiny settlements perched at elevations of nearly 6,000 feet (1,830 m). As modern development reaches these rural villages, increasing numbers of huts sport a satellite dish. But many women still practice the traditional arts of intricate needlework and handmade jewelry, often found in the popular night markets of larger villages. Like other Thai,

they love children and welcome visitors with brilliant smiles and innate courtesy.

■ **PLANNING Thailand** www.tourismthailand.org. The Population and Community Development Association of Chiang Rai offers daily treks to hill-tribe villages and other tours, from $60 per person. Visit www.pdacr.org for more information. Several operators also offer package tours of the region: See www.chiangmai elephants.com, www.azuretours.com, and www.thailandhilltribe holidays.com for sample itineraries.

## ⌁ IN THE KNOW ⌁
### TASTE THE LOCAL COMFORT FOOD

Northern Thailand's *khao soi,* a coconut-milk stew, is a beloved regional specialty, sold in night markets and cafés throughout the region. The traditional recipe always includes red curry paste, egg noodles, and a squeeze of fresh lime, with a ladle of chicken or beef. This is comfort food Chiang Rai–style, served on the street or at home, as breakfast, lunch, or dinner *(www .chiangraiprovince.com).* Or learn to cook the dish for yourself at the **Asia Scenic Thai Cooking School** in Chiang Rai. Visit www .asiascenic.com for a list of available courses.

Northern Thailand's mountains are home to diverse ethnic groups, including the Hmong.

AUSTRALIA

# TASMANIA
Rough it in the wilderness.

ustralia's smallest state sits at the edge of the world. The next stop south is Antarctica, 1,537 miles (2,473 km) away. Yet it seems as if bits from the entire globe have been assembled in one place to create this far-off destination, inspiring Mark Twain to remark, "How beautiful is the whole region, for . . . variety of color, and grace and shapeliness of the hills, the capes, the promontories." Tasmania is small enough that you may be tempted to do a quick day's sample platter—but you would miss so much. The heart-shaped island is compact yet encompasses secluded beaches, more than 200 vineyards, snowcapped mountains, a temperate rain forest, and Australia's second oldest city and smallest capital, Hobart. An idea: Give a few days over to Hobart and a vineyard or two and then, if you're hearty, head into the wilderness.

Experienced bush walkers fly into Southwest National Park, part of the 3.46-million-acre (1.38 million ha) Tasmanian Wilderness World Heritage Area, to tackle some of the most challenging and remote hikes on the planet. Low on bush-walking miles? Hire a guide or consider less strenuous fly/cruise excursions so you can experience the solitude and isolation of a primeval world so fresh and new it seems to have the first dew still on it.

■ **PLANNING Tasmania** www.discovertasmania.com.au. **Southwest Wilderness Tours** Par Avion *(www.paravion.com.au)* offers half- and full-day fly/cruise tours. Daylong excursions include wilderness walks where you may spot the rare orange-bellied parrot.

## ❦ BEST OF THE BEST ❦
### Tasmanian Ferry

Flying is the fastest way to get from Melbourne to Tasmania, but cruising aboard the *Spirit of Tasmania* means the trip there becomes an exquisite starting point for your post-Tasmania story—but only consider it if rough seas don't throw you. The only smooth portion of the 9- to 11-hour voyage is in placid Port Phillip Bay. After that it's a choppy, if not downright rough, passage through Bass Strait, known for some of the world's stormiest seas. The ride gives you a taste of the Roaring Forties—the region of heavy westerly winds between latitudes 40° and 50° south—which old mariners wrote about and feared. The payoff is the first glimpse of Tasmania's rocky coastline and green hills. Visit www.spiritoftasmania.com.au to make a reservation.

# WORLD WONDERS

*Mankind's Most Tantalizing Creations*

Outstanding man-made structures are found the world over. While some stand out for a time, most are soon eclipsed by the latest and greatest. Only a small number have proved enduringly fascinating. These world wonders excite us with their artistry, ingenuity, or sheer size—and thrill us with the mystery of their creation.

The domes that dominate the view in Moscow's Red Square weren't always such lookers. Final touches on St. Basil's Cathedral were added 300 years after construction.

The Tiwa people
still call Taos
Pueblo home.

## NEW MEXICO
# TAOS PUEBLO
Step back in time to a thousand-year-old way of life.

Taos Pueblo doesn't try too hard to impress. Located just a few miles north of the bustle of Taos plaza, the pueblo offers simple buildings made from clay, straw, and the mica-flecked dirt beneath your feet. Red Willow Creek, fed by a hidden mountain lake sacred to the Pueblo people, runs through the village and still provides its drinking water.

Several U.S. Native American sites enjoy World Heritage site status, but only Taos Pueblo is a living community. The Tiwa still live here, their rituals unchanged for centuries. Blue smoke from their cooking fires still mingles with the scents of piñon pine, juniper, and sage. Learn about life in this sovereign nation on a free, guided walking tour of the pueblo led by a local resident. Tours typically leave on the half hour from San Geronimo Chapel. As you wind through the maze of adobe dwellings built in the late 13th and early 14th centuries, savor the comforting fragrance of baking bread rising from clay ovens shaped into smooth domes.

■ **PLANNING** Taos Pueblo www.taospueblo.com. The pueblo is generally open to visitors daily 8 a.m.–4:30 p.m., except when tribal rituals require it to close. It closes for about ten weeks from late winter to early spring, so call ahead (575-758-1028) if you'll be visiting during this time. Admission and camera fees.

## ～ IN THE KNOW ～
### TAOS PUEBLO CEMETERY

A low wall surrounds the small cemetery just outside the pueblo buildings. Within are the ruins of a mission church tower surmounted by a mute bell and a field of handmade wooden crosses. The little plot is decorous and quiet now, but the history it represents, like so much of the early history of native peoples facing European settlers, is sad and violent. The bell tower is all that remains of the 1706 church of San Geronimo, which was destroyed, with pueblo women and children inside, to quell an 1847 revolt. Today the wooden crosses and little bell tower watch over the remains of those victims of the often repeated clash of old and new cultures in early America.

# COLORADO
# MESA VERDE

Experience the mysterious aura of the ancients.

Where the long fingers of the Mesa Verde reach deep into southwestern Colorado, ancestral Puebloans, once known as the Anasazi, or "ancient ones," built some 600 sandstone dwellings in the sheltering alcoves of steep canyon walls. Scarcely a hundred years later, at the end of the 13th century, the pueblos were abandoned, and they stood forgotten until 1874, when cowboys spied a crumbling ruin in what is now Mesa Verde National Park.

Standing 1,000 feet (305 m) above the Montezuma Valley, the 52,074-acre (21,073 ha) park creates a prevailing feeling that one must be near the rim of the world. Mesas, canyons, and purple shadows melt into the horizon. Protected within the cliff-rock alcoves are approximately 4,000 prehistoric sites built over a period ranging from about A.D. 550 to 1300.

Tourists flock to North America's largest cliff dwelling, the 150-room Cliff Palace. To truly experience the mysterious aura of the ancients, head first instead to Wetherill Mesa in the park's less traveled western portion. Accessible only in summer, Wetherill is home to the second largest cliff dwelling,

Long House. The ranger-led site tour is strenuous, requiring climbing two 15-foot (4.5 m) ladders and navigating 50 steps. After the hike, walk the leisurely trails threading through pit houses and pueblos cloaked in seven centuries of silence.

■ **PLANNING** Mesa Verde www.nps.gov/meve. Cliff dwellings can be visited only via ranger-led tour. Purchase tickets early at the Far View Visitor Center, open at 8 a.m., early April–mid-Oct.

The Cliff Palace is impressive, though Wetherill Mesa is less crowded.

# NATIVE AMERICAN SITES

From the struggle of survival to ecstatic spiritual celebrations, delve into Native American culture.

## 1 HEAD-SMASHED-IN
### Alberta, Canada

Where the foothills of the Rocky Mountains meet the great plains is a 36-foot-high (11 m) cliff used for 5,500 years by Alberta's indigenous Blackfoot tribe to kill bison by driving them off it. Today the site is also home to information about Blackfoot heritage.
www.head-smashed-in.com

## 2 LITTLE BIGHORN
### Montana

Nearly 150 years after the Battle of the Little Bighorn, the poignancy of the epic struggle of the Great Sioux War remains palpable. Explore the scene of Custer's Last Stand against the Lakota and Cheyenne on horseback, led by native horsemen in the footsteps of Crazy Horse and White Bull.
www.westernromancecompany.com

## 3 UNITED TRIBES INTERNATIONAL POWWOW
### North Dakota

Currently in its 44th year, this four-day event attracts thousands of visitors from more than 70 Indian tribes. They come to watch and participate in dance, drumming, singing, horseback-riding performances, and a prestigious beauty pageant.
www.unitedtribespowwow.com

## 4 THE BLACK HILLS
### South Dakota

Visiting the Lakota's most sacred sites, such as Wind Cave and Place of the Thunders, enjoying authentic fireside storytelling, and seeking out the few remaining herds of buffalo, revered by the Lakota, enables appreciation of their extraordinary spirituality and heritage.
www.gonativeamerica.com

## 5 MEDICINE WHEEL MOUNTAIN
### Big Horn, Wyoming

The ancient Bighorn Medicine Wheel, a stone structure 75 feet (23 m) in diameter, has been used for centuries by the Cheyenne for medicinal and ceremonial plant gathering, prayers, fasting, and vision ceremonies.
www.wyoshpo.state.wy.us

## 6 HOPI LAND
### Arizona

Considered the oldest of the native peoples, the Hopi reside in traditional villages on land that their ancestors inhabited 100 generations ago. Visitors to Hopi Land can watch time-honored dance ceremonies and admire artisans crafting their celebrated jewelry, pottery, coiled baskets, and *katsina* dolls.
www.hopiculturalcenter.com

## 7 CHACO CANYON
### New Mexico

For 400 years, Chaco was the hub of ancient Puebloan civilization—an unequaled urban, commercial, and cultural center in the arid high-desert landscape. Explore more remote parts of the canyon by following one of four backcountry hiking trails, passing ancient roads, petroglyphs, stairways, and dramatic desert viewpoints.
http://www.nps.gov/chcu

## 8 SAN FELIPE PUEBLO
### New Mexico

Although only 26 miles (42 km) from Albuquerque, San Felipe doesn't generally encourage visitors. However, each June, Katishtya (the pueblo's traditional name) welcomes outsiders to its celebrations of San Pedro's Day, with traditional dancing and singing performed in the dramatic sunken bowl of the village plaza. The Green Corn dances on May 1 is another popular festival where visitors are welcome.
www.indianpueblo.org

## 9 GREAT SERPENT MOUND
### Ohio

The largest earthwork of its kind in the world, the 1,370-foot-long (420 m) Great Serpent Mound curves and slides across the landscape of southwestern Ohio, its grass-covered humps meant to represent a snake with an egg in its mouth. Originally believed to be a burial place for the Adena Nation, recent evidence places the mound as the work of the later Fort Ancient culture.
www.ohiohistory.org/places/serpent

## 10 MUSEUM OF THE CHEROKEE INDIAN
### North Carolina

The museum is an official Park Service interpretive site for the Trail of Tears National Historic Trail. A powerful exhibit about the 1,200-mile (1,900 km) forced march (one in four marchers died along the way) details how the Eastern Band of Cherokee Indians was formed from those who remained in their ancestral homeland.
www.cherokeemuseum.or

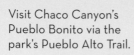

Visit Chaco Canyon's
Pueblo Bonito via the
park's Pueblo Alto Trail.

# OLD QUEBEC CITY

Have a taste of Canada's oldest and most fashionable city.

The oldest city in Canada, 400-plus-year-old Quebec City combines the romance of Paris and the charm of a provincial village. The first settlement in New France, Quebec City was founded in 1608 as a fur-trading post by Samuel de Champlain. A vertiginous staircase (dubbed L'Escalier Casse-Cou, or Breakneck Staircase) links the cliff-top Upper Town (historically home to political dignitaries, nuns, and Jesuits) and Lower Town (a riverside knot of narrow streets, once home to merchants and tradesmen).

But the truest—and tastiest—way to partake in the city is to feast your way through it. Rue St.-Jean, the city's premier boulevard of Gallic gastronomy, excels at what Quebecers do best: romance and fattening food. Pop into North America's oldest grocery store, J. A. Moisan, founded in 1871, for picnic-ready savories like salamis, pâtés, and ice cider, Quebec's sweet elixir. Continue on to Épicerie Européenne with its lusty selection of raw-milk artisanal cheeses.

End the day at Auberge Saint-Antoine's Panache restaurant, located in a 19th-century maritime stone warehouse in the city's Vieux Port. The menu changes daily based on what's in season. Chef François Blais is so serious about his farm-to-fork philosophy that he won't allow a freezer in the kitchen.

■ **PLANNING** **Quebec City** www.quebecregion.com. **J. A. Moisan** www.jamoisan.com. This Quebec institution also operates as a B&B. **Épicerie Européenne** www.epicerie-europeenne. com. **Panache** www.saint-antoine.com.

Pair wine with views of the city at Château Frontenac.

The main hall's mosaics and murals befit the grandeur of the building's collections.

WASHINGTON, D.C.

# LIBRARY OF CONGRESS

Uncover the symbolic secrets of the world's largest temple of learning.

With 838 miles (1,349 km) of shelves holding a mind-boggling 33 million-plus books, the Library of Congress is the world's largest library and houses such treasures as a rare Gutenberg Bible. The original library, started in 1800 as a reference collection for Congress, was housed in the U.S. Capitol. After the 1814 British burning of the Capitol destroyed all the books, Thomas Jefferson sold his eclectic personal library of 6,487 tomes to reestablish the nation's temple of learning.

It's fitting, then, that the library's main building, the Italian Renaissance–style Thomas Jefferson Building, houses what many regard as Washington's most beautiful space—the opulent yet tasteful Great Hall. Reminiscent of a Mediterranean palazzo, it dazzles with an abundance of intricate mosaics, architectural flourishes, and overhead murals.

Take a free, hour-long walking tour to hear the stories behind the Great Hall's symbolic art and architecture, such as the 12 brass inlays in the marble entrance floor representing the signs of the zodiac. As you climb the grand staircases, try to identify all of the occupations depicted by the whimsical marble cherubs decorating the railings. Pause at the elevated Visitors Gallery for unobstructed views of the sanctum santorum, the circular Main Reading Room.

## PLACES THAT CHANGED ME

### James H. Billington, Librarian of Congress

There are enough opportunities for quiet contemplation in the Library to last a lifetime, in a building with iconography so rich in meaning. A large mosaic of Minerva, the classical Goddess of Wisdom, dominates the Great Hall. The Goddess of Human Understanding looks down from the domed ceiling of the Main Reading Room as she lifts the veil of ignorance from humanity. Time slows down here, allowing silent reading and reflection to help us find the wisdom and understanding we all need.

■ **PLANNING** Library of Congress www.loc.gov. **Great Hall Tours** Public tours of the Jefferson Building, including the Great Hall, are offered Mon. through Sat. No reservations required.

The Aztec thought Teotihuacán was a "place of the gods."

## MEXICO
# TEOTIHUACÁN
Glide over the streets of the Western Hemisphere's first great city.

Rising above a gold, grassy plain about 30 miles (48 km) to the northeast of Mexico City are the ruins of the Western Hemisphere's first true metropolis. When the Aztecs visited this ancient center—abandoned just a few centuries after it reached its golden age—they found a ruined city dominated by a hulking pair of terraced pyramids, the largest one rising more than 200 feet (60 m) and covering an area of 10 acres (4 ha).

Concluding that mere humans could not build on such a grand scale, the Aztecs called the city Teotihuacán—Place of the Gods. But humans did, of course, build the city. Founded 2,000 years ago, the city spread across 8 square miles (20.7 sq km) and supported a population of, most likely, 200,000. At its peak around A.D. 600, the city controlled a powerful state that was probably larger than imperial Rome.

Most visitors climb up the 244 steps of the Pirámide del Sol (Pyramid of the Sun) to survey the site, but the ultimate view is from the sky. Outfitters like Viator Tours offer a combination hot-air balloon ride and walking tour, so that you can both glide over and stroll down the Avenida de los Muertos (Avenue of the Dead), the volcanic stone street aligned with the stars.

### ∼ IN THE KNOW ∼
#### THE STORIES THAT GRAVES TELL

While there are still endless mysteries about the lives of the people who walked Avenida de los Muertos 2,000 years ago, their graves also tell tales. Some graves were used several times. Others were looted long before the Aztecs ever arrived. Many contained figurines, their purposes still unknown. And others contained the remains of human sacrifices. One, a bound male figure discovered by Arizona State University archaeologist Saburo Sugiyama, was surrounded by burial offerings of obsidian blades, figurines, shells, and animals—including jaguars—that might have been buried alive.

■ **PLANNING** Teotihuacán www.visitmexico.com. Plan to spend a full day. Remember to take along sunscreen, an umbrella, and plenty of water. **Viator Tours** www.viator.com.

# PANAMA CANAL

Walk—or float—through this eco-hot spot, where wildlife fill thriving rain forests.

A man, a plan, a canal, Panama. So goes the palindrome that sums up the genesis of this artificial body of water, which took ten years (1904–1914) and 250,000 people (5,600 of whom died) to build. The canal stretches from Panama City's Miraflores Locks, on the Pacific coast, to Colón on the Atlantic coast, and it provides transcontinental passage for more than 14,000 oceangoing vessels per year.

But the Panama Canal, which had been off the tourist radar until only recently, is not just a significant engineering marvel. It's also a stunning 50-mile (80 km) strip that traverses biodiversity hot spots like Gatun Lake, the rain forests of Soberanía and Camino de Cruces National Parks, Espíritu Santo Gold Mine, and Bocas del Toro, an archipelago made up of 68 islands. The strip is home to endangered leatherback turtles, jaguars, ocelots, and orchids, not to mention more than 500 species of birds. To get up close and personal with some of this amazing wildlife, head to Gamboa Rainforest Resort, a luxury resort and spa that overlooks the Río Chagres. Here, a variety of nature experiences are offered, including boat safaris and nature walks, providing you plenty of opportunities to spot Panama flycatchers, howler monkeys, and sloths.

■ **PLANNING** **Panama Canal** www.visitpanama.com, www.pan canal.com. **Gamboa Rainforest Resort** www.gamboaresort.com.

## ~ IN THE KNOW ~
### CANAL EXPANSION

In 2006, Panamanian president Martín Torrijos proposed the expansion of the Panama Canal, and Panama's citizens approved it. Though some environmentalists have expressed opposition, the plan is considered ecologically sound, with minimum impact on existing wildlife and human communities. When it is complete, the expansion, whose excavation stage was completed in late 2011, will add a third lane and a set of locks to the existing site and double the canal's cargo ship capacity by 2015. The levels of Lake Gatun, Panama's source of drinking water, will rise by 1.6 feet (0.5 m), and 2 miles (3.2 km) of navigational channels will be built.

A cargo ship passes through Gatun Lake, a biodiversity hot spot.

Visitors must hike 12 miles (19 km) to reach the ruins of Ciudad Pérdida.

# COLOMBIA
# CIUDAD PÉRDIDA

Take the pilgrimage up the rugged Sierra Nevada de Santa Marta to this "lost city."

Parts of Colombia have long been off-limits to travelers due to the violence of the country's drug wars. Among the no-go regions was Ciudad Pérdida, the pre-Inca Lost City. But that is slowly changing. Often compared to Machu Picchu in Peru, Ciudad Pérdida is unlike that famous destination: You'll find few tourists along its verdant ridges—for now.

Ciudad Pérdida sits in a cloud forest on the Sierra Nevada de Santa Marta in northern Colombia. Discovered by treasure hunters in the 1970s, this romantic site demands a bit of a commitment from its suitors: It's a 12-mile (19 km) slog just to get there, much of it muddy and frequently uphill. A round-trip visit can take up to six days, during which time you'll sleep in hammocks and bathe in rivers. The payoff for all this effort, however, is worth it: breathtaking ruins of homes, a drainage system, bridges, and experimental farming terraces, all built sometime between the 700s and the 1300s. Along the way you pass several indigenous villages—and keep an eye out for the region's plentiful hummingbirds.

■ **PLANNING Ciudad Pérdida** www.colombia.travel. The mosquitoes in this region are notorious; make sure to bring repellent. Hikes can be arranged in the nearby tourist towns of Santa Marta and Taganga. **Adventure Associates** www.adventure-associates .com/lostcity. Among several outfitters offering guided treks.

## ≫ BEST OF THE BEST ≪
### Swimming & Camping Around Santa Marta

The town of Santa Marta is blessed with one of the loveliest bays in the Americas. Head first for **El Rodadero** and its pleasant stretch of white sand. You can go for a swim in the warm water here or simply lounge in the sun and rest your weary muscles. **Tayrona National Park** is also home to some wonderful beaches, with ample opportunity for swimming. Take a dip at **Bahía Concha,** or prepare to sleep under the stars at the park's **Neguanje** or **Cañaveral Beaches;** you will find campgrounds at both.

CHILE

# EASTER ISLAND

Face the island's mysteries from the sea.

Their backs to the sea, they stand watch with long faces and searching eyes. These are the *moai,* the immense stone figures thought to represent sacred chiefs and gods. They've come to symbolize the triangular, windswept island that the locals call Rapa Nui and that the Dutch named Easter Island after the day they reached it in 1722.

Visit this place, some 2,200 miles (3,500 km) west of Chile, with no plans to fully understand it. Only 14 miles (22.5 km) across, the salty island has air thick with mysteries that only the sealed lips of the moai could explain.

We know that between 800 and 1,200 years ago, a group of Polynesians pulled their canoes ashore. But no one can say for sure what drove them to carve into the volcanic rock and create about 900 stone figures, or why they placed the statues along the island's coast. The only way to see the etched stone faces from the first mariners' perspective is by sea. Stay overnight at Explora's Posada de Mike Rapu, the island's

luxury LEED-certified lodge, where the rate includes guided tours along the coastline in traditional local boats, as well as scuba and snorkeling excursions.

■ **PLANNING** **Easter Island** www.chile.travel/en. Easter Island is about a five-hour flight from Santiago, Chile. **Posada de Mike Rapu** www.explora.com/explora-rapa-nui.

## PLACES THAT CHANGED ME
*Pico Iyer, author of* **The Open Road & other books**

The wind was whistling in my ears, and the sea pounded against the black volcanic rocks. The nearest inhabited place was Pitcairn Island, 1300 miles away. My mother and I watched a few fireworks go up into the sky, and then walked across the wide, near-empty lawns back to our hotel. It was now January 1, 2000—we had come to the home of large stone heads, or moai, to see the new millennium—and in the haunting quiet, we learned, a 21st-century luxury was a simple piece of wood.

The moai stand tall, unwilling to share their secrets.

The ancient Inca city of
Machu Picchu continues
to draw modern-day
travelers from around
the world.

# MACHU PICCHU

*In the variety of its charms and the power of its spell, I know of no place in the world which can compare with it. Not only has it great snow peaks looming above the clouds . . . [I]t has also, in striking contrast, orchids and tree ferns, the delectable beauty of luxurious vegetation, and the mysterious witchery of the jungle.*

—HIRAM BINGHAM, *INCA LAND*, 1922

# STONEHENGE

Let Europe's famed prehistoric monument enthrall you.

A sanctuary of stone standing on Salisbury Plain still casts a spell on visitors after nearly four millennia. Unique today, Stonehenge was probably also unique in its own time—a stone monument modeled on timber precedents. Indeed, its massive lintels are bound to their uprights by mortise-and-tenon joints, an eloquent indication of just how radically new this hybrid monument must have been.

Its rich trove of artifacts continues to draw study. Barrows, or mounds for collective burials, pre-date even the first stage of Stonehenge's construction. Its largest stones, the sarsens, were somehow dragged 20 miles (32 km) from the Marlborough Downs; others were quarried in Wales. The astonishing result has attracted visitors ever since. Bronze coins from the fourth century A.D., found at the site, imply that even Roman legionnaires came for a look.

To experience the mystical power that the Bronze Age craftsmen, who finished this site in 1600 B.C., vested in this silent place, approach these 26-ton (23 mt) megaliths at the winter solstice, when the rays of the setting sun shine straight into the monument's center. You won't be alone, however; all kinds of Druids and other revelers convene to celebrate this magical occurrence.

■ **PLANNING** **Stonehenge** Visit www.english-heritage.org.uk for a downloadable activity pack before your visit. Access inside the stone circle must be reserved and paid for far in advance of your travel dates. Touching the stones is forbidden.

## ~ IN THE KNOW ~
### AVEBURY STONE CIRCLE

At Stonehenge, monoliths command a deserted grassland; at Avebury, they enclose a charming village with its own thatch-roofed pub. The much larger Neolithic circle, considered part of the Stonehenge World Heritage site, lies 29 miles (47 km) north of Stonehenge; unlike at Stonehenge, however, visitors can wander and explore at will. With its small museum and within an easy hike of the West Kennet Long Barrow, a vast 5,000-year-old communal tomb, Avebury offers a rich context for considering Wiltshire's prehistoric building boom. See www.nationaltrust.org.uk for more information.

The mysteries of Stonehenge have been confounding visitors for centuries.

Pilgrims to Mont St.-Michel have added their own layers of history—and architecture—to the islet.

## FRANCE
# MONT ST.-MICHEL
Spend the night among pilgrim spirits of the past.

At Mont St.-Michel, perched just off the coast of Normandy, follow the Grande Rue skyward, beyond the mount's secular hubbub and commercialism, to the medieval abbey that sits at its pinnacle. Linking sea and sky, earth and heaven, this soaring masterpiece exudes piety with marble cloisters, magnificent rib vaulting and capitals in the knights'

room, and a terrace with stunning views of the bay.

In 708, according to legend, the archangel Michael commanded a bishop to raise a chapel on the summit of the islet here. Over the centuries, the faithful piled upon it even grander churches and cloisters, creating a labyrinth of foundations and crypts from different ages. Pilgrims, joined by the scholarly and the curious, flocked to seek the archangel's blessing. The masses still swarm here, mingling in the souvenir shops and restaurants (including famous omelet maker La Mère Poulard) before trekking up more than 900 steps.

To truly experience the mount, however, you must stay overnight in one of the island's several inns. After the crowds have dispersed back to their buses and the shops have shuttered their doors, silence reigns in this timeless, windswept niche. For a special twist, plan a visit during high tide, when the waters come surging in and surround the lonely mount.

■ **PLANNING** Mont St.-Michel www.ot-montsaintmichel.com. Access to the island of Mont St.-Michel is free, but there is a fee for parking. In summer, it is best to park on the mainland and walk across the causeway.

## ～ IN THE KNOW ～
### HIGH TIDE AT MONT ST.-MICHEL

Europe's greatest tides occur at the Bay of Mont St.-Michel. To see the highest tides, which rely on the moon's gravitational pull, visit during the full moon. They are at their highest in spring, when a 60-foot (18 m) difference between low and high water is common, and the sea surges out 28 miles (45 km) from the coast only to turn around and surge back in at a force of more than 3 feet (0.9 m) per second. You can take guided hikes on the flats when the tide is out, but never venture out alone—quicksand and a quick incoming tide are constant threats. Visit www.ot-montsaintmichel.com for a tide schedule.

# VERSAILLES

*The beauty of Versailles for me has always been the juxtaposition of the pretty gardens with the grandiose château, letting you believe that the courtiers, with all their constraints and corsets, could try to lose themselves among the deceptively natural-seeming flowers scattered there as if strewn by nature. Marie-Antoinette carried the notion of the simple life farther, with lambs and milkmaids in sight of the forbidding, angular palace.*

—DIANE JOHNSON, AUTHOR OF *LE DIVORCE, LE MARIAGE, L'AFFAIRE, INTO A PARIS QUARTIER,* & OTHER BOOKS

The gardens tickle the eye. Stories of palace intrigue treat the brain.

Expect changes with each visit: The cathedral is still under construction.

BARCELONA, SPAIN

# SAGRADA FAMILIA

Scale the lofty walkways of Gaudí's heavenly vision.

The Expiatory Temple of the Holy Family is unlike any other church in Barcelona—or the world. Nearly nine decades after his death, local architect Antoni Gaudí's masterwork, crowned with 8 of 18 planned towers, is still under construction, with elongated pillars and twirl-a-whirl stone flourishes that seem to defy gravity. Rising among the ubiquitous construction cranes, it is the proud emblem of Barcelona's individualism.

The music inside this cathedral is a choir of hammers and saws, as workmen dart past the visitors who pour through the nave. Gaudí, who took over the construction of Sagrada Familia in 1882, worked without blueprints and continuously revised as construction progressed. The result is a psychedelic interpretation of traditional spiritual symbols, including elongated, El Greco–style saints, Christ's astrological signs, and a spiraling sacred dome. Gothic rose windows and the modern Passion facade complete the time warp.

Walk the church-tower walkways. Festooned with mosaics, they overlook a skyline shaped in Gaudí's image—his Parc Güell and Casa Milà are icons in this playful Catalonian city. Take an elevator to a steeple overlook, and then descend to a ground-floor gallery that interprets how Gaudí used natural forms, such as eucalyptus trees, for inspiration.

■ **PLANNING Barcelona** www.barcelonaturisme.com. **Sagrada Familia** www.gaudisagradafamilia.com. The cathedral is located on Carrer de Sardenya in Barcelona.

## ∽ IN THE KNOW ∾
### CASA MILÀ

Though Gaudí is buried in the crypt of Sagrada Familia, his life and career are best interpreted ten blocks away in the heart of the Eixample neighborhood. Casa Milà (also known by the nickname La Pedrera, or Stone Quarry), an innovative block of flats built in 1906, houses the Espai Gaudí on its top floor. Stop by for a brilliant interactive display of Gaudí's designs and models—and bring your camera to the extraordinary roof terrace, crowned with organically shaped sculptures. Casa Milà is located on Carrer de Provença and is open year-round. Hours vary, and there is an admission fee. See www.lapedreraeducacio.org for more information.

# THE ALHAMBRA

Submerge your senses into a sublime Islamic oasis.

Allah cast the Moors out of the Alhambra, legend says, because they dared to make it too much like Paradise. But the Alhambra complex sprang from earthly beginnings: a modest fortress the Moors built to protect themselves, set on a spur of the Sierra Nevada overlooking the city of Granada. Expanded at the height of 13th-century Moorish power in Spain, this hilltop palace is one of the finest examples of Islamic architecture in Europe.

The palaces and fortress of the Alhambra are a sophisticated oasis in the arid Andalusian Plain. The 35-acre (14 ha) site includes a labyrinth of shimmering ponds, trickling fountains, and gardens fragrant with honeysuckle and jasmine. You can easily spend a day exploring here: climbing to the roof of the Alcazaba, the ninth-century military fortress and oldest part of the complex, for a panoramic view; enjoying flamenco performances in the narrow lanes of the city's Albaicín district and the nearby Gypsy quarter; and dining on fried *berenjenas*—the region's signature eggplant dish—at the tiny Casa Julio off the Plaza Nueva. Linger into the evening on one of the famous patios. After the guided tours have departed, glowing floodlights accent the subtle and sensual atmosphere.

■ **PLANNING** Alhambra www.alhambra.org. The Alhambra is located on Avenida de los Alixares in Granada, Andalusia. Guided tours of the site are offered daily at 10 a.m., and an admission fee is charged.

## ∼ IN THE KNOW ∼
### WASHINGTON IRVING'S *TALES OF THE ALHAMBRA*

He was not the first or last person to be enamored of the Alhambra, but Washington Irving was the first writer to bring its legends to life. In 1829, he installed himself in the governor's apartments overlooking the orange trees and fountains of the garden of Daraxa to pen *Tales of the Alhambra*. The collection of essays and sketches influenced other writers, including Alexander Pushkin, and revived American interest in the grand palace, but Irving nearly despaired of doing it justice. "How unworthy is my scribbling of the place!" he wrote. Look for the wall plaque that commemorates his stay.

The Alhambra provides a master course in Islamic architecture.

# VATICAN CITY

See the pope in person and retrace the footsteps of the masters in rooms where their frescoes were born.

A statue of the mythical figure of Laocöon awaits in the Vatican Museums.

The ancient Romans believed that every place had a *genius loci*, a guardian deity that made extraordinary things happen. One such place had to be the Vatican Hill—its name a derivation of *vaticinium*, the prophecy of future things. Over the past 2,000 years, a succession of popes has made this center of faith on the Tiber River's western bank into a center of culture and art as well. Guarded by the papal Castel Sant'Angelo, the 109-acre (44 ha) Vatican City is the smallest state in the world, one-eighth the size of Central Park in New York City.

## PAPAL AUDIENCE

Pilgrims for nearly two millennia have been visiting Rome to visit the seat of Christianity and, if possible, see the pope and obtain a papal blessing. You can too. The Vatican offers free tickets to anyone who requests them. At the appointed time, you'll file into the spacious hall and take your seat among lay people, clerics, and nuns from all over the world. The ceremony begins with the papal address, followed by songs and dances performed by representatives of different groups. The two-hour meeting—a cross between a revival meeting and a pop concert—ends with a solemn blessing.

## TOP-DRAWER ARTWORK

There are two distinctions that make the 14 Vatican Museums different from other museums. First, the vast collections of world-class artworks—including the Greek "Laocöon" and "Apollo Belvedere" sculptures—are grouped with masterpieces that literally were born in these rooms, like Raphael's frescoes in the Raphael Rooms, Michelangelo's frescoes in the Sistine Chapel, and frescoes by Beato Angelico in the Niccoline Chapel. Second, a number of the masterpieces created here were inspired by artworks already in the collection—for example, the Belvedere Torso, on which Michelangelo modeled his portrayal of Christ in "The Last Judgment." But other treasures fill the Vatican rooms as well, including Egyptian and Etruscan offerings, ancient maps, precious manuscripts, medieval furniture, tapestries, and jewels and

---

### ❧ BEST OF THE BEST ❧
#### Underground Tombs

Consecrated in 1626, St. Peter's Basilica occupies the site of a fourth-century basilica erected by Rome's first Christian emperor, Constantine. Deep beneath the soaring bronze canopy that protects the high altar lie more than 20 mausoleums excavated in the 1950s, including the sacred tomb of St. Peter the Apostle. The other ancient Roman graves, all richly embellished with ancient art—frescoes, an early Christian mosaic, and statues—represent a hodgepodge of cults: dancing satyrs and deities ranging from Apollo to Isis. "Romans of those days took no chances," one priest observed.

chalices representing thousands of years of papal power.

Since seeing the entire collection means walking 5 miles (8 km), it's wise to visit the obvious highlights first: the Museo Pio-Clementino, with its classical sculpture, the Sistine Chapel, Raphael's Rooms, and the Pinacoteca (picture gallery), where the cream of the collection's Renaissance and baroque paintings are on display. Then, branch off to museums that reflect your own interests.

■ **PLANNING** **St. Peter's Basilica & Square** www.saintpeters basilica.org. Several Masses are held daily. The dress code stipulates no shorts, miniskirts, or bare shoulders. For information or tickets visit www.vatican.va. **Vatican Museums** http://mv.vatican .va. The museums are closed on Sun.

St. Peter's—the church built over the tomb of the Apostle Peter—is the center of Roman Catholicism.

# BREATHTAKING PAINTINGS

Transcend the mundane through the power of art.

---

**1 GEORGIA O'KEEFFE, "BLACK HOLLYHOCK, BLUE LARKSPUR"**
Georgia O'Keeffe Museum, Santa Fe, New Mexico
Georgia O'Keeffe pushed flower imagery to new places, and her "Black Hollyhock, Blue Larkspur"—bold and sexy—was no slacker on that front. And in 1930, too? So forward!
www.okeeffemuseum.org

**2 DIEGO RIVERA'S FRESCOES**
Detroit Institute of Arts
Detroit, Michigan
Diego Rivera's mid-20th-century frescoes honor the industry—and people—that once made Detroit a powerhouse. The 27 panels took 11 months to complete and are considered the finest example of Mexican mural art in the U.S.
www.dia.org

**3 "JACKIE ROBINSON" MURAL**
2803 N. Broad St.
Philadelphia, Pennsylvania
Many of Philadelphia's murals hit it out of the park, but the one of baseball player Jackie Robinson stealing home in the World Series is special. All energy and strength, it's a fitting tribute to a man whose spirit was just as tall as the painting that honors him.
http://muralarts.org/explore/projects/jackie-robinson

**4 MARK ROTHKO, "NO. 4"**
National Gallery of Art
Washington, D.C.
Oh, to really *see* a Rothko for the first time. His work, often dismissed by kids on field trips with a "What's the big deal? I could paint that," starts to pulse and pull you in if you just stand, wait, and look for long enough. It's all emotion. The effect is most startling with his darker pieces, like "No. 4."
www.nga.gov

**5 PICASSO, "GUERNICA"**
Museo Naciional Centro de Arte Reina Sofia, Madrid, Spain
Pablo Picasso's "Guernica," which he painted during the Spanish Civil War, will always stand as one of the finest examples of antiwar art. It is absolutely heart wrenching—yet it's nearly impossible to turn away.
www.museoreinasofia.es

**6 MONET'S WATER LILIES**
Musée de l'Orangerie
Tuileries Garden, Paris, France
Claude Monet is so easy to like that he's also easy to overlook. We're just used to his work. The Musée de l'Orangerie's water lily–filled rooms will make you see his creative genius anew. With eight of the giant murals spread between two oval rooms open to natural light, you'll feel like you're swimming in those ponds.
www.musee-orangerie.fr

**7 MASACCIO, "HOLY TRINITY"**
Basilica of Santa Maria Novella, Florence, Italy
Masaccio helped give a flat world some depth. His painting of the Holy Trinity was one of the first to put perspective to work.
www.firenzeturismo.it

**8 VINCENT VAN GOGH, "FIELD WITH FLOWERS NEAR ARLES"**
Van Gogh Museum
Amsterdam, Netherlands
It's the rare van Gogh that makes you want to leap inside the moody work. "Starry Night" may indeed welcome your gaze, but his 1888 "Field With Flowers Near Arles" positively invites you to dive in and run through that field.
www.vangoghmuseum.nl

**9 SAN BUSHMAN ROCK PAINTINGS**
Bushmans Kloof, Cederberg Mountains, South Africa
They wanted to leave their mark. The San Bushmen who lived in the Cederberg Mountains of western South Africa up to 120,000 years ago turned nature into paint and put their stories on the rocks all around them. There are more than 130 rock art canvases in the region around Bushmans Kloof—beholding the images, the mind reels thinking of their age.
www.bushmanskloof.co.za/rock_art.php

**10 YAYOI KUSAMA, "NET ACCUMULATION"**
National Museum of Art
Osaka, Japan
The work is both manic and quiet. Reflecting her recurring psychiatric issues, Yayoi Kusama's "Net Accumulation" (1958) is a deep dive into the artist's obsessive thinking. Her "net" works, with their apparently undulating fields of painted loops, are often immense, some stretching 33 feet (10 m) long.
www.osaka-info.jp

There's no traveling show for Diego Rivera's Detroit frescoes. Visit Motor City to get a close-up of their power.

# MILAN CATHEDRAL

*For some, Milan means fashion. For me, it means Saint Ambrose, the fourth century bishop of this "Ambrosian" city. Under the cathedral, an archeological find of the 1940s contains the pool where Ambrose baptized an African visitor named Augustine, later to be Saint Augustine, determining the future history of Europe.*

—GARRY WILLS, JOURNALIST, HISTORIAN, AND
PULITZER PRIZE–WINNING AUTHOR

The Duomo di
Milano dominates
the view in its
namesake square.

# RILA MONASTERY

Spend the night in a medieval monastic refuge.

On a steep mountain slope in the wilderness of western Bulgaria stands a secluded retreat that once held the heart of a nation. Fortresslike walls enclose an inviting arcade of colorful arches and a treasure trove of paintings and wood carvings. For much of its history, Rila Monastery has been stronghold and art repository, monastic refuge, and cradle of national consciousness.

The monastery was founded near the cave that sheltered the religious hermit St. John of Rila in the tenth century. After the 1396 invasion of Bulgaria by the Ottomans, the buildings slid into disrepair, although the Rila monks continued to pursue their religious and literary activities. When the nation began its struggle for independence in the early 1800s, the monastery found itself the symbolic center of a cultural and spiritual awakening. A fire soon ravaged the complex, but Bulgarian master craftsmen lovingly rebuilt it.

Most visitors spend a few hours touring the complex, but the best way to experience life in this functioning monastery is to spend the night in one of the spartan guest rooms. It's only after the tourists leave (monastery doors are locked promptly at 7 p.m.) that you can truly begin to appreciate the serenity and wonder of monastic silence.

■ **PLANNING** Rila Monastery www.rilamonastery.pmg-blg.com. Visit the reception desk when you arrive at the monastery to ask about room availability and rates. For more background information on the monastery, visit http://whc.unesco.org.

## ∼ IN THE KNOW ∼
### SNOWSHOE BULGARIA

A short two-hour drive from Sofia, the ski resort Bansko is Bulgaria's equivalent of Zermatt, bristling with newfangled ski lifts and luxury lodges. But to really see its wild mountain valleys, consider trading in the skis for a pair of snowshoes. Inteco Travel (www.intecotravel.com) offers snowshoe tours through the Rila and Pirin Mountains. Far from the madness of the booming ski towns, these tours show off the silent, monochromatic beauty of Bulgaria's mountain ranges. The guides also offer ice climbing, bear-watching (there are more than 700 bears in the Balkans), archaeological outings, and horseback-riding tours.

The monastery's guest rooms and monastic quarters feature elaborate murals.

# ATHENS, GREECE
# ACROPOLIS

Let the Acropolis surprise you, no matter how many times you've seen it.

This massive rock, rising more than 500 feet (156 m) from the plain, was a natural fortress for prehistoric settlers. It still looks impregnable, and it still inspires awe. Think of the work that went into its temples—getting the immense marble beams and column drums down from the quarries on Mount Penteli and then up the sacred rock with only mules, ramps, and pulleys as tools. Think of Pheidias's craftsmen, hundreds of them, chiseling the elements of the Parthenon with subtle imperfections—swellings, tiltings, curvings, to offset its symmetry—that engineers today can barely duplicate with their computers. Or consider Pericles, Athens's ruler after the fifth-century B.C. Persian invasion, who consciously erected the Parthenon as a monument to Athenian glory.

The Acropolis today is very different from what it was in antiquity. Back then its buildings were painted, and it was littered with statues. We might have thought it vulgar or cluttered. Time, plunder, and reverence for the classical world have cleansed it of "foreign" influences: a Frankish tower, a Byzantine church, a mosque. And for the past 20 years the cranes and scaffolding of restoration projects mask our view. Even so, whether we walk its slippery stones with hundreds of others or gaze up at it from a busy street below, the Acropolis is like Shakespeare's Cleopatra: "age cannot wither her nor custom stale her infinite variety."

■ **PLANNING Acropolis** www.culture.gr. Arrive early, wear non-slip shoes, and take a hat and a water bottle. Your admission ticket is valid for four days and will get you into other sites on the antiquities trail.

## ☙ BEST OF THE BEST ☙
### Acropolis Museum

The stunning Acropolis Museum (*www.theacropolismuseum .gr*) features more than 150,000 square feet (14,000 sq m) of exhibition space—ten times larger than the old museum—in an airy, ultramodern building filled with light. Glass floors allow visitors a glimpse at the ongoing excavations beneath the museum, while an enormous glass wall affords a stunning view of the Parthenon. The museum's permanent collection includes statues and objects removed from the Acropolis during excavations, as well as friezes from the Parthenon. There is no public parking; take metro line 2 to the Akropoli station. Small admission fee.

POLAND
# WIELICZKA SALT MINE

Attend a subterranean concert in an ancient salt mine.

You won't find many salt mines on UNESCO's coveted list of World Heritage sites, but then again, Wieliczka, just on the outskirts of the ancient Polish capital of Kraków, is no ordinary salt mine. Since the 17th century, the miners here have used the skills of their trade to carve masterpieces into the walls of Europe's oldest saltworks, which date back a thousand years. During the Middle Ages, the mines provided Polish kings with up to a quarter of the state income.

Wieliczka's 2,000 grottoes stretch some 180 miles (290 km) on nine levels. Perhaps to ward off evil spirits—or, more likely, given the country's deep Catholic faith—most of the carvings reflect religious motifs, including altars, biblical bas-reliefs, and statues of the saints.

Access to the mine is by guided tour only. During the summer, tours in English depart every half hour or so. At other times, expect six to eight English tours daily. In addition to the tour, try to attend one of the many concerts staged here to fully experience both the sights and sounds of the subterranean chambers. If you can arrange a visit on Miner's Day (December 4), you'll be treated to the thunderous sounds of the Wieliczka Salt Mine Brass Band, whose current members continue a mining musical tradition dating back to 1830.

■ **PLANNING** **Wieliczka Salt Mine** www.kopalnia.pl. Plan on spending around two hours on the tour. Wear comfortable shoes and be sure to pack a jacket, since the year-round temperature in the mine is a chilly 57°F (14°C).

## ~ IN THE KNOW ~
### MYTH & HISTORY OF THE MINE

Europe's oldest salt mine is filled with its share of legend and mystery. Many stories involve St. Kinga, a 13th-century former grand duchess of Poland and daughter of Hungarian King Bela IV. Kinga is best known for her chastity and charity. Legend says she once tossed her engagement ring into a briny spring in her native Hungary and magically retrieved it in Wieliczka, thus bringing salt to Poland as a queenly dowry. During World War II, the Nazis paved the floor of one grotto with concrete and set up a secret aircraft engine factory, safe from Allied bombing runs.

# TSARSKOYE SELO

Explore Romanov riches away from the crowds.

Lauded as one of the 18th century's most glorious works of art and architecture, the magnificent Catherine Palace, located 17 miles (27 km) south of St. Petersburg, celebrates flamboyant rococo to the extreme. Beginning in 1743, Empress Elizabeth built the elaborate, turquoise-and-white palace, with its glittering, statue-studded exterior, as her summer residence. Her daughter, Catherine the Great, embellished the structure to the point of self-indulgence. Today crowds flock here to see the Great Hall, featuring intricately carved golden decor; the Picture Hall, its walls a jigsaw of canvases by 17th- and 18th-century masters; and the Amber Room, dubbed the eighth wonder of the world. Treat yourself to a private guide, who will lead you into empty rooms as if you are wandering the halls in search of Catherine the Great herself.

Catherine Palace is the high point of Tsarskoye Selo, a spectacular ensemble of palaces, parks, and a model town. After leaving the palace, stroll through monument-dotted Catherine Park and untamed Alexander Park. Nearby, Alexander Palace is where Nicholas II, aka the last tsar of Russia, installed his family in 1905. Recently renovated, its rooms seem haunted with the past: Bearskin rugs, children's toys, and black-and-white family portraits remain just as they were before the family was taken away on their last journey to Siberia.

■ **PLANNING** Catherine Palace www.saint-petersburg.com. The palace is closed Tues. and the last Mon. of each month.

## ⁂ BEST OF THE BEST ⁂
### Agate Rooms

The Amber Room at Catherine Palace has long been revered for its stunning *richesse*. Several other stone-embossed rooms recently stepped into the limelight to rival its magnificence. Located in the summer pavilion, where Catherine the Great kept her personal apartments, the Agate Rooms were created to match the splendor of Versailles. In the process of meticulous reconstruction by master craftspeople, these violet-hued rooms showcase Russia's mineral wealth with touches of malachite, lapis lazuli, porphyry, and alabaster. Gilded ceilings and masterful paintings complement the dramatic work.

Free concerts of Russian folk and religious music take place daily at the pretty Grotto pavilion.

# ST. BASIL'S CATHEDRAL

Be bowled over by Red Square's boisterous cathedral.

Moscow's exuberant St. Basil's Cathedral is an instantly recognizable icon of the Russian capital, Moscow. The cathedral's famous onion domes, more like psychedelic baubles, are an eye-catching swirl of textures, patterns, and colors that lend an undeniably comic feel to the impressive but otherwise austere Red Square.

Ivan the Terrible built the church between 1555 and 1561 to commemorate the taking of Kazan in battle against the Mongol horde, but precious little information about its origins has survived. The church miraculously survived Napoleon's onslaught, World War II, and the Soviet period. Even Stalin, who reputedly loathed St. Basil's, could not bring it down.

A tour of the interior is worth the ticket price to admire the icons, the frescoes, and the central church's soaring ceiling. But exterior views are free and should be frequent to fully appreciate this masterpiece of Orthodox art. Visit at different times of day to see how the sun, moon, stars, and elements alter the look and feel of one of the world's most iconic sacred places. St. Basil's appears at its most magical on winter evenings when a light dusting of snow makes the central church and its eight surrounding chapels look like a sugar-frosted, fairy-tale castle.

■ **PLANNING** St. Basil's Cathedral www.moscow.info.

## ～ IN THE KNOW ～
### ALSO IN RED SQUARE

Though St. Basil's dominates Red Square with its inspired exuberance, this dramatic public plaza is filled with many other must-sees. First on the list would have to be **Lenin's Mausoleum.** Communism as an ideology arguably may have been relegated to the scrap heap of history, but the embalmed body of the leader of the 1917 Russian Revolution remains open for public viewing (though there are plans afoot to bury him next to his mother in St. Petersburg). The **State Historical Museum,** at the northern end of the square, is a romp through centuries of history of the Russian Empire. Find more details at www.shm.ru.

St. Basil's interior is as vivid as its carnival-bright onion domes.

# SAMARKAND & BUKHARA

Follow in the footsteps of ancient traders to two of the greatest cities on the Silk Road.

Despite being the cradle of the world's greatest civilizations (China, India, ancient Egypt, Persia, Arabia, and ancient Rome), the Silk Road remains unknown to all but the most intrepid Western travelers. Stretching some 4,000 miles (6,500 km), the historical network of trade routes linking Africa and Asia laid the foundations of the modern world. Uzbekistan exemplifies the rich cultural, artistic, and religious tapestry woven by the Silk Route traders. The two great cities of Samarkand and Bukhara are among the finest along the route.

An important crossroads on the Silk Road, Samarkand is one of the world's most ancient cities, a contemporary of Rome, whose inhabitants also left their mark, evidenced in jewels and pieces of gold and silver. Here, in the lovely blue-hued Registan Square, take time to sip Persian tea from Chinese porcelain while marveling at the towering madrassas (religious schools) adorned with mosaics and crowned with turquoise cupolas. Bukhara, nicknamed "the Divine" for its proliferation of mosques and madrassas, is equally awe-inspiring.

## ∾ IN THE KNOW ∾
### GARDENS OF SAMARKAND

Amir Timur, the 14th-century conqueror of West, South, and Central Asia who founded Samarkand more than 2,500 years ago, was unaware that his demand for a green belt around the city would influence horticulture across the world. The gardens of Samarkand, with plantations of fruit and decorative trees, flower gardens, pools, and fountains, were so tall and dense that visitors to the city couldn't see its houses from outside. Timur's gardeners channeled water in geometric quadrants, symbolizing the rivers of paradise referenced in the Koran, symmetry that so impressed his international visitors that it was copied across Asia and India. Today, Samarkand is one of Uzbekistan's greenest cities, and its gardens are still tended daily.

■ **PLANNING** Samarkand & Bukhara www.samarkand-bukhara-travel.com, www.sambuh.com. Trains link both cities to the capital Tashkent, but traveling solo in Uzbekistan is challenging. Leave the logistics to a Central Asian tour specialist like East-Site Travel (www.east-site.com).

# BEST OF THE WORLD

✦

# HOUSES OF WORSHIP

Allow peace and tranquillity to take over in the sacred spaces both ancient and modern.

## 1 BAHÁ'Í HOUSE OF WORSHIP
Wilmette, Illinois

The five million adherents of Bahá'í believe in the oneness of humankind. Their North American temple, located north of Chicago on a bluff overlooking Lake Michigan, promotes unity through its nine-sided design, surrounding gardens, and intricate, lacelike ornamentation.
www.bahai.us/bahai-temple

## 2 SANCTUARY OF OUR LADY OF LAS LAJAS
Ipiales, Colombia

According to legend, in the 18th century an image of the Virgin Mary appeared on a rock above the Guáitara River. Worshippers built a fairy-tale Gothic-style stone church that rests on a bridge spanning the river gorge. The miraculous rock serves as the church's high altar.
www.colombia.travel

## 3 SEVILLE CATHEDRAL
Seville, Spain

The tomb of Christopher Columbus is housed in this immense cathedral, the largest Gothic building in Europe. Founded in 1403 on the site of a former mosque, it harmoniously blends Gothic, Renaissance, and Moorish styles.
www.andalucia.org

## 4 THE GREAT SYNAGOGUE
Budapest, Hungary

Europe's largest synagogue is the focal point of Budapest's vibrant Jewish community. Designed like a basilica, its vast interior features ornate Byzantine and Moorish architectural details, and holds up to 3,000 worshippers. The Memorial Garden commemorates the millions who died in the Holocaust.
http://hungary.com/budapest

## 5 SHEIKH ZAYED GRAND MOSQUE
Abu Dhabi, United Arab Emirates

Completed in 2008, the UAE's largest mosque boasts a 27-story main dome and can accommodate 41,000 worshippers. The complex dazzles with marble mosaics, crystal-encrusted chandeliers, and columns inlaid with mother-of-pearl and semiprecious stones.
http://szgmc.ae

## 6 TEMPLE OF SETI I
Abydos, Egypt

The sacred city of Abydos, just north of Luxor, was a necropolis for the earliest Egyptian rulers and a pilgrimage destination for the ancient Egyptians who worshiped Osiris. The uniquely L-shaped Temple of Seti I has chapels dedicated to Osiris, Isis, and Horus, with well-preserved hieroglyphs and painted carvings.
www.egypt.travel

## 7 GOLDEN TEMPLE
Amritsar, India

Also known as the Harmandir Sahib, this 400-year-old temple in northwestern India is the holiest site for Sikhs. The structure's glowing patina of gold foil is reflected in the surrounding waters of the Amrit Sarovar, or Pool of Nectar, which symbolizes external purity and spiritual unity.
www.punjabtourism.gov.in

## 8 JOKHANG TEMPLE
Lhasa, Tibet

Jokhang is the most sacred place of worship for Tibetan Buddhists. Pilgrims travel to the seventh-century temple from all across Tibet, usually on foot. After prostrating themselves in the temple plaza, they pray in the main hall before the life-size Sakyamuni Buddha statue, one of Tibet's most venerated relics.
www.cnto.org/lhasa.asp

## 9 BOROBUDUR TEMPLE
Java, Indonesia

This monumental temple, hidden in the jungle of central Java, was built by a king of the Sailendra dynasty during the eighth and ninth centuries—300 years before Cambodia's Angkor Wat. The walls and balustrades of the three-tiered structure are decorated with thousands of masterful relief panels and stupas honoring the Buddha that extend for more than 3 miles (6 km).
www.borobudurpark.com

## 10 ISE SHRINES
Ise, Japan

The simple structures of these two shrines—Geku and Naiku—in Ise, located about 180 miles (290 km) southwest of Tokyo, are virtually unchanged from when they were first built nearly 1,500 years ago. They are completely reconstructed every 20 years, in keeping with Shinto beliefs of renewal and the preservation of traditional Japanese culture.
www.isejingu.or.jp

The Pool of Nectar at Harmandir Sahib, also known as the Golden Temple, symbolizes spiritual unity.

All that's left of the Roman emperor Septimius Severus's great city is ruins and sand.

LIBYA

# LEPTIS MAGNA

Wander the streets that Emperor Septimius Severus loved to call home.

Once one of the richest trading centers in the world, Leptis Magna is now partially buried in sand. In fact, many of the architectural wonders from this remnant of the Roman Empire lay hidden from the world for more than 1,400 years. The visible sections of the UNESCO World Heritage site tell the story of a city that advanced thinking on urban planning and architecture, that pulsed with life, that celebrated its emperors . . . a place where Medusa looks on from the stone of the forum.

Wander through the city's grid and you'll pass places where, more than 1,800 years ago, men relaxed at therapeutic baths and gathered at the local amphitheater, where servants shopped for meals fit to serve Septimius Severus, the emperor who was born there in A.D. 145. Leptis Magna was the emperor's great pride, and he was determined to turn it into a seaside version of Rome.

While under his control, the city's port took shape. Here modern-day travelers go slack-jawed trying to imagine the place filled with workers building a dam and a canal that could control the Wadi Lebda, the fierce waterway that spills into the Mediterranean a short distance away.

■ **PLANNING Leptis Magna** http://whc.unesco.org/en/list/183. The site lies about 80 miles (130 km) east of Tripoli, Libya's capital city. For current travel conditions, consult the U.S. Department of State travel site for Libya at www.travel.state.gov.

## PLACES THAT CHANGED ME
### Andrew Cockburn, journalist & documentary producer

I walk down long-silent streets, past buildings complete enough to suggest that the 100,000 inhabitants who once thronged them have only just gone away . . . Most of all Leptis is a monument to the mighty Septimius Severus, a well-connected local boy who made very good by seizing control of the entire Roman Empire in A.D. 193 . . . As Severus's reign declined, the markets for the olive oil exports responsible for the city's wealth gradually dried up. The city shrank in the face of enemy tribes and the ever encroaching sand, until it was empty and all but forgotten. Thus undisturbed, it has survived as a portal to a glorious empire past.

# EGYPT
# PYRAMIDS

Crawl and climb inside narrow pyramid passageways.

Monuments for the ages to ponder, the pyramids of Egypt have fascinated people for 5,000 years. In fact, of the seven wonders of the ancient world, the three pyramids of the Giza Plateau are the only survivors. They've braved looting, dismantling, and pollution. Today, suburban Cairo creeps up to the paws of the Sphinx, and one of the best photo ops of the pyramids is at sundown . . . from the roof of a Pizza Hut. Yet somehow the Giza Pyramids still spark our imagination and provide us with a link to Egypt's powerful past and to those who achieved one of the greatest engineering feats of all time.

The pyramid credited to King Khufu—Cheops in Greek—is the biggest, its square base covering 13.1 acres (5.3 ha). Constructed around 2055 B.C., the Great Pyramid's original apex towered 50 stories high. If you're not claustrophobic, don't miss the opportunity to crawl inside. Entering the pyramid is truly like stepping back in time 4,500 years. A narrow, ascending corridor leads to makeshift stairs. From there, you're forced to hunch nearly in half to navigate a tight tunnel. After more climbing and scrambling you reach the king's chamber where Khufu's robbed and emptied sarcophagus still rests.

■ **PLANNING** **Pyramids** www.egypt.travel. The Giza Plateau is a large site; bring water, sunscreen, and comfortable shoes. There is an admission fee to the plateau and another fee if you want to crawl inside any of the pyramids.

## PLACES THAT CHANGED ME
*Zahi Hawass, former director general of the Giza Pyramids*

It never ceased to amaze me that every day I looked at the pyramid, I saw a different image . . . The first time I entered the Great Pyramid and gazed upward toward the grand gallery, I felt as though it went straight up to the sky. I began to climb the ascending corridor, stopping to touch the polished limestone sides of the pyramid, where centuries before a great pharaoh may have passed. Reaching the king's burial chamber, I stood in silence. I could feel the spirits of ancient Egyptians. And I wanted to know more about this amazing structure.

Of the seven wonders of the ancient world, only Giza's Pyramids still stand.

# JORDAN
# PETRA

Peer through a rock-hewn window of the past and camp Bedouin-style under the stars.

Bedouin traditions continue to flourish around the ancient city of Petra.

Carved into sheer cliffs of sunset-hued sandstone, Jordan's rose-red city of Petra once commanded the respect of traders from Rome to China. Like ancient caravan traders, today's visitors must enter Petra via a mile-long (1.6 km) ravine called the Siq. In places the chasm walls soar to 328 feet (100 m) and nearly close overhead. Plan to visit early or late in the day when the light creates the most colorful effects on Petra's ubiquitous stone.

## PATH INTO THE PAST
Suddenly, through a towering, shadow-shrouded opening in the Siq barely wide enough for two horses, appears a lofty, 13-story facade in a shaft of light. Pale pink Grecian columns

and sharp pediments—a temple, a tomb, who knows? This mysterious structure, called the Treasury, was probably built between 100 B.C. and A.D. 200. Some say a band of pirates stashed their loot on the second floor. Others say Egyptian pharaohs used it as a treasury. Moviegoers these days might know it better for serving as the final resting place of the Holy Grail in the 1989 movie *Indiana Jones and the Last Crusade*. Continue your explorations with empty caves, visit the archaeological and Nabataean museums, and hike 800 steps up to the top of Al-Dier (the Monastery).

## NABATAEAN LIFE
Petra—which means "rock" in Greek—is the legacy of a nomadic Arab tribe called the Nabataeans, who settled in this hidden valley 2,000 years ago to exploit the site's strategic location at the nexus of six ancient caravan routes. "The camel caravans crossing the country were like armies on the march," wrote the Greek geographer Strabo of the traffic in frankincense, spices, silks, gold, and ivory.

Open to new ideas and careful stewards of their environment, the Nabataeans were a remarkable people. Because their society was built on trade, Petra's residents had to be outwardly focused. This open-minded attitude helped them improve

## ⌁ IN THE KNOW ⌁
### BRINGING WATER TO AN ANCIENT DESERT CITY

Environmentalists by necessity, the Nabataeans worked diligently to ensure their desert city and trade routes never lacked for water. Using an ingenious hydraulic engineering system, they dug hidden cisterns along their parched trade routes and within their city. The system, some of whose features pre-date Western techniques by 2,000 years, brought water from nearby springs into Petra via clay pipes and channels, serving 30,000 inhabitants during Petra's ancient apogee. Every drop of water was preserved. The Nabataeans also developed a diversified economy based on husbandry of their grazing ranges, arable agricultural land, and mining resources.

their position in a commercial network that included Greece, Persia, Rome, India, Arabia, and ultimately China.

Retrace their routes on a camel caravan north from Wadi Rum (Valley of the Moon), the desert valley setting for *Lawrence of Arabia,* to Petra. You'll ride camels by day and sleep under the stars at night in Bedouin-style tents. En route, you'll visit the Red Sand Dunes and the spectacular Seven Pillars of Wisdom rock formation named for T. E. Lawrence's autobiography.

■ **PLANNING** **Petra** www.petrapark.com. The ancient site and its visitor center are open on a daily basis 6 a.m.–6 p.m. in summer and 6 a.m.–4 p.m. in winter. The visitor center sells tickets, arranges for guides, and provides information and help to visitors. **Kensington Tours** www.kensingtontours.com. Adventure tours including camel treks.

Dating to the first century B.C., the Monastery tomb is Petra's largest monument.

# ANCIENT DAMASCUS

Navigate the narrow lanes of one of the world's oldest cities.

The wall around the heart of Damascus lets visitors know they are about to enter a special place. Founded in the third millennium B.C., the Old City of Damascus goes back much further, perhaps as many as 10,000 years, making this metropolis, the capital of modern Syria, one of the oldest continually inhabited cities on Earth.

To enter the Old City, you must pass through the citadel, guarded by a statue of Saladin. Inside is a world alive with ruins, a great contrast to the mid-20th-century socialist architectural style of modern Damascus. Much of the Old City dates from the medieval period and is a mix of half-timbered structures, their waddle-and-daub exteriors dissolving. Narrow alleyways accumulated layer upon layer of buildings, so that now one facade nearly touches the next.

Old Damascus's winding lanes are best explored on foot, and a leisurely pace allows ample time to explore the city's ageless charms—including frequent stops at enticing restaurants and cafés. Among the most impressive sights is the temple dedicated to the Roman god Jupiter. The temple became a church in the late fourth century, and later, in the early eighth century, it was converted into the Umayyad Mosque. Inside, gentle light pours from above and causes the mosque's gold and green mosaics to gleam.

■ **PLANNING** **Ancient Damascus** www.syriatourism.org. Be sure also to check with the U.S. Department of State (*www.state.gov*) for current travel conditions.

---

## ✤ BEST OF THE BEST ✤
### Al-Hamidiyah Souk

The Old City boasts the largest suq, or marketplace, in Syria. Al-Hamidiyah Souk—a sprawling river of smells, sights, and sounds—stretches about a third of a mile (0.5 km) from Al-Thawra Street to the plaza outside the Umayyad Mosque. Inside the covered suq you'll find everything you can imagine for sale, including antiques, textiles, spices, candies, toys, and carpets. The cries of the merchants vying for your attention bounce off old stone walls, and the result can be deafening. Make your way through the hawkers and buy what you want before plunging into the Umayyad Mosque's peaceful surroundings.

The Dome of the Treasury was erected in the courtyard of the Umayyad Mosque in the eighth century.

## ESFAHAN, IRAN
# MEIDAN-E-SHAH

Listen for the sounds of the past in a palatial Persian music room.

Esfahan is half the world," the city's poets once proclaimed. So it must have seemed in the 17th century after Shah Abbas I moved his capital to this oasis city in central Iran. Among tree-lined avenues and gardens, a French chronicler counted 102 mosques, 273 public baths, and 1,802 caravansaries—courtyarded inns where travelers and traders stayed the night and told stories of their long journeys.

At the center of Esfahan lies the Meidan-e-Shah, or Royal Square, one of the world's largest plazas and most beautiful places. A showcase for the 17th-century Persian Renaissance, the square is most notable for the architecture that surrounds it. Monumental buildings, which line all sides, are linked one to another by graceful two-story arcades filled with shops. No facade here has been left untouched: Ceramic tiles painted with yellow, turquoise, and cobalt-blue floral themes adorn every surface. On the square's west side, enter the pavilion of Ali Qapu and climb the spiral staircase to the palace's sixth-floor Music Room. Shaped like a cross, the room has painted, stucco ceiling cutouts shaped like ancient ceramics and glassware. The intricate honeycomb design was created to enhance the vaulted room's acoustics, but today you're more likely to hear a public concert in the royal gardens behind the palace.

■ PLANNING Meidan-e-Shah http://whc.unesco.org/en/list/115. For current travel conditions in Iran, check with the U.S. Department of State at www.state.gov.

### ~ IN THE KNOW ~
#### SKIING IN IRAN

Few people know it, but this beautiful city in Iran is also a gateway to the country's best kept secret: skiing. Reminiscent of the Rockies, Iran's Zagros Mountains overlook the metropolitan region and are dotted with winter resorts, and the slopes here climb as high as 9,843 feet (3,000 m). Prices for a ski vacation in Iran tend to be significantly lower than getaways in Europe and North America. The season runs from December to as late as May, depending on snow conditions. Check www.iranskiresort.com for a list of resorts and hotels.

Restored in the 16th century, Djingareyber, or the Great Mosque, is the world's largest mud building.

# TIMBUKTU

Tour a priceless treasure trove of ancient African manuscripts.

Where the great sands of the Sahara meet the savannas of North Africa lies the legendary "ends of the Earth," Timbuktu. Founded in the 11th century by the "blue men of the desert"—Tuareg nomads known for their indigo robes and dye-tinged skin—the fabled Niger River Delta city became a major stop for trans-Saharan salt and gold caravans, as well as a center of Islamic scholarship.

By the late 16th century, European seafaring merchant ships made desert trade routes obsolete, rendering the once glorious cultural crossroads a lost city. For most people, this humble adobe outpost is but a mirage of the imagination, forgotten for centuries to the sands of the Sahara. Yet hidden in the UNESCO World Heritage site is a treasure trove of African history that scholars are feverishly scrambling to preserve.

Most of the region's remaining priceless sacred manuscripts—estimated to number more than 700,000—are in private hands. The largest (30,000-volume) collection, some texts written on tree bark, lamb, and gazelle skin, is protected and preserved in Timbuktu's Ahmed Baba Institute library, supported by the Tombouctou Manuscripts Project. Take a guided tour of the library to witness ongoing efforts to reclaim the written legacy of Timbuktu's respected Islamic scholars, revered throughout North Africa as Ambassadors of Peace.

■ **PLANNING Timbuktu** http://whc.unesco.org/en/list/119. The Ahmed Baba Institute (*www.tombouctoumanuscripts.org*) contains state-of-the-art preservation resources, research facilities, a public library, and a lecture hall. Monitor regional conflicts at www.state.gov.

## ❧ BEST OF THE BEST ❧
### Mosques of Timbuktu

Timbuktu's former status as an Islamic oasis is echoed in its three great mud-and-timber mosques: Djingareyber, Sankore, and Sidi Yahia. Restored by Imam Al Aqib in the 16th century, these 14th- and 15th-century places of worship are part of a wider UNESCO World Heritage site. The **Mosque of Djingareyber**'s central minaret is the urban landscape's most visible landmark. The **Mosque of Sankore**'s sanctuary was rebuilt to the measurements of the Kaaba at Mecca, after Al Aqib's pilgrimage there. The **Mosque of Sidi Yahia** was erected in expectation of a holy person who arrived four decades later.

# ETHIOPIA
# LALIBELA

Meet the resident monks of monolith cathedral masterpieces.

Considered the eighth wonder of the world, Lalibela, a small town in the Ethiopian Highlands, is home to 11 churches hewn from red volcanic rock. According to legend, King Lalibela saw a vision of them while lying unconscious after having been poisoned. When he recovered, he vowed to replicate the vision on Earth. (Another story says that Lalibela sought to build a new Ethiopian Jerusalem. This would explain why you'll find an Ethiopian River Jordan, a grave of Abraham, and a tomb of Adam.) Whatever the impetus, construction was carried out at such great speed that the churches were thought to be the work of angels.

Carved as monoliths from the top down, the churches of Lalibela are masterpieces of architectural ingenuity. Go slowly on the steep, rocky stairs leading down into the site, and hire a local guide to navigate the network of tunnels and underground passageways linking all the churches. As you tread lightly through medieval grottoes, crypts, and galleries, you'll pass the kinds of watercolors and oils that you would expect to see in a European cathedral (renderings of Jesus, Mary, the Crucifixion, and the Last Supper). Stop to greet each church's resident monk—some bedecked in fuchsia capes, white robes, turbans, and Coptic crosses the size and shape of a shield.

■ **PLANNING** **Lalibela** www.tourismethiopia.org. Ethiopian Airlines *(www.flyethiopian.com)* flies once daily from Addis Ababa to Lalibela. The city comes to life the third week in Jan. during the local festival known as Timkat, the celebration of Epiphany.

## ~ IN THE KNOW ~
### HISTORIC ROUTE

Ethiopia's Historic Route connects the country's great cities of antiquity. Lalibela may be the most famous stop, but it is by no means the only one worth exploration. The route escorts you to medieval castles and churches, a walled Muslim city, and ruins from the Queen of Sheba's tenth-century B.C. capital. Fly into Addis Ababa, and then head to Aksum, legendary home of the Ark of the Covenant. En route, enjoy a coffee ceremony and sample local fare, such as *doro wat* with *injera* (spicy chicken and a pancake) and *tej*, a refreshing honey wine. For a sample itinerary, consult www.awazetours.com.

Lalibela is home to 11 churches carved from red volcanic rock.

INDIA

# TAJ MAHAL

*I had been skeptical about the visit . . . The building itself left my skepticism in shreds, however . . . The beauty of beautiful things is still able, in these image-saturated times, to transcend imitations. And the Taj Mahal is, beyond the power of words to say it, a lovely thing, perhaps the loveliest of things.*

—SALMAN RUSHDIE, AUTHOR OF *THE ENCHANTRESS OF FLORENCE* & OTHER BOOKS

The instantly recogniz-
able Taj Mahal mauso-
leum, built in the first
half of the 17th century

# PLACES OF REVERENCE & REFLECTION

Voyage deep within the soul of humanity.

## 1 9/11 MEMORIAL
### New York, New York

The National September 11 Memorial solemnly bows its head to a painful, gaping void. Two reflecting pools occupy the footprints of the fallen towers, and the names of the 2,983 victims are inscribed on seemingly endless panels of bronze. www.911memorial.org

## 2 CHICHÉN ITZÁ
### Yucatán, Mexico

The most renowned of the Maya pyramids on the Yucatán Peninsula, Chichén Itzá is powerful testimony to the mystical rites of pre-Columbian worship. Built between A.D. 1000 and 1200, the temple of El Castillo probably served as a calendar. www.chichenitza.com

## 3 D-DAY MEMORIALS
### Normandy, France

On June 6, 1944, some 45,000 Allied troops landed on beaches near Bayeux, Normandy, launching the historic invasion to break Nazi Germany's stranglehold on Europe. The beautifully maintained Normandy American Cemetery and Memorial at Colleville-sur-Mer contains the marked graves of 9,387 military dead; 18 Commonwealth cemeteries trace the lines of advance of British and Canadian troops. www.abmc.gov

## 4 METÉORA MONASTERIES
### Greece

Peering down on the city of Kalambaka, steep sandstone pinnacles are crowned with six monasteries and convents, home to Eastern Orthodox monks and nuns since the ninth century. Metéora, or Suspended Rocks, were once scaled by rope ladders, although it is said that St. Athanasius, the founder, was carried by an eagle. www.meteora-greece.com

## 5 GALLIPOLI MEMORIALS
### Turkey

Sailing north through the Dardanelles, the straits that separate the Asian and European sides of Turkey, you can find dozens of sober marble and bronze monuments to the Gallipoli Campaign in 1915 to 1916, when a staggering 100,000 lives were lost. www.gallipoli.com.tr

## 6 VICTORIA FALLS
### Zimbabwe/Zambia

This legendary waterfall is among the most awe-inspiring sights on the planet. The Zambezi River, more than a mile (1.6 km) wide at the falls, cascades over a large plateau and plunges around 350 feet (107 m), generating clouds of rainbow-tinged mist. Explorer David Livingstone reported that islands on the lip of the falls were sacred worship places for ancient Batoka chiefs. www.zambiatourism.com

## 7 YAD VASHEM
### Israel

A glass-covered spear boring through a hillside, a cattle car, a soaring dome covered with the faces of victims—nowhere are the horrors of the Holocaust recalled more poignantly. The centerpiece is the new Holocaust History Museum, an exhibition walkway that leads visitors through light to darkness and back to light. www.yadvashem.org

## 8 ELEPHANTA CAVES
### Gharapuri Island, India

Carved out of a hillside in the fifth century, the Hindu deities in these temples seem to be swaying to the drone of Indian instruments. The sinuous curves of Shiva Nataraja and the three faces of Trimurti, the creator, preserver, and destroyer aspects of the god Shiva, are as expressive today as they were centuries ago. www.maharashtratourism.gov.in

## 9 BAGAN
### Myanmar (Burma)

With more than 2,000 temples in an area the size of downtown Manhattan, you could easily mistake Myanmar's (Burma's) lost city for a vast mirage, its spires and mountains of red sandstone shimmering in the dusty, rising heat. Elaborate carved doorways of *zedis* (chapels) lead to towering Buddhas, glinting altars, and 800-year-old murals. www.ancientbagan.com

## 10 HIROSHIMA PEACE MEMORIAL
### Japan

Covering an area flattened by the atomic explosion, Hiroshima's Peace Memorial Park is a quiet tract of gardens dedicated to a horrifying legacy. The memorial contains the official registry of the victims of the A-bomb, now listing over 269,000 names. Nearby, the eerie Atomic Bomb Dome is the city's only bomb-seared building left standing. www.pcf.city.hiroshima.jp

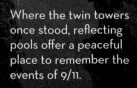

Where the twin towers once stood, reflecting pools offer a peaceful place to remember the events of 9/11.

## CHINA
# TERRA-COTTA ARMY

Look in the eyes of lifelike legions of clay.

Just imagine it. More than two millennia ago, the fearsome emperor whose army unified China for the first time dragooned 700,000 men to labor 36 years on building a life-size army garrison of clay to accompany him in the afterlife. Stashed in a vast mausoleum outside of Xi'an, China, the 8,000 terra-cotta warriors and their hundreds of clay steeds slumbered until 1974. That's when a Chinese farmer, while digging a well, unearthed the first traces of Emperor Qin Shi Huang's ancient burial ground, among the most awesome archaeological discoveries of all time.

They're eerily lifelike, recalls China scholar Albert Dien: "Turning a corner, we came upon the figure of an archer. It was kneeling, half turned, eyes gazing into the distance. It was such a shock to see this startlingly lifelike figure that I had to sit and rest awhile." Stationed in three underground vaults covering close to 6 acres (2.4 ha), each terra-cotta soldier has a different face, with individual features hand sculpted by skilled craftsmen. To protect the warriors while allowing visitors to view the ongoing excavation, the Museum of the Terra-cotta

Warriors and Horses of Qin Shihuang was erected over the site. Arrive early to stake out a viewing spot before the huge tour groups arrive.

■ **PLANNING** Museum of the Terra-cotta Warriors & Horses of **Qin Shihuang** www.bmy.com.cn. The site is located about 19 miles (30 m) east of the city of Xi'an. Bus Nos. 306, 914, and 915 run to the site from the city, or take a taxi. There is an admission fee.

> ## ~ IN THE KNOW ~
> ### HANYANGLING MUSEUM
>
> In north Xi'an, the Hanyangling Museum is devoted to more than 1,700 Han dynasty relics from a royal tomb. Apparently this Han emperor, who lived from 188 B.C. to 141 B.C., thought plump-faced dancers and kneeling servants, in addition to soldiers, would be needed for the afterlife. Dramatically lit displays, including fully enclosed burial pits, give a complete overview of the Han period. Excavation is ongoing, and visitors can watch archaeologists at work. If you want to get your hands dirty, reserve in advance to participate in one of the simulated excavation workshops. Visit www.hylae.com for more information.

The warriors have stood at the ready for more than two millennia.

Avoid large crowds by hiking the Juyong Guan section.

## CHINA
# GREAT WALL
Get a rare glimpse at Chinese life in the slow lane.

Contrary to popular belief, China's Great Wall is not visible from space, but it is the longest fortress on the planet. This spectacular marvel stretches from Shanhaiguan on the Bo Hai Sea just north of Beijing to Fort Jiayu Guan in the Gobi Desert, a distance of 3,890 miles (6,260 km), roughly the same as the distance from Oslo, Norway, to Abu Dhabi. Construction on the wall began in the fifth century B.C. Made from earth, stones, and wood, it has survived wars, storms, and dynasty and regime changes, all the while having an enormous impact on the movement of humans and animals within China.

A hike along one of the Great Wall's many sections is like time travel and offers a rare glimpse of rural China and the ancient, slower pace from which this rapidly changing society evolved. For a more intimate or extreme experience with the wall, sign up for one of William Lindesay's WildWall excursions. The conservationist, author, and academic has devoted his life to studying the Great Wall, and he has been organizing walks along it for the past 30 years. His intrepid outings encourage travelers to discover sections beyond the tourist spots and often lead travelers to unofficial sections.

■ **PLANNING** **Great Wall** www.cnto.org. Other just as spectacular sites along the wall include the misty, wooded, and photogenic Mutianyu, 56 miles (90 km) northeast of Beijing; desolate Jin Shan Ling, 56 miles (90 km) southwest of Chengde; and the dangerously vertiginous Simatai. **WildWall Excursions** www.wildwall.com.

---

### ☙ BEST OF THE BEST ☙
#### Great Wall Marathon

Runners in the annual Great Wall Marathon describe it as the experience of a lifetime. Flat terrain in the countryside gives way to more than 5,164 steps along a remote, 2.17-mile (3.5 km) section of the Great Wall at Huangyaguan, northeast of Beijing. The May event, which also includes a half marathon, 10K, and 5K, is more steeplechase than marathon. Navigating the course requires fast footwork and dexterity on narrow goat paths and steep staircases and over loose pebbles and crumbling bricks. Everyone who finishes the race in eight hours or less receives a medal. Visit the marathon site (*www.great-wall-marathon .com*) for dates and registration information.

A 14th-century idea remains a modern reality.

KYOTO, JAPAN

# SAIHO-JI MOSS GARDEN

Tread lightly through what may just be paradise on Earth.

Stroll. Stop. Observe. These are the keys to attaining garden nirvana in Japanese landscapes like the one at Saiho-ji Buddhist Temple outside of Kyoto. On these moss-blanketed grounds, absorb the sheer sensual perfection of nature groomed to its highest degree: a universe in a tuft of moss, a man-made world expressing nature's simple essence, the 4.5-acre (1.8 ha) vision of a 14th-century Zen priest transmitted to us today.

To the east of the main temple, called Saiho-ji, one path leads into the shady garden grove, a circular promenade around a pond studded with three islands. As the path winds among dark tree trunks, radiant green moss of a single, luxuriant texture unfolds, carpeting every surface, dappled with sunlight, softening edges and blending rock with soil. Draw near, and the verdant blanket separates into distinct patches, each its own shade of green, with tiny, flowerlike shoots of various hues. Unlike aristocratic gardens, which were designed to be viewed from a single vantage point, Saiho-ji yields ever changing vistas: a bamboo grove, a moss-covered stone, a group of artfully arranged rocks, a mirror of water reflecting lacy branches. You will see no flowers. Instead, try appreciating 120 varieties of humble moss. Rich in both illusion and allusion, Saiho-ji encourages the viewer to see large within small, a whole universe within the bounds of a garden.

## ∽ IN THE KNOW ∽
### FATHER OF THE JAPANESE TEA CEREMONY

The tea ceremony was developed during the 16th century as an arcane art form by tea masters, notably Sen-no-Rikyu. Spurning ostentation to seek refinement in simplicity, Rikyu became the highest arbiter of Japanese aesthetics. Courted as such by the shogun Toyotomi Hideyoshi, whose tastes were decidedly ostentatious, Rikyu walked on thin ice. Inevitably he fell from the jealous shogun's favor, and in 1591, Hideyoshi forced Rikyu to commit seppuku (suicide). Today, millions seek to follow Rikyu's vision through the tea ceremony and other acts of simple beauty.

■ PLANNING **Moss Garden of Saiho-ji** Access to the garden is restricted to entry by appointment only. There is an admission fee. For the most recent information, check with the Kyoto Tourism Council (*www.pref.kyoto.jp*).

CORDILLERA, PHILIPPINES

# RICE TERRACES

Hike through terraced mountainside masterpieces of agrarian art.

Nothing can prepare you for the sight of the sinuous, bright green terraces stepping down from steep tropical mountainsides. The rice terraces of the Cordillera Mountain region, on the main Philippine island of Luzon, are natural poetry. They turn entire mountains into sculptures. Here, landscape and culture are woven together seamlessly. For generations, the planting, cultivating, and harvesting of rice have been the foundation of local culture and the central focus for its communities.

Legend has it that the gods from the Skyworld gave the first sacred rice to the original builders of the terraces. These fields, and the knowledge to farm and sustain them, have been passed down from generation to generation for centuries. The Banaue paddies are the most famous of the lot. Banaue is some 216 miles (348 km) north of Manila (perhaps eight to ten hours with stops and mountainous terrain), and daily buses make the trip. To see multiple terraces, take a guided trek, which generally include terrace hiking plus village and waterfall tours. It's better to visit in winter, since abundant summer and fall rains can cloud views of the slopes.

■ **PLANNING** Cordillera Rice Terraces www.tourism.gov.ph. **Adventure Bound Asia** www.adventureboundasia.com. Among the companies that offer treks to the terrace. The cities of Banaue and Batad make excellent bases for exploring the area.

---

### ⚜ BEST OF THE BEST ⚜
#### Heirloom Rice Varieties

They are not the easiest rice crops to grow. But for the people who have tended the Cordillera Terraces for 2,000 years, they are some of the most important. Tinawon and unoy are two of the area's heirloom rice varieties. **Tinawon,** which produces a crop just once each year, is a white rice that throws off a wonderfully rice-y smell while cooking but has a mild flavor. Traditionally used for festivals and ceremonies, **unoy,** a red rice, has a nutty flavor; its popcorn scent is a signal that it's time to gather.

---

UNESCO's protection helps maintain an ancient way of life.

# CAMBODIA
# ANGKOR WAT

Get a rare bird's-eye view of Cambodia's vanished Khmer Empire.

Sleeping in the humid embrace of banyan trees and moss-covered moats, Angkor Wat is a humbling and exhilarating world monument. Like Stonehenge, it is a sophisticated engineering project, harnessing the waters of Southeast Asia's monsoons for a mighty ninth-century civilization; like St. Peter's Basilica, it has witnessed the worship of deities of successive religions, adorning its facades with beatific images carved by ancient craftsmen; and like Versailles, it is adorned with more than a thousand images of celestial maidens, representing the pleasures of paradise. As poetically put by

The mysterious world of Angkor Wat is an engineering marvel that was way ahead of its time.

university professor and author Eleanor Mannikka, Angkor Wat is a place where "time stops, divinity and space merge." To explore this 120-square-mile (400 sq km) kingdom, the region's most important archaeological site, is a sublime visual privilege.

A World Heritage site since 1992, Angkor Wat is slowly being restored. As peace returns to Cambodia after decades of suffering under the Khmer Rouge, the nearby town of Siem Reap has become a popular tourist destination, with a modern airport and 900,000 residents. Hire a *tuk-tuk* (motorcycle taxi)

Repeat visits to Angkor Archaeological Park are a must—especially to witness traditional folk dancing.

or hail a *song teaw,* a truck with wooden benches, to travel to Angkor. In town, hire a bicycle to pedal among the various sites.

Tall trees along the quiet roads and canals of Angkor Wat are home to monkeys that swing above visitors' heads. The fearless primates are even more aggressive than the vendors and souvenir sellers—adults and children alike—who cheerfully crowd the perimeter of the site.

The heat and the immensity of Angkor Wat make it imperative for visitors to pace themselves. Consider making several shorter trips to the Angkor Archaeological Park (choose from one-, three-, and seven-day admission passes). Time at least one visit to coincide with sunrise or sunset, when the dancing *nagas* (serpents), elephants, and maidens of this sacred site glow with mysterious light.

## Bird's-eye View

Many people believe that a powerful spirit resides in Angkor Wat and prevents birds from flying over it. The Cambodian government does likewise for commercial aircraft. But a half mile (0.8 km) west of the temple, Angkor Balloon ascends a 650-foot (198 m) tether to put the vast complex in perspective. Looking down on Prasat Phnom Bakheng, its seven levels crowned with a dozen towers, gives a bird's-eye view of the complex and its geometric enclosure within restored moats. The balloon ascends every ten minutes; arrive early to purchase tickets for sunrise and sunset flights.

## Angkor Thom

Angkor Wat itself, with its towers symbolizing the five peaks of Mount Meru, home of the Hindu gods, should be any visitor's first stop. But make sure to explore Angkor Thom, with its Terrace of the Elephants and the Gate of the Dead, and Bayon, the only Angkorian state temple to be built primarily as a Buddhist shrine. The 37 massive face towers of the Angkor Thom complex, all bearing the meditative "Angkor Wat smile," rise above stone pyramids. At Ta Prohm, towering silk-cotton trees and strangler figs perch on the temple, their tentacle-like roots crawling along the crumbling stone walls. A former Buddhist monastery, it is the least restored site in the complex, providing a glimpse of the Herculean tasks involved in raising the massive stone walls and an unparalleled photo opportunity.

■ **PLANNING** **Angkor Wat** www.tourismcambodia.com/attractions/angkor.htm. The site opens daily at 5 a.m., and there is an admission fee. **Angkor Balloon** Email sokhasr@camintel.com for details and advance reservations. **Angkor Thom** www.tourismcambodia.com.

## ∼ In the Know ∼
### HISTORY OF DISCOVERY

When French naturalist Henri Mouhot crashed through the dense jungle along the shores of Tonle Sap in 1845 to rediscover Angkor Wat, the site had been hidden for centuries. Between the 9th and 13th centuries, more than a dozen Khmer kings built their palaces and temples—Hindu, then Buddhist—at Angkor, in northern Cambodia. To honor Vishnu, the Hindu ruler of the western quarter of the compass, the main temple faced west. After the defeat of the Khmer Empire in 1431, Buddhist monks worshipped here.

André Malraux, the French writer and culture minister, visited the area in 1923, but not as an observer. He was apprehended while stealing temple artifacts at Banteay Srei, about 15 miles (24 km) from the main temple.

Figures of apsaras, the dancing girls of Hindu myth, can be found on temples throughout Angkor Wat.

# INDEX

**Boldface** indicates illustrations.

# ILLUSTRATIONS CREDITS

2-3, Daryl Benson/The Image Bank/Getty Images; 4, Norbert Wu/Minden Pictures/National Geographic Stock; 6, Richard Nowitz/National Geographic Stock; 10-11, Chris Johns/National Geographic Stock; 12, Michael Nichols/National Geographic Stock; 13, Norbert Rosing/National Geographic Stock; 14-15, Michael Collier/National Geographic My Shot; 16, Daniel R. Westergren/National Geographic Stock; 17, Michael Melford/National Geographic Stock; 18, Pgiam/iStockphoto; 19, James Randklev; 21, Russell Kord/Alamy; 22-23, Kevin Ebi/Alamy; 24, John Burcham/National Geographic Stock; 25, Thomas Ferrell/National Geographic My Shot; 27, James D. Balog; 28, Paul Chauncey/Alamy; 29, DEA/C.SAPPA/Getty Images; 30, Steve Bly/Alamy; 31, Michael Melford/National Geographic Stock; 32-33, Linda Mirro/iStockphoto; 34, Burt Johnson/iStockphoto; 35, Frans Lanting/National Geographic Stock; 36, Kevin Schafer; 37, Eugene Berman/Shutterstock; 39, Radius Images/Alamy; 40, Joel Sartore/National Geographic Stock; 41, Mike Theiss/National Geographic Stock; 42-43, Volodymyr Goinyk/Shutterstock; 45, Kevin Schafer/Minden Pictures/National Geographic Stock; 46, Yva Momatiuk & John Eastcott/MI/National Geographic Stock; 47, Peter Essick; 48, Pavel Svoboda/Shutterstock; 49, Guido Cozzi/SIME; 50, Martin McCarthy/iStockphoto; 51, Antony Spencer/iStockphoto; 52-53, Funkyfood London - Paul Williams/Alamy; 55, Colin Monteath/Minden Pictures/National Geographic Stock; 56, Aaron Huey/National Geographic Stock; 57, Stephen Alvarez/National Geographic Stock; 58, Annie Griffiths/National Geographic Stock; 59, George Steinmetz/National Geographic Stock; 60-61, Danita Delimont/Alamy; 62, Shin Yoshino/Minden Pictures/National Geographic Stock; 63, Beverly Joubert/National Geographic Stock; 64, Carsten Peter/National Geographic Stock; 65, Gordon Wiltsie/National Geographic Stock; 66, Ira Block/National Geographic Stock; 67, Lynn Johnson/National Geographic Stock; 68-69, Stocktrek Images, Inc./Alamy; 71, Jason deCaires Taylor; 72-73, Rob Rayworth/Alamy; 74, Nico Smit/iStockphoto; 75, Panoramic Images/National Geographic Stock; 76-77, Susan Seubert; 78, Colin Sands/Getty Images; 79, Susan Seubert; 80,

Andy Z./Shutterstock; 81, Robert Harding World Imagery/Alamy; 82, Richard Nowitz/National Geographic Stock; 83, Songquan Deng/Shutterstock; 84-85, SeanPavonePhoto/iStockphoto; 86, Randy Duchaine/Alamy; 87, Ilja Mašík/Shutterstock; 89, Scott S. Warren/National Geographic Stock; 90, Ulita/Dreamstime.com; 91, Jon Hicks/Corbis; 92, Philippe Cohat/Getty Images; 93, Mike Theiss/National Geographic Stock; 94, Stefgo/Dreamstime.com; 95, Maurizio Rellini/SIME; 96-97, Tupungato/Shutterstock; 98-99, Luciano Mortula/Shutterstock; 100, Massimo Ripani/SIME; 101, Justin Foulkes/4Corners/SIME; 103, An Qi/Alamy; 104-105, Stephen L. Alvarez/National Geographic Stock; 106, AISPIX by Image Source/Shutterstock; 107, Hemis/Alamy; 108, Jim Webb/National Geographic Stock; 109, Aleksandar Todorovic/Shutterstock; 110-111, LOOK Die Bildagentur der Fotografen GmbH/Alamy; 113, John Kernick; 114, Kevin Galvin/Alamy; 115, Kenneth Garrett/National Geographic Stock; 116-117, Sam Abell/National Geographic Stock; 118, Bjorn Holland/Alamy; 119, Heracles Kritikos/Shutterstock; 120-121, David Noton Photography/Alamy; 122, Diak/Shutterstock; 123, Paul Murtagh/Shutterstock; 124, Liz Gilbert/Redux; 125, Günter Gräfenhain/Huber/SIME; 126, Gordon Wiltsie/National Geographic Stock; 127, Stefano Amantini/SIME; 128-129, Paul/Chesley/National Geographic Stock; 131, David Noton Photography/Alamy; 132, Stefano Cellai/SIME; 133, Justin Guariglia/National Geographic Stock; 134-135, Hideaki Tanaka/Getty Images; 136, Reinhard Schmid/Huber/SIME; 137, Robert Harding World Imagery/Alamy; 138, Lawrence Wee/Shutterstock.com; 139, David Joyner/iStockphoto; 140-141, Chad Ehlers/Alamy; 142-143, Brian Raisbeck/iStockphoto; 144, Pete Ryan/National Geographic Stock; 145, Steve and Donna O'Meara/National Geographic Stock; 146, Phil Schermeister/National Geographic Stock; 147, Tui de Roy/ Minden Pictures/National Geographic Stock; 148, Mike Theiss/National Geographic Stock; 149, Orietta Gaspari/iStockphoto; 150-151, fotokik_dot_com/Shutterstock; 152, Tim Laman/National Geographic Stock; 153, Lonely Planet Images/Alamy; 155, Bertl123/Shutterstock; 156-157, Tim Fitzharris/Minden Pictures/National Geographic Stock; 158, Nikki Bidgood/iStockphoto; 159, Robert Harding Picture Library Ltd./Alamy; 160, Mlenny

Photography/iStockphoto; 161, Amit Erez/iStockphoto; 163, John Peter Photography/Alamy; 164-165, Pietro Canali/SIME; 166, Bon Appetit/Alamy; 167, Massimo Borchi/SIME; 168, traveler1116/iStockphoto; 169, Olimpio Fantuz/SIME; 171, Eric Nathan/Alamy; 172-173, Richard Nowitz/National Geographic Stock; 174, Maynard Owen Williams/National Geographic Stock; 175, Giovanni Simeone/SIME; 176, Luis Filipe Catarino/4SEE/Redux; 177, Jonathan Tichon/Alamy; 178, Paul Souders/CORBIS; 179, Jad Davenport/National Geographic Stock; 180-181, Bill Curtsinger/National Geographic Stock; 182, Alison Wright/National Geographic Stock; 183, Norbert Wu/Minden Pictures/National Geographic Stock; 185, Guido Cozzi/SIME; 186, J Marshall - Tribaleye Images/Alamy; 187, Kris LeBoutillier/National Geographic Stock; 188, Tbradford/iStockphoto; 189, Kris LeBoutillier/National Geographic Stock; 190, fototrav/iStockphoto; 191, Mike Veitch/Alamy; 192-193, Hemis/Alamy; 194, Marc van Vuren/Shutterstock; 195, Przemyslaw Skibinski/Shutterstock; 196-197, Fotis Mavroudakis/National Geographic My Shot; 198, onepony/iStockphoto; 199, Alison Cornford-Matheson/iStockphoto; 200, Bryce Pincham/Corbis; 201, Tim Fitzharris/Minden Pictures/National Geographic Stock; 202, Catherine Karnow; 203, Andrew Penner/iStockphoto; 205, Liz Leyden/iStockphoto.com; 206, Andre Jenny/Alamy; 207, Larry William Richardson, Inner Visions; 208, Kenneth Wiedemann/iStockphoto; 209, rabbit75_ist/iStockphoto.com; 210, Tina Manley/Alamy; 211, John Coletti/Getty Images; 213, TAO Images Limited/Alamy; 214-215, Robert Harding Picture Library Ltd/Alamy; 216, Seb Agudelo/Alamy; 217, Hemis/Alamy; 218, Pablo Corral Vega; 219, Yadid Levy/Alamy; 220-221, John Butterfield/iStockphoto; 222, Steven Gillis hd9 imaging/Alamy; 223, Ian Dagnall/Alamy; 225, Taylor S. Kennedy/National Geographic Stock; 226-227, Douglas Pearson/4Corners; 228, Robert van Beets/iStockphoto; 229, James A. Sugar/National Geographic Stock; 230, Jeppe Wikstrom/Getty Images; 231, Luis Pedrosa/iStockphoto; 232-233, Matt Propert; 234, Benozzo di Lese di Sandro Gozzoli/The Bridgeman Art Library/Getty Images; 235, Floriano Rescigno/iStockphoto.com; 236, Fesus Robert/Shutterstock; 237, Manfred Mehlig/Huber/SIME; 239, Antony McAulay/Shutterstock; 240, Gilbert M. Grosvenor/

National Geographic Stock; 241, Andreas Karelias/iStockphoto; 242-243, Dieter Roeseler/laif/Redux; 244, FotoS.A./Corbis; 245, Hemis/Alamy; 246, Sandy Chestnut/Liquid Light/arabianEye; 247, Nikki Bidgood/iStockphoto; 248, Floris Leeuwenberg/Hollandse Hoogte/Redux; 249, Jeremy Horner/Corbis; 251, Martin Harvey/Alamy; 252, Nick Spannagel/iStockphoto; 253, KingWu/iStockphoto; 254, Flash/Parker/Getty Images; 255, JTB Photo Communications, Inc./Alamy; 257, Mark A. Johnson/Alamy; 258, VasikO/Shutterstock; 259, Ashley Whitworth/Alamy; 260-261, Gordon Wiltsie/National Geographic Stock; 262, Dick Durrance II/National Geographic Stock; 263, Helena Lovincic/iStockphoto; 265, George H.H. Huey/Alamy; 266, Pietro Canali/SIME; 267, Rena Schild/Shutterstock; 268, Vadim Petrakov/Shutterstock; 269, Christian Ziegler/Minden Pictures/National Geographic Stock; 270, urosr/Shutterstock; 271, James P. Blair/National Geographic Stock; 272-273, Mike Theiss/National Geographic Stock; 274, Joe McNally; 275, efesan/iStockphoto; 276-277, Lyubov Timofeyeva/Shutterstock.com; 278, elifranssens/iStockphoto; 279, Raymond Choo/National Geographic My Shot; 280, didon/Shutterstock; 281, Daniella Nowitz/National Geographic Stock; 283, Diego Rivera (1886-1957)/Detroit Institute of Arts, USA/Gift of Edsel B. Ford/The Bridgeman Art Library; 284-285, Tips Images/Tips Italia Srl a socio unico/Alamy; 286, Plamen/Shutterstock; 287, Nick Pavlakis/Shutterstock; 288, Jan Wlodarczyk/Alamy; 289, DIMUSE/iStockphoto; 290, Danita Delimont/Alamy; 291, Robert Preston Photography/Alamy; 293, Holger Mette/iStockphoto.com; 294, John Copland/Shutterstock; 295, sculpies/Shutterstock; 296, Joel Carillet/iStockphoto; 297, OPIS/Shutterstock; 298, Mysa Kafil Hussain/National Geographic My Shot; 299, dbimages/Alamy; 300, oversnap/iStockphoto; 301, George Steinmetz/National Geographic Stock; 302-303, Suman Bajpeyi/National Geographic My Shot; 305, Jon Hicks/Corbis; 306, Lukas Hlavac/Shutterstock; 307, Ronald Sumners/Shutterstock; 308, Justin Guariglia/National Geographic Stock; 309, Aaron Joel Santos/Alamy; 310-311, Paul Chesley/National Geographic Stock; 312, W. Robert Moore/National Geographic Stock; 313, Paul Chesley/National Geographic Stock.

**World's Best Travel Experiences**
400 Extraordinary Places

**Prepared by the Book Division**
Hector Sierra, Senior Vice President and General Manager
Anne Alexander, Senior Vice President and Editorial Director
Jonathan Halling, Design Director, Books and Children's Publishing
Marianne R. Koszorus, Design Director, Books
Barbara A. Noe, Senior Editor
R. Gary Colbert, Production Director
Jennifer A. Thornton, Director of Managing Editorial
Susan S. Blair, Director of Photography
Meredith C. Wilcox, Director, Administration and Rights Clearance

**Staff for This Book**
Lawrence M. Porges, Editor
Mary Stephanos, Project Editor
Elisa Gibson, Art Director
Nancy Marion, Illustrations Editor
Carl Mehler, Director of Maps
Michael McNey and Martin S. Walz, Map Research and Production
Mark Baker, Mary Budzik, Karen Carmichael, Maryellen Duckett,
    Adam Graham, Jeremy Gray, Rachael Jackson, Tim Jepson,
    Gabriella Le Breton, Diana Farr Louis, Michael Luongo, Jennifer
    Michels, Ceil Miller-Bouchet, Meghan Miner, Barbara A. Noe,
    Christine O'Toole, Jenna Schnuer, Olivia Stren, Contributing
    Writers
Judith Klein, Production Editor
Mike Horenstein, Production Manager
Galen Young, Rights Clearance Specialist
Katie Olsen, Design and Production Assistant

**Manufacturing and Quality Management**
Phillip L. Schlosser, Senior Vice President
Chris Brown, Vice President, NG Book Manufacturing
George Bounelis, Vice President, Production Services
Nicole Elliott, Manager
Rachel Faulise, Manager
Robert L. Barr, Manager

Since 1888, the National Geographic Society has funded more than 13,000 research, exploration, and preservation projects around the world. National Geographic Partners distributes a portion of the funds it receives from your purchase to National Geographic Society to support programs including the conservation of animals and their habitats.

National Geographic Partners
1145 17th Street NW
Washington, DC 20036-4688 USA

Get closer to National Geographic explorers and photographers, and connect with our global community. Join us today at national geographic.com/join

For information about special discounts for bulk purchases, please contact National Geographic Books Special Sales: specialsales@natgeo.com

For rights or permissions inquiries, please contact National Geographic Books Subsidiary Rights: bookrights@natgeo.com

Library of Congress Cataloging-in-Publication Data
National Geographic Society (U.S.)
 World's best travel experiences : 400 extraordinary places / by National Geographic.
    p. cm.
ISBN 978-1-4262-0959-8 (hardcover : alk. paper)
1. Voyages and travels. I. Title.
G465.N365 2012
910.4--dc23

                                      2012016594

Printed in Hong Kong
18/PPHK/4